A Struggle to Survive

SEVENTEENTH ANNUAL YEARBOOK
OF THE AMERICAN EDUCATION FINANCE ASSOCIATION
1996

A Struggle to Survive

Funding Higher Education in the Next Century

Editors

David S. Honeyman
James L. Wattenbarger
Kathleen C. Westbrook

CORWIN PRESS, INC.
A Sage Publications Company
Thousand Oaks, California

For information address:

Corwin Press
A Sage Publications Company.
2455 Teller Road
Thousand Oaks, California 91320
E-mail: order@sagepub.com

SAGE Publications Ltd.
6 Bonhill Street
London EC2A 4PU
United Kingdom

SAGE Publications India Pvt. Ltd.
M-32 Market
Greater Kailash I
New Delhi 110048 India

Printed in the United States of America

Library of Congress Cataloging-in-Publication Data

Main entry under title:

A struggle to survive: funding higher education in the next century/
    editors, David S. Honeyman, James L. Wattenbarger, Kathleen C.
Westbrook.
        p. cm.—(Annual yearbook of the American Education Finance
Association; 17th)
    Includes bibliographical references and index.
    ISBN 0-8039-6530-3 (acid-free paper)
    1. Education, Higher—United States—Finance. 2. State aid to
higher education—United States. I. Honeyman, David Smith.
II. Wattenbarger, James Lorenzo, 1922-   . III. Westbrook, Kathleen
C. IV. Series.
LB2342.S856   1996
379.1'18'0973—dc20   96-25275

98 99 00 01 02 03 10 9 8 7 6 5 4 3 2

Production Editor:	Diana E. Axelsen
Typesetter/Designer:	Danielle Dillahunt
Cover Designer:	Marcia R. Finlayson

Contents

Preface

The Seventh Annual Yearbook of the American Education Finance Association was published in 1986 and was titled *Values in Conflict: Funding Priorities for Higher Education.* Ten years later, we present the Seventeenth Annual Yearbook that continues and updates that discussion on higher education funding.

In the preface to the 1986 volume (p. xv), Mary P. McKeown wrote the following observations:

> In the 1980s, educational reform has focused on both higher education and elementary and secondary education. Facing the need for improved quality of higher education, increased competition for resources at the state and federal levels, and declining enrollments at many institutions, institutions of higher education, state coordinating and governing boards, legislators, and others have been forced to reexamine the roles and missions of institutions of higher education. Critical issues include the sources of funding, the levels of funding, and the very existence of the institutions. Education is a key contributor to continued U.S. economic growth and to maintaining the current U.S. position in the world economy.

As we discuss the current issues in higher education funding, we must ask, "What has changed?" We are still directed at reform efforts, competition has sharpened, the roles and missions of many institutions have changed, and *survival* is the operative phrase for many administrators and faculty of the community colleges, four-year schools, and universities across the country.

This yearbook is the result of the work of many writers who have struggled throughout their collective 200 years of experience in post-secondary education to indicate the routes of change for higher education to follow. Performance-based accountability standards, decentralization of control, the increasing use of business and private sectors in underwriting development, and alternate revenue sources are issues that greatly influence the operation of colleges and universities.

Overview of Contents

The opening chapter gives an overview of the issues involved in financing higher education and serves to introduce the book. David S. Honeyman and Megan Bruhn, University of Florida, detail the changing environment of the 1990s and the challenges presented to postsecondary institutions. Diminished revenue sources, changing student demographics, accountability, and the increasing demands for outcome-based assessment systems have all gained greater importance in the successful operations of the college and university.

In Chapter 2, Terry G. Geske, Louisiana State University, reviews the return through monetary benefit and increased productivity outside the labor market for higher education. He indicates that the true value of the nonmonetary benefits is still elusive and more work needs to be done.

The need for a new paradigm for funding higher education is discussed in Chapter 3. Mary P. McKeown, Arizona Board of Regents, continues her detailed discussion of state formulas and observes that the formulas will never resolve all the resource problems in higher education. Even though they may be objective in nature, they remain entrenched in the political process operating in every state. She concludes with a question concerning a change in the promise of higher education.

Accountability and the evaluation of quality are elusive concepts. John V. Lombardi, President of the University of Florida, and Elizabeth D. Capaldi, Provost and Vice President for Academic Affairs, describe the Florida Quality Evaluation Project. This project has been a major initiative to assess productivity and quality by measuring resources, expenditures, productivity, and quality. The model is designed to assist in planning and helping in the process of accounting to the university's many publics, including the state legislature.

In Chapter 5, Jay L. Chronister, University of Virginia, discusses faculty compensation issues in higher education. Trends in benefits and retirement are major concerns for the fiscal health of every postsecondary institution. He details the aging of the faculty, the increased pressure to modify fringe benefits, and the issues that surround retirement. Controlling the cost of benefits, and health care in particular, will continue to be a challenge to colleges and universities.

Responsibility-centered decentralized management is the theme covered in Chapter 6. Edward L. Whalen, recently from Indiana University, details the benefit and potential weakness of the process of implementing responsibility-centered management within the major research university. He contends that it is imperative that major universities need new management arrangements that facilitate effective governance, management, and control.

In Chapter 7, Susan Robinson Summers, a research associate with the Center for the Study of Education Finance at the University of Florida and Dean of Extended Services at Lake City Community College, challenges the idea that lottery revenues benefit higher education. Lotteries have existed since colonial times, and their popularity continues to grow. Although several states have developed innovative methods to distribute funds that benefit higher education, most have been failures. As she notes, lotteries are inefficient, compromise political morality, and, in general, fail to improve the fiscal health of the beneficiary.

Chapters 8, 9, and 10 specifically address community college funding issues. In Chapter 8, Dale F. Campbell, Lynn H. Leverty, and Karen Sayles, Institute of Higher Education, University of Florida, discuss community college funding issues from 1990 to 1995. Their work indicates that, nationally, funding has not kept pace with enrollment and that community colleges, like their sister institutions, are relying on tuition as an increasing funding source.

In Chapter 9, James C. Palmer, Illinois State University, describes the funding of multipurpose community colleges and details the mix and conflicts of the scholastic and social service philosophies of the community college. He notes that, in additon to the academic function, community colleges are positioned to be effective brokers for a variety of programs in economic development and workforce training within the community setting.

Concluding Chapter 10 describes the growing conflict within the community college movement competing with sister institutions for limited resources. Richard L. Alfred, University of Michigan, identifies the realities, problems, and prospects for enhancing the financial competitiveness of the community college.

Acknowledgments

As always, the editors wish to thank each of the authors who worked to develop this yearbook. Thanks to all the staff of Corwin Press for their continued support of the process.

David S. Honeyman
James L. Wattenbarger
Kathleen C. Westbrook

About the Authors

Richard L. Alfred is Associate Professor in the School of Education, University of Michigan, Ann Arbor, Michigan.

Megan Bruhn is Assistant Director of Housing at the University of Florida. She also is a research associate with the Center for the Study of Education Finance for Florida.

Elizabeth D. Capaldi is Provost and Vice President for Academic Affairs at the University of Florida. Previously, she was a faculty member at Purdue University, serving as chair of the Department of Psychological Sciences and assistant dean of the graduate school.

Dale F. Campbell is Professor and Director, Institute of Higher Education, University of Florida, and Executive Director, Community College Business Officers.

Jay L. Chronister is Professor at the Curry School of Education, University of Virginia, Charlottesville, Virginia.

Terry G. Geske is Professor of Educational Administration at Louisiana State University. He has published extensively in the areas of the economics of education and education finance policy. His major publications include *Financing Education: Overcoming Inefficiency and Inequity* (with Walter McMahon) and *The Economics of Education* (with Elchanan Cohn).

David S. Honeyman is Professor of Education Leadership at the University of Florida and serves as the director of the Center for Educational Finance for Florida. He also is technical advisor and expert witness for the Governor and Commissioner of Education for Florida on school finance issues, and he is Past President of the American Education Finance Association (AEFA). He is coauthor of a textbook on educational finance, and has written over 90 articles, monographs, and book chapters on education finance and school facilities in both the K-12 public school and post-secondary higher education.

Lynn H. Leverty is Associate Director, Askew Institute on Politics and Society, and Visiting Assistant Professsor, Department of Political Science, University of Florida.

John V. Lombardi is President of the University of Florida. A historian, teacher, administrator, and author, he came to the University of Florida from Johns Hopkins University, where he was Provost and Vice President for Academic Affairs.

Mary P. McKeown is Associate Executive Director for Financial Affairs for the Arizona Board of Regents. Her primary research interests are the economics and finance of higher education, budgeting, equity analysis, and strategic planning. She has been an expert witness in federal higher education equity cases, has published widely, and has served as a consultant to numerous school districts, universities, and municipalities.

James C. Palmer is Associate Professor of Educational Administration and Foundations at Illinois State University (ISU). He previously was on the staffs of George Mason University's Center for Community College Education, the American Association of Community Colleges, the ERIC Clearinghouse for Community Colleges, and the Center for the Study of Community Colleges.

Karen Sayles is Manager of Financial Planning, Santa Fe Community College, Gainesville, Florida.

Susan Robinson Summers is Division Chair, Extended Studies, Lake City Community College, and a research associate for the Center for

Florida Education Finance, College of Education, University of Florida. Her area of interest is community college finance.

James L. Wattenbarger is Distinguished Professor Emeritus in the Department of Education Leadership at the University of Florida. He has been an active contributor to the community college movement in Florida and the United States. A recipient of the Leadership Award from the American Association of Community Colleges (AACC), he was the first director of the Division of Community Colleges for Florida and served as Director of the Institute of Higher Education at the University of Florida for 24 years. He is the author of more than 200 articles, books, monographs, and other publications on issues influencing higher education in the United States and abroad.

Kathleen C. Westbrook is Science and Technology Associate, Division of Educational Programs, Argonne National Laboratory-East. Her current teaching and research includes K-12 teacher Internet training in the Systemic Reform Initiative of the Illinois State Board of Education through the Educational Networking Consortium in the Chicago area.

Edward L. Whalen is Vice President for Program and Member Services, National Association of College and University Business Officers. He is the author of *Responsibility Center Budgeting, an Approach to Decentralized Management for Institutions of Higher Education* (1991) and of articles related to incentive-based systems for colleges and universities.

ONE

The Financing
of Higher Education

DAVID S. HONEYMAN

MEGAN BRUHN

Higher education is a costly enterprise. In 1993, the National Center for Education Statistics (NCES) reported that the total revenues for higher education in the United States exceeded $170 billion, a 6% increase over the previous year. These revenues supported programs that educated almost 15 million students in undergraduate, graduate, and professional programs.

Higher education is also a complex operation funded by a delicate balance of revenue sources. These sources are diverse and differ in each state. In 1993, public tax-supported revenue accounted for almost 40% of all revenues and were derived from a combination of federal, state, and local sources. Additional revenues were generated by tuition and fee payments (26.5%), gifts and grants (5.7%), and sales and services (23.3%). The amounts and percentages of each revenue source are reported in Table 1.1.

1

TABLE 1.1 Revenue Breakdown for All Higher Education, 1993 (in billions)

| | Total | | Public | | Private | |
	%	($)	%	($)	%	($)
All revenues		$170.8		$108		$62
Federal	12.3	(21)	10.8	(12)	15	(9.3)
Fees/Tuition	26.5	(45)	18	(19)	41	(25)
State	24.1	(41)	36.8	(40)	2.3	(1.5)
Local						
government	2.6	(4.5)	3.7	(4)	0.6	(1.4)
Gifts/grants	5.7	(9.6)	4	(4)	4.1	(5.3)
Sales service	23.3	(40)	23.4	(25)	23	(14.5)
Other	3	(5)	2.7	(3)	4	(2.8)

SOURCE: National Center for Education Statistics, *Current Revenues and Expenditures for Institutions of Higher Education: Fiscal 1984 to 1992* (NCES Document No. 94-036).

One of the primary sources of funding for higher education has been the federal government. Federal funds expended on all education exceeded $18 billion in 1990 and grew to approximately $21 billion in 1993. However, this was a 14.3% reduction in federal support when measured in (constant) (1980) dollars (see Table 1.2). As a result of the reduced support of the federal government, almost every institution of higher education is struggling to operate effectively with diminished resources. One of the key factors in the current fiscal crisis is the decrease in federal support to college students in higher education. Since 1990, federal funds to higher education have increased slightly (15%), but there has been a reduction in assistance to college students (−8.3%). In addition, most federal funds for education have flowed as block grants to the individual states with no guarantee that the funds are spent on higher education. These funds to "state agencies" increased almost 98% from 1980 to 1994 (see Table 1.3).

Coupled with an understanding of the costs of higher education, attention continues to be focused on the economic and social outcomes of higher education. During the decades of the 1980s and early 1990s, this interest was driven by institutional survival needs and by the public expectation that colleges and universities contribute to the economic well-being of our nation by producing a highly trained and skilled workforce. Projections concerning the composition of the stu-

TABLE 1.2 Estimated Federal Tax Expenditures for Education: Fiscal Years 1975 to 1990 (amounts in billions of current and constant FY 1994 dollars)

Estimated federal tax expenditures	FY 75	FY 80	FY 85	FY 89	FY 90	Percent change, FY 80 to FY 90	Percent change, FY 89 to FY 90
In current dollars	$8.6	$13.3	$18.0	$16.9	$18.1	36.2	7.4
In constant dollars	23.4	24.2	24.6	20.2	20.8	−14.3	2.9

SOURCE: U.S. Department of Education, National Center for Education Statistics, various contractor reports, FYs 1975-1990.
NOTE: Percentages based on unrounded numbers. Because of rounding, details may not add up to totals.

TABLE 1.3 Total Federal Support for Education, by Type of Ultimate Recipient: Fiscal Years 1980, 1990, and 1994 (amounts in billions of current dollars)

Ultimate recipient	FY 80 Amount	FY 80 Percent	FY 90 Amount	FY 90 Percent	FY 94[1] Amount	FY 94[1] Percent	Percent change, FY 80 to FY 94[1]	Percent change, FY 90 to FY 94[1]
Total	$39.3	100.0	$62.8	100.0	$87.6	100.0	122.5	39.4
Local education agencies	10.9	27.8	13.9	22.1	20.0	22.9	83.0	44.1
State education agencies	1.4	3.5	3.3	5.2	5.0	5.7	259.5	52.4
College students[2]	9.1	23.2	10.5	16.8	15.2	17.4	66.7	44.3
Institutions of higher education	11.2	28.6	20.4	32.5	27.1	30.9	141.1	32.7
Federal government	1.4	3.5	2.4	3.9	3.0	3.5	120.7	25.8
Multiple types	2.5	6.4	5.5	8.8	10.1	11.6	302.9	83.2
Other	2.8	7.0	6.7	10.7	7.1	8.1	156.7	5.3

(amounts in billions of constant FY 94 dollars)

Ultimate recipient	FY 80 Amount	FY 80 Percent	FY 90 Amount	FY 90 Percent	FY 94[1] Amount	FY 94[1] Percent	Percent change, FY 80 to FY 94[1]	Percent change, FY 90 to FY 94[1]
Total	$71.6	100.0	$71.9	100.0	$87.6	100.0	22.4	21.8
Local education agencies	19.9	27.8	15.9	22.1	20.0	22.9	0.6	25.9
State education agencies	2.5	3.5	3.7	5.2	5.0	5.7	97.7	33.2
College students[2]	16.6	23.2	12.1	16.8	15.2	17.4	−8.3	26.1
Institutions of higher education	20.4	28.6	23.4	32.5	27.1	30.9	32.6	15.9
Federal government	2.5	3.5	2.8	3.9	3.0	3.5	21.4	9.9
Multiple types	4.6	6.4	6.3	8.8	10.1	11.6	121.6	60.1
Other	5.0	7.0	7.7	10.7	7.1	8.1	41.2	−8.0

SOURCE: U.S. Department of Education, National Center for Education Statistics, compiled from data appearing in U.S. Office of Management and Budget, *Budget of the United States Government*, FYs 1982-1995; National Science Foundation, *Federal Funds for Research and Development*, FYs 1980-1994; unpublished data obtained from various federal agencies; and U.S. Department of Education, Office of Management and Budget, unpublished data.
NOTE: Excludes estimated federal tax expenditures. Percentages are based on unrounded numbers. Because of rounding, details may not add to totals.
1. Estimated.
2. This includes estimated off-campus spending by students.

dent body in the future were daunting for higher education leaders. Research conducted in the early 1990s indicated that by the turn of the century students would likely be older, non-Anglo, poorer both financially and educationally, and limited in numbers. Changes in the composition of students on campus signified many challenges for college and university leaders. Student enrollment forecasts in several southern and western states were formidable. Issues of resource constraint, accountability, and outcomes all emerged as important when predicting the financial stability of the institution. Both student and institutional factors interacted to create an evolving dynamic that has resulted in the diminished support of postsecondary education in the mid-1990s.

Demographic Projections

The student body attending higher education institutions across the country have experienced dramatic changes heading for the end of the 20th century. Garcia (1994) contends that the changing composition of the student bodies may be responsible for lengthening the actual time necessary to complete a baccalaureate degree program and commensurably increase the cost of education.

The percentage of the population classified as white declined relative to the percentage of people of color due to low birth rates among whites and changing immigration patterns (Renner, 1993, p. 44). Population projections indicated that in the period from 1985 to 2000 the nation's youth population would rise by 2.4 million Hispanics, 1.7 million blacks, 483,000 other ethnic children, and only 60,000 Caucasians (Hodgkinson, 1990, p. 12). By the year 2000, whites are projected to compose a little more than two thirds of the pool of college applicants, blacks 17%, Hispanics 12%, and Asians about 4% (Levine, 1990, p. 26).

The early 1990s saw the socioeconomic status and family backgrounds of students entering higher education also shifting. More and more children were being born into poverty. Hodgkinson (1990) reported that almost 15 million children were growing up in single-parent homes. Hispanics and blacks, the largest of the nonwhite groups, had the highest rates of poverty and the lowest rates of educational attainment (Levine, 1990).

By the mid-1990s, the number of traditional age students entering postsecondary education, those in the 18- to 24-year-old cohort, had declined while the population of students over the age of 25 was growing significantly. In 1994, O'Connor reported that about 43% of all college students were age 25 or older. The number of students over the age of 30 more than doubled in the period from 1974 to 1994, and growth of 16% is projected by the year 2000, with growth in the traditional student group projected to remain constant (O'Connor, 1994, p. 84). Primarily women and minorities comprised the adult learner population.

Demographic information indicates that approaching the year 2000, students are likely to be older, non-Anglo, and poorer both financially and educationally. The lower socioeconomic status of students coupled with changes in financial aid policies and a shift from grants to loans have made it necessary for many student to work, either full- or part-time, often interrupting or delaying degree attainment. The proportion of students in four-year institutions attending part-time increased from 26.7% in 1970 to 31.4% in 1989 (Tinto, 1993). However, this trend is expected to decline into the year 2000 (see Table 1.4). At the start of the 1990s, demographic information indicated changes in racial and ethnic composition, socioeconomic status and family background, age, and gender of the student body.

While the demographics of the student body attending higher education will continue to change, total enrollment is expected to increase through the year 2005. High-end projections for enrollment growth in all institutions of higher education expect the student population to exceed 16 million by the year 2005 (see Table 1.4). The largest growth in public-supported higher education is anticipated in the four-year institutions (8.8% growth for 1994 to 2005), whereas two-year schools will grow at approximately 7.6% for the same period. Private undergraduate education will grow at 10.9% (see Tables 1.5 through 1.8).

The Economic Effects on Education

In addition to demographic projections, the changing economics of higher education have had a strong effect on students' decisions to

TABLE 1.4 Total Enrollment in All Institutions of Higher Education, by Sex, Attendance Status, and Control of Institution, With Alternative Projections: 50 States and Washington, D.C., Fall 1980 to Fall 2005 (in thousands)

Year	Total	Sex		Attendance status		Control	
		Men	Women	Full-time	Part-time	Public	Private
1980	12,097	5,874	6,223	7,098	4,999	9,457	2,640
1981	12,372	5,975	6,397	7,181	5,190	9,647	2,725
1982	12,426	6,031	6,394	7,221	5,205	9,696	2,730
1983	12,465	6,024	6,441	7,261	5,204	9,683	2,782
1984	12,242	5,864	6,378	7,098	5,144	9,477	2,765
1985	12,247	5,818	6,429	7,075	5,172	9,479	2,768
1986	12,504	5,885	6,619	7,120	5,384	9,714	2,790
1987	12,767	5,932	6,835	7,231	5,536	9,973	2,793
1988	13,055	6,002	7,053	7,437	5,619	10,161	2,894
1989	13,539	6,190	7,349	7,661	5,878	10,578	2,961
1990	13,820	6,284	7,535	7,821	5,998	10,845	2,975
1991	14,359	6,502	7,857	8,115	6,244	11,310	3,049
1992	14,492	6,526	7,966	8,167	6,325	11,389	3,103
1993 *	14,762	6,643	8,119	8,220	6,542	11,569	3,193
Middle alternative projections							
1994	14,889	6,669	8,220	8,212	6,677	11,675	3,214
1995	15,159	6,705	8,454	8,388	6,771	11,883	3,276
1996	15,006	6,699	8,307	8,198	6,808	11,779	3,227
1997	15,090	6,737	8,353	8,240	6,850	11,850	3,240
1998	15,192	6,780	8,412	8,327	6,865	11,931	3,261
1999	15,352	6,859	8,493	8,467	6,885	12,055	3,297
2000	15,522	6,948	8,574	8,624	6,898	12,187	3,335
2001	15,665	7,028	8,637	8,755	6,910	12,296	3,369
2002	15,796	7,111	8,685	8,879	6,917	12,396	3,400
2003	15,848	7,165	8,683	8,930	6,918	12,435	3,413
2004	15,976	7,231	8,745	9,053	6,923	12,529	3,447
2005	16,077	7,300	8,777	9,149	6,928	12,607	3,470
Low alternative projections							
1994	14,329	6,416	7,913	7,950	6,379	11,232	3,097
1995	14,439	6,387	8,052	8,074	6,365	11,311	3,128
1996	14,246	6,381	7,865	7,898	6,348	11,172	3,074
1997	14,295	6,410	7,885	7,943	6,352	11,212	3,083
1998	14,427	6,483	7,944	8,069	6,358	11,312	3,115
1999	14,582	6,553	8,029	8,216	6,366	11,433	3,149
2000	14,747	6,646	8,101	8,374	6,373	11,557	3,190
2001	14,888	6,720	8,168	8,513	6,375	11,664	3,224
2002	15,010	6,802	8,208	8,637	6,373	11,754	3,256
2003	15,079	6,847	8,232	8,709	6,370	11,805	3,274
2004	15,163	6,897	8,266	8,798	6,365	11,868	3,295
2005	15,251	6,955	8,296	8,884	6,367	11,934	3,317
High alternative projections							
1994	15,431	6,853	8,578	8,505	6,926	12,101	3,330
1995	15,589	6,933	8,656	8,533	7,056	12,233	3,356
1996	15,627	6,956	8,671	8,542	7,085	12,265	3,362
1997	15,705	7,011	8,694	8,592	7,113	12,330	3,375
1998	15,815	7,068	8,747	8,685	7,130	12,417	3,398
1999	15,980	7,140	8,840	8,836	7,144	12,545	3,435
2000	16,150	7,232	8,918	8,992	7,158	12,675	3,475
2001	16,307	7,311	8,996	9,134	7,173	12,795	3,512
2002	16,444	7,394	9,050	9,262	7,182	12,898	3,546
2003	16,525	7,450	9,075	9,340	7,185	12,958	3,567
2004	16,630	7,516	9,114	9,439	7,191	13,035	3,595
2005	16,726	7,584	9,142	9,529	7,197	13,109	3,617

SOURCE: U.S. Department of Education, National Center for Education Statistics, "Fall Enrollment in Colleges and Universities" surveys and "Integrated Postsecondary Education Data System (PEDS)" surveys. (Table was prepared August 1994.)
NOTE: Projections are based on data through 1992. Because of rounding, details may not add to totals.
*Projected.

attend college and the financing of higher education. The late 1980s and 1990s were a difficult time for higher education and its relationship with the public. Colleges and universities experienced significant

TABLE 1.5 Total Enrollment in Two-Year Institutions of Higher Education, by Sex, Attendance Status, and Control of Institution, With Alternative Projections: 50 States and Washington, D.C., Fall 1980 to Fall 2005 (in thousands)

Year	Total	Sex		Attendance status		Control	
		Men	Women	Full-time	Part-time	Public	Private
1980	4,526	2,047	2,479	1,754	2,772	4,329	198
1981	4,716	2,124	2,591	1,796	2,919	4,481	236
1982	4,772	2,170	2,602	1,840	2,932	4,520	252
1983	4,723	2,131	2,592	1,827	2,897	4,459	264
1984	4,531	2,017	2,514	1,704	2,827	4,279	252
1985	4,531	2,002	2,529	1,691	2,840	4,270	261
1986	4,680	2,061	2,619	1,696	2,983	4,414	266
1987	4,776	2,073	2,703	1,709	3,068	4,541	235
1988	4,875	2,090	2,785	1,744	3,132	4,615	260
1989	5,151	2,217	2,934	1,856	3,295	4,884	267
1990	5,240	2,233	3,007	1,884	3,356	4,996	244
1991	5,652	2,402	3,250	2,075	3,577	5,405	247
1992	5,724	2,414	3,310	2,083	3,641	5,486	238
1993 *	5,689	2,379	3,310	2,034	3,655	5,434	255
			Middle alternative projections				
1994	5,763	2,394	3,369	2,037	3,726	5,506	257
1995	5,856	2,412	3,444	2,080	3,776	5,594	262
1996	5,844	2,419	3,425	2,048	3,796	5,585	259
1997	5,889	2,442	3,447	2,070	3,819	5,628	261
1998	5,928	2,462	3,466	2,096	3,832	5,664	264
1999	5,983	2,491	3,492	2,135	3,848	5,715	268
2000	6,037	2,521	3,516	2,176	3,861	5,766	271
2001	6,078	2,545	3,533	2,206	3,872	5,804	274
2002	6,115	2,570	3,545	2,235	3,880	5,839	276
2003	6,124	2,585	3,539	2,241	3,883	5,847	277
2004	6,158	2,606	3,552	2,269	3,889	5,878	280
2005	6,190	2,630	3,560	2,295	3,895	5,908	282
			Low alternative projections				
1994	5,536	2,309	3,227	1,979	3,557	5,288	248
1995	5,555	2,302	3,253	2,009	3,546	5,304	251
1996	5,519	2,305	3,214	1,982	3,537	5,272	247
1997	5,542	2,319	3,223	2,003	3,539	5,293	249
1998	5,581	2,340	3,241	2,036	3,545	5,329	252
1999	5,635	2,366	3,269	2,080	3,555	5,378	257
2000	5,684	2,395	3,289	2,120	3,564	5,422	262
2001	5,719	2,413	3,306	2,150	3,569	5,455	264
2002	5,750	2,435	3,315	2,178	3,572	5,483	267
2003	5,762	2,445	3,317	2,190	3,572	5,495	267
2004	5,782	2,459	3,323	2,209	3,573	5,513	269
2005	5,807	2,477	3,330	2,232	3,575	5,536	271
			High alternative projections				
1994	5,972	2,452	3,520	2,101	3,871	5,707	265
1995	6,059	2,488	3,571	2,114	3,945	5,791	268
1996	6,085	2,504	3,581	2,125	3,960	5,816	269
1997	6,126	2,534	3,592	2,150	3,976	5,854	272
1998	6,166	2,555	3,611	2,178	3,988	5,892	274
1999	6,222	2,581	3,641	2,220	4,002	5,944	278
2000	6,275	2,610	3,665	2,260	4,015	5,993	282
2001	6,319	2,632	3,687	2,291	4,028	6,035	284
2002	6,356	2,656	3,700	2,319	4,037	6,069	287
2003	6,373	2,670	3,703	2,332	4,041	6,085	288
2004	6,400	2,689	3,711	2,352	4,048	6,109	291
2005	6,427	2,711	3,716	2,374	4,053	6,135	292

SOURCE: U.S. Department of Education, National Center for Education Statistics, "Fall Enrollment in Colleges and Universities" surveys and "Integrated Postsecondary Education Data System (PEDS)" surveys. (Table was prepared August 1994.)
NOTE: Projections are based on data through 1992. Because of rounding, details may not add to totals.
*Projected.

tuition increases. With these tuition increases, however, higher education did not see a commensurate growth in financial aid. Colleges and universities charged higher prices with no noticeable change in the

TABLE 1.6 Total Enrollment in Four-Year Institutions of Higher Education, by Sex, Attendance Status, and Control of Institution, With Alternative Projections: 50 States and Washington, D.C., Fall 1980 to Fall 2005 (in thousands)

Year	Total	Sex		Attendance status		Control	
		Men	Women	Full-time	Part-time	Public	Private
1980	7,571	3,827	3,743	5,344	2,226	5,129	2,442
1981	7,655	3,852	3,805	5,387	2,270	5,166	2,489
1982	7,654	3,861	3,793	5,381	2,273	5,176	2,478
1983	7,741	3,893	3,849	5,434	2,307	5,223	2,518
1984	7,711	3,847	3,864	5,395	2,317	5,198	2,513
1985	7,716	3,816	3,900	5,385	2,331	5,210	2,506
1986	7,824	3,824	4,000	5,423	2,401	5,300	2,524
1987	7,990	3,859	4,131	5,522	2,468	5,432	2,558
1988	8,180	3,912	4,268	5,693	2,487	5,546	2,634
1989	8,388	3,973	4,414	5,805	2,582	5,694	2,693
1990	8,579	4,052	4,528	5,937	2,642	5,848	2,731
1991	8,707	4,100	4,607	6,041	2,666	5,905	2,802
1992	8,768	4,112	4,656	6,084	2,684	5,903	2,865
1993 *	9,073	4,264	4,809	6,186	2,887	6,135	2,938
				Middle alternative projections			
1994	9,126	4,275	4,851	6,175	2,951	6,169	2,957
1995	9,303	4,293	5,010	6,308	2,995	6,289	3,014
1996	9,162	4,280	4,882	6,150	3,012	6,194	2,968
1997	9,201	4,295	4,906	6,170	3,031	6,222	2,979
1998	9,264	4,318	4,946	6,231	3,033	6,267	2,997
1999	9,369	4,368	5,001	6,332	3,037	6,340	3,029
2000	9,485	4,427	5,058	6,448	3,037	6,421	3,064
2001	9,587	4,483	5,104	6,549	3,038	6,492	3,095
2002	9,681	4,541	5,140	6,644	3,037	6,557	3,124
2003	9,724	4,580	5,144	6,689	3,035	6,588	3,136
2004	9,818	4,625	5,193	6,784	3,034	6,651	3,167
2005	9,887	4,670	5,217	6,854	3,033	6,699	3,188
				Low alternative projections			
1994	8,793	4,107	4,686	5,971	2,822	5,944	2,849
1995	8,884	4,085	4,799	6,065	2,819	6,007	2,877
1996	8,727	4,076	4,651	5,916	2,811	5,900	2,827
1997	8,753	4,091	4,662	5,940	2,813	5,919	2,834
1998	8,846	4,143	4,703	6,033	2,813	5,983	2,863
1999	8,947	4,187	4,760	6,136	2,811	6,055	2,892
2000	9,063	4,251	4,812	6,254	2,809	6,135	2,928
2001	9,169	4,307	4,862	6,363	2,806	6,209	2,960
2002	9,260	4,367	4,893	6,459	2,801	6,271	2,989
2003	9,317	4,402	4,915	6,519	2,798	6,310	3,007
2004	9,381	4,438	4,943	6,589	2,792	6,355	3,026
2005	9,444	4,478	4,966	6,652	2,792	6,398	3,046
				High alternative projections			
1994	9,459	4,401	5,058	6,404	3,055	6,394	3,065
1995	9,530	4,445	5,085	6,419	3,111	6,442	3,088
1996	9,542	4,452	5,090	6,417	3,125	6,449	3,093
1997	9,579	4,477	5,102	6,442	3,137	6,476	3,103
1998	9,649	4,513	5,136	6,507	3,142	6,525	3,124
1999	9,758	4,559	5,199	6,616	3,142	6,601	3,157
2000	9,875	4,622	5,253	6,732	3,143	6,682	3,193
2001	9,988	4,679	5,309	6,843	3,145	6,760	3,228
2002	10,088	4,738	5,350	6,943	3,145	6,829	3,259
2003	10,152	4,780	5,372	7,008	3,144	6,873	3,279
2004	10,230	4,827	5,403	7,087	3,143	6,926	3,304
2005	10,299	4,873	5,426	7,155	3,144	6,974	3,325

SOURCE: U.S. Department of Education, National Center for Education Statistics, "Fall Enrollment in Colleges and Universities" surveys and "Integrated Postsecondary Education Data System (PEDS)" surveys. (Table was prepared August 1994.)
NOTE: Projections are based on data through 1992. Because of rounding, details may not add to totals.
*Projected.

services provided, causing the American public to become skeptical of higher education's objectives and the efficiency with which institu-

TABLE 1.7   Undergraduate Enrollment in Public Institutions, by Sex and Attendance Status, With Alternate Projections: 50 States and Washington, D.C., Fall 1980 to Fall 2005 (in thousands)

Year	Total	Men Full-time	Men Part-time	Women Full-time	Women Part-time
1980	8,441	2,426	1,588	2,334	2,093
1981	8,648	2,452	1,639	2,373	2,185
1982	8,713	2,487	1,653	2,373	2,201
1983	8,697	2,482	1,635	2,385	2,195
1984	8,494	2,390	1,600	2,325	2,179
1985	8,478	2,357	1,596	2,331	2,193
1986	8,661	2,351	1,652	2,367	2,291
1987	8,919	2,375	1,701	2,449	2,393
1988	9,103	2,399	1,714	2,550	2,439
1989	9,488	2,470	1,801	2,663	2,553
1990	9,710	2,527	1,826	2,734	2,623
1991	10,148	2,610	1,921	2,851	2,766
1992	10,220	2,603	1,936	2,885	2,796
1993 *	10,313	2,624	1,947	2,861	2,881
			Middle alternative projections		
1994	10,396	2,613	1,972	2,859	2,952
1995	10,594	2,620	1,990	2,984	3,000
1996	10,491	2,610	2,001	2,865	3,015
1997	10,562	2,629	2,016	2,888	3,029
1998	10,646	2,659	2,024	2,929	3,034
1999	10,773	2,712	2,035	2,984	3,042
2000	10,907	2,775	2,044	3,041	3,047
2001	11,020	2,831	2,051	3,086	3,052
2002	11,122	2,887	2,060	3,122	3,053
2003	11,167	2,920	2,068	3,130	3,049
2004	11,254	2,960	2,077	3,171	3,046
2005	11,330	3,000	2,089	3,199	3,042
			Low alternative projections		
1994	10,005	2,515	1,900	2,788	2,802
1995	10,089	2,500	1,895	2,900	2,794
1996	9,956	2,502	1,892	2,779	2,783
1997	10,000	2,526	1,894	2,798	2,782
1998	10,100	2,578	1,896	2,840	2,786
1999	10,226	2,635	1,899	2,900	2,792
2000	10,351	2,700	1,904	2,952	2,795
2001	10,460	2,757	1,905	2,999	2,799
2002	10,552	2,815	1,908	3,031	2,798
2003	10,604	2,846	1,911	3,051	2,796
2004	10,666	2,881	1,914	3,078	2,793
2005	10,730	2,918	1,920	3,102	2,790
			High alternative projections		
1994	10,776	2,689	2,015	2,973	3,099
1995	10,891	2,713	2,048	2,968	3,162
1996	10,923	2,714	2,065	2,981	3,163
1997	10,987	2,739	2,085	3,001	3,162
1998	11,075	2,777	2,092	3,037	3,169
1999	11,206	2,829	2,099	3,101	3,177
2000	11,336	2,891	2,107	3,154	3,184
2001	11,458	2,945	2,114	3,207	3,192
2002	11,562	2,998	2,123	3,247	3,194
2003	11,618	3,030	2,131	3,266	3,191
2004	11,693	3,067	2,140	3,296	3,190
2005	11,762	3,105	2,151	3,320	3,186

SOURCE: U.S. Department of Education, National Center for Education Statistics, "Fall Enrollment in Colleges and Universities" surveys and "Integrated Postsecondary Education Data System (PEDS)" surveys. (Table was prepared August 1994.)
NOTE: Projections are based on data through 1992. Because of rouding, details may not add to totals.
*Projected.

tions fulfilled these objectives. Two themes received increased attention in American higher education: institutional accountability and educational quality. State legislatures challenged public institutions

TABLE 1.8 Undergraduate Enrollment in Private Institutions, by Sex and Attendance Status, With Alternate Projections: 50 States and Washington, D.C., Fall 1980 to Fall 2005 (in thousands)

Year	Total	Men		Women	
		Full-time	Part-time	Full-time	Part-time
1980	2,033	800	185	801	246
1981	2,106	809	209	816	272
1982	2,112	812	219	811	270
1983	2,149	823	219	824	283
1984	2,124	805	212	827	280
1985	2,120	800	210	832	278
1986	2,137	796	219	839	284
1987	2,128	788	204	850	286
1988	2,213	807	217	886	304
1989	2,255	808	231	899	316
1990	2,250	810	217	905	317
1991	2,291	825	215	935	316
1992	2,320	823	222	937	338
1993 *	2,373	844	233	945	351
			Middle alternative projections		
1994	2,379	840	237	942	360
1995	2,435	841	240	987	367
1996	2,389	838	240	943	368
1997	2,403	842	242	950	369
1998	2,426	851	243	963	369
1999	2,465	869	244	983	369
2000	2,504	888	244	1,003	369
2001	2,541	907	245	1,019	370
2002	2,571	925	245	1,032	369
2003	2,589	937	246	1,037	369
2004	2,617	950	248	1,050	369
2005	2,639	963	249	1,059	368
			Low alternative projections		
1994	2,296	807	228	919	342
1995	2,330	801	228	960	341
1996	2,282	801	227	915	339
1997	2,293	807	227	921	338
1998	2,324	824	227	935	338
1999	2,363	842	227	955	339
2000	2,404	863	228	974	339
2001	2,440	882	228	991	339
2002	2,472	902	228	1,003	339
2003	2,490	912	229	1,010	339
2004	2,511	924	229	1,020	338
2005	2,530	935	229	1,028	338
			High alternative projections		
1994	2,467	865	242	982	378
1995	2,482	872	246	979	385
1996	2,487	871	248	983	385
1997	2,501	878	250	988	385
1998	2,525	889	251	1,000	385
1999	2,564	906	251	1,022	385
2000	2,603	926	251	1,041	385
2001	2,641	944	252	1,059	386
2002	2,676	963	253	1,074	386
2003	2,694	973	253	1,082	386
2004	2,719	986	255	1,093	385
2005	2,738	997	256	1,100	385

SOURCE: U.S. Department of Education, National Center for Education Statistics, "Fall Enrollment in Colleges and Universities" surveys and "Integrated Postsecondary Education Data System (PEDS)" surveys. (Table was prepared August 1994.)
NOTE: Projections are based on data through 1992. Because of rounding, details may not add to totals.
*Projected.

with new performance-based accountability demands. Heavy competition with other government agencies for state funding made it necessary for colleges and universities across the country to demonstrate to lawmakers the value of an education to both the individual and to society. With high tuition charges and decreased financial aid, students and parents needed information on both the economic value of an education and how colleges and universities spent the funds allocated to them.

Recent discussion of the value of an education has focused on costs and benefits. The individual and the public have a clear understanding of the financial investments and sacrifices committed to higher education. Indeed, the cost side of the equation gained a great deal of attention in the early part of the decade of the 1990s. During this time period, as the job market became increasingly competitive and employment prospects for college graduates were bleak, both the individual and society questioned their investment in education, and pressure mounted for the benefits of this investment to be better articulated. Productivity demands by policy makers and the public meant the higher education institutions had to make adjustments to increase financial and educational yields on taxpayers' investments.

Alexander (1993) stated that the benefits of education

> may be broadly categorized as anything which (a) increases production through income in the capacity of the labor force, (b) increases efficiency by reducing unnecessary costs, thereby reserving resources for the enhancement of human productivity—for example the release of public resources from law enforcement to more productive pursuits—and (c) increases the social consciousness of the community so living conditions are enhanced. (p. 86)

In general, the explanations of the value of an education can be divided into four basic categories:

- Economic value expressed as monetary value to the individual
- Economic value expressed as monetary value to society
- Social value expressed as skills, sensitivities, and knowledge provided to the individual
- Social value as a contribution to the efficient functioning of society.

These four explanations frequently overlap as do the benefits associated with education, and they often drive decisions concerning attendance made by students and their parents.

Monetary Value of Higher
Education to the Individual

There are three ways to estimate the monetary yield of a college education to the individual: earnings differentials; the net present value of a college education (the present value of a college education after costs are subtracted and corrections are made to adjust for the changing value of money over time); and traditionally calculated private rates of return (Becker & Lewis, 1992; Leslie & Brinkman, 1988).

The earnings differentials concept has been identified as the most rudimentary approach for estimating the pecuniary value of a college education. The earnings measure indicates how much more, on average, a college graduate earned than other individuals with less education. This measure has been used because it is easy to calculate and generally less contentious than more complex measures. A drawback to the earnings differentials is that the measure identifies only benefits and omits costs. Because of this, earnings differentials are of little value when comparing the yield on an investment in education with other investment alternatives. The measure also fails to account for preexisting differences between college attendees and nonattendees.

Despite the weaknesses of this measure, it is widely used as a method for quantifying the value of a college education to the individual. In 1972, the income per year of male high school graduates averaged $10,433 in comparison to the average yearly income of $16,201 for male college graduates (Alexander, 1993). Comparative data reveal the mean annual income for male high school graduates in 1939 was about 60% of the mean annual income for male college graduates—a percentage that had not changed significantly by 1972. In 1983, the median income of college graduates was more than $6,000 greater than the median income of high school graduates for males aged 25-34 (Leslie & Brinkman, 1988). Further, it was noted that, although education did not pay as well for black males or for women, all groups realized a substantial rise in income with progressive education. The ratio of median college to high school graduate earnings stood at 1.47 for white males, 1.94 for white females, 1.76 for black males, and 2.04 for black females in 1990 (Becker & Lewis, 1992).

Net present value (NPV) is a second measure for quantifying the economic value of an education to the individual. NPV estimates the present value of an education by subtracting costs from benefits adjusted to reflect the changing value of a dollar over time. For example, based on 1979 data, the benefits of education for male college graduates relative to high school graduates were $60,000, net of forgone earnings. This research also revealed that for males the present value of benefits exceeds the present value of costs by $23,000; for females, the difference was only $7,000. A dollar investment in four years of college yields, on average, $1.62 for men and $1.19 for women in benefits (Cohn & Geske, 1990).

One drawback to net present value analysis is the sensitivity of the measure to discount rate selection. Questions often arose as to the determination of the discount rate and whether the real or nominal interest rate was a better measure. A slight change in the magnitude of the discount rate has produced large changes in the size of the net present value. Higher lifetime earnings are indicated when a person completes more years of schooling and a lower discount rate is chosen.

By the mid-1990s, the internal rate of return was the most broadly used measure for estimating the value of an education. This measure relates total resource costs of education to income benefits and was derived by projecting a lifetime stream of earnings and the costs of attendance. Costs, corrected to current dollars, are used in calculating the interest or discount rate that sets the earnings value equal to the cost value. The internal rate of return is the discount rate at which the net present value calculation equals zero. The net present value analysis is heavily influenced by discount rate selection; this measure is not. Additionally, the internal rate of return is more widely understood by the general public. Rate of return measures are highly sensitive to cost fluctuations. Because of this, private rates of return to elementary and secondary education are much higher than those to postsecondary education due to the relatively low costs to the individual associated with K-12 schooling and the reduced forgone earnings resulting from the earlier return to the workforce. In 1990, it was reported that the private rate of return for four years of higher education to be between

10% and 15%. The private rate of return was somewhat higher for white males than it was for females and African Americans (Cohn & Geske, 1990).

Monetary Benefits of Higher Education to Society

Three methods are commonly used in the calculation of the economic benefits of education to society: the social rate of return, growth accounting studies that assess the percentages of national income growth derived from education, and economic impact studies.

Social rates of return are calculated in the same way as private rates of return. This measure differs from the private rate of return in that it uses costs to society for supplying educational services in the calculation. These costs, in most cases, are specified as the educational and general (E&G) expenditures of institutions plus all or part of the student's forgone earnings. E&G expenditures have grown consistently over the past 15 years. In 1980, E&G expenditures were $44 billion, or approximately $10,993 per full-time-equivalent student. Recent projections indicate that E&G expenditures will exceed $92 billion, or $17,234 per full-time student, by the year 2004 (see Table 1.9). Because benefits are assessed by the pretax wages and earnings a student accrues over one's lifetime, the rate of increase of E&G expenditures would have a negative effect on the rate of return calculation.

Social rates of return are often used to guide policy makers as they make decisions concerning fiscal allocations. Over time, social rates of return have typically been a few percentage points below private rates of return because of the manner in which higher education is subsidized; students pay only a fraction of the total costs of educating them, and the remainder is borne by society.

A variety of studies found social rates of return to range from 11% to 15% during the period 1965-1990. The drawbacks to the social rate of return analysis is that the measure excludes both monetary benefits that spill over to others and all nonmonetary benefits of education. The interpretation of social rates of return presents similar limitations to private rates of return and is also highly sensitive to costs.

TABLE 1.9 Educational and General Expenditures and Educational and General Expenditures per Full-Time-Equivalent (FTE) Student of Public Four-Year Institutions, With Alternative Projections: 50 States and Washington, D.C., 1979-1980 to 2004-2005

Year ending	Full-time-equivalent enrollment (in thousands)	Current-fund expenditures			
		Constant 1992–93 dollars[1]		Current dollars	
		Total (in billions)	Per student in FTE	Total (in billions)	Per student in FTE
1980	4,059	$44.6	$10,993	$24.3	$5,985
1981	4,158	44.6	10,723	27.1	6,515
1982	4,209	44.5	10,579	29.4	6,986
1983	4,221	45.6	10,796	31.4	7,434
1984	4,266	47.3	11,087	33.8	7,917
1985	4,238	50.3	11,859	37.3	8,800
1986	4,240	53.2	12,545	40.6	9,580
1987	4,295	55.7	12,976	43.5	10,130
1988	4,396	57.8	13,143	47.0	10,686
1989	4,506	59.7	13,252	50.8	11,270
1990	4,620	62.1	13,433	55.3	11,968
1991	4,740	63.1	13,302	59.3	12,504
1992	4,796	64.2	13,392	62.3	12,988
1993[2]	4,800	66.1	13,769	66.1	13,769
1994[2]	4,935	67.8	13,747	69.7	14,116
Middle alternative projections					
1994	4,942	70.0	14,155	74.1	14,998
1995	5,044	72.2	14,304	79.1	15,676
1996	4,942	74.4	15,062	84.4	17,074
1997	4,962	76.7	15,464	90.1	18,162
1998	5,006	78.9	15,758	96.0	19,184
1999	5,077	81.1	15,969	—	—
2000	5,158	83.2	16,135	—	—
2001	5,230	85.3	16,319	—	—
2002	5,294	87.5	16,520	—	—
2003	5,326	89.6	16,827	—	—
2004	5,390	91.9	17,041	—	—
Low alternative projections					
1994	4,942	69.9	14,152	74.7	15,115
1995	5,044	71.9	14,249	80.6	15,970
1996	4,942	74.0	14,967	87.2	17,643
1997	4,962	76.2	15,366	94.6	19,062
1998	5,006	78.4	15,656	102.4	20,455
1999	5,077	80.5	15,856	—	—
2000	5,158	82.6	16,015	—	—
2001	5,230	84.7	16,198	—	—
2002	5,294	86.8	16,399	—	—
2003	5,326	89.0	16,705	—	—
2004	5,390	91.2	16,916	—	—
High alternative projections					
1994	4,942	70.0	14,158	73.9	14,952
1995	5,044	72.5	14,369	78.8	15,614
1996	4,942	75.0	15,177	83.8	16,952
1997	4,962	77.3	15,585	88.9	17,919
1998	5,006	79.5	15,891	94.3	18,836
1999	5,077	81.8	16,113	—	—
2000	5,158	84.0	16,293	—	—
2001	5,230	86.2	16,484	—	—
2002	5,294	88.4	16,694	—	—
2003	5,326	90.6	17,008	—	—
2004	5,390	92.9	17,234	—	—

SOURCE: U.S. Department of Education, National Center for Education Statistics, "Financial Statistics of Institutions of Higher Education" and "Fall Enrollment in Colleges and Universities" surveys. (Table was prepared September 1994.)
NOTE: Projections in current dollars are not shown after 1999 due to the uncertain behavior over the long term.
1. Based on the Consumer Price Index for all urban consumers (from Bureau of Labor Statistics, U.S. Department of Labor).
2. Projected.

One approach to overcoming the benefits omissions of social rate of return studies is to analyze the proportion of economic gain attributable to higher education and related activities. National income growth is used as the dependent variable and classic measures of production—land, labor, and capital—as the independent variable. Educational outlays are treated as influencing a portion of labor's contribution to the national economy's growth. Again, various studies reveal estimates generally in the 15%-20% range, with approximately one fourth of this economic growth assigned to education. In 1992, it was reported that although higher education directly connected to only 4%-5% of the national income growth it was probably indirectly linked to another 20%-40% of this growth (Becker & Lewis, 1992).

Economic impact studies are designed to measure the increase in a region's economic activity attributable to the presence of a college or university. Economic impact studies are viewed as studies of externalities because they draw attention to the value added by colleges to their communities to prove the social benefits to education. Economic impact studies traditionally have examined short-term benefits of higher education but not the long-term quantifiable investment benefits of education.

The traditional method of economic impact assessment was developed by Caffrey and Isaacs in 1971 and rests on the economic base approach. Studies that modeled the Caffrey and Isaacs framework isolated economic gains attributable to the presence of a college or university. These analyses attempted to factor out consumption activities that merely recycled community funds and focused on economic gains represented by the export of goods and services in exchange for outside revenues.

Using the Caffrey and Isaacs framework, economic impact studies assess the impact of postsecondary institutions on three regional components: local business, local government, and local individuals. The major analytical task of these studies was to distinguish between expenditures representing actual gains to the local economy and those that were recycled funds. Economic impact studies of this nature have ignored long-range economic impacts such as the enhancement of workers' skills and the relationship between research and local industry.

Despite these shortcomings, economic impact studies are widely used to highlight higher education's economic contributions to society. For community colleges, the type of institution most frequently considered in an economic impact assessment, studies revealed that the mean business volume to college budget ratio was 1.6 and the jobs created to budget ratio, in millions of dollars, was about 55, expressed in 1988-1989 dollars for the period 1985-1986. This meant that a community college annual budget of $10 million generated $16 million in business volume and created 550 jobs in 1988-1989. For four-year institutions in the same time period, the business volume to budget ratio was 1.8 and the jobs to budget ratio, in millions of dollars, was 53% (Becker & Lewis, 1992; Leslie & Brinkman, 1988).

An alternative approach to economic impact studies focuses on input-output analysis and uses information about transactions with local industries. A regional input-output model was "designed to estimate the indirect impact of properly and carefully specified direct or initial impact experienced in one or more industry sectors within a region" (Goldstein, 1990, p. 53). For example, this method was used to estimate the impact of the University of North Carolina at Chapel Hill's sponsored research budget on the state. It was concluded that for fiscal year 1983 the university's total sponsored research funds of $52.5 million resulted in $26.6 million in direct in-state expenditures and in $26.8 million in indirect and induced expenditure in the state economy, yielding a total output impact of $53.4 million. The drawbacks to this type of economic impact analysis are the time and costs associated because of the enormous data requirements and the failure to account for the nonmonetary stimulus that colleges and universities provide to local economies.

Current Institutional Revenue and Expenditure Patterns

In the 1980s, American higher education enjoyed a substantial increase in its revenues from each of the major sources of revenues: state and local funding, tuition and fees, annual gifts and endowment income, and federal funds. The increase in revenue resulted in increased expenditures for all higher education from $104.5 billion in 1980 to an estimated $151 billion in 1990 (in constant 1992 dollars; see Table 1.10). The seeming intent of colleges and universities to maximize revenues in the 1980s from any and all sources contributed to the erosion of public trust and confidence in American higher education and set the stage for the push on accountability and the careful scrutiny of resource allocation that occurred in the 1990s. Postsecondary education leaders focused on increasing quality by spending more instead of spending differently, creating the public perception that program quality and student learning had not kept pace with resource increases. The increases in expenditures were most notable in the public four-year sector, which experienced a 35% growth (from $14,019 to $18,011) in per-student expenditure from 1980 to 1994, whereas two-year institutions experienced a 12.7% growth (from $5,345 to $6,028) for the same period (see Tables 1.11 and 1.12).

Hauptman (1993) suggested that the financial issues facing postsecondary institutions in the 1990s be divided into two basic questions:

- How do colleges and universities finance themselves?
- How is the money spent?

From a financing perspective, the most pressing challenge facing public institutions during this era was what to do about state cutbacks brought about by the recession and increased competition for state resources from prisons, health care providers, K-12 education, and other state agencies.

For private institutions, the most prominent issue was the question of the limits of the high tuition/high aid strategy that worked so well in the 1980s. Students in private four-year and two-year schools depended on financial assistance to offset the high tuition charged by these institutions. Private institutions had seen the greatest increase in expenditures during the 1980s. Expenditures increased approximately 49% (from $17,009 to $25,451) per full-time student from 1980 to 1994 (see Table 1.13). Almost 70% of private school students received some form of financial assistance by 1993 (see Table 1.14). The projected decrease in tuition/student assistance from federal sources would greatly influence the ability of students to attend these schools.

The environment of limited resources and public accountability pressures on colleges and universities that surrounded higher education institutions in the early 1990s led to considerable concern over how colleges and universities spent the funds they received. Although higher education consumers were still interested in the monetary and nonmonetary returns of a college degree, more interest was focused

TABLE 1.10   Current-Fund Expenditures of Public and Private Institutions of Higher Education, With Alternative Projections: 50 States and Washington, D.C., 1979-1980 to 2004-2005

Year ending	Constant 1992–93 dollars [1] (in billions)			Current dollars (in billions)		
	Total	Public	Private	Total	Public	Private
1980	$104.5	$69.4	$35.2	$56.9	$37.8	$19.1
1981	105.4	69.6	35.8	64.1	42.3	21.8
1982	106.5	70.0	36.5	70.3	46.2	24.1
1983	110.3	72.0	38.3	75.9	49.6	26.4
1984	114.8	74.3	40.5	82.0	53.1	28.9
1985	121.2	78.6	42.6	90.0	58.3	31.6
1986	127.7	82.8	45.0	97.5	63.2	34.3
1987	135.5	86.7	48.8	105.8	67.7	38.1
1988	139.9	89.3	50.6	113.8	72.6	41.1
1989	145.7	92.8	52.8	123.9	78.9	44.9
1990	151.1	96.3	54.9	134.7	85.8	48.9
1991	155.4	98.9	56.5	146.1	93.0	53.1
1992	161.1	101.9	59.2	156.2	98.8	57.4
1993 [2]	165.8	104.5	61.3	165.8	104.5	61.3
1994 [2]	171.1	107.3	63.7	175.6	110.2	65.5
Middle alternative projections						
1995	176.0	110.3	65.7	186.5	116.9	69.6
1996	181.7	114.2	67.5	199.1	125.2	73.9
1997	186.6	116.8	69.8	211.5	132.4	79.1
1998	192.1	120.3	71.8	225.6	141.3	84.3
1999	197.5	123.6	73.9	240.4	150.5	89.9
2000	203.0	127.2	75.9	—	—	—
2001	208.5	130.6	77.8	—	—	—
2002	213.7	134.0	79.7	—	—	—
2003	218.8	137.2	81.6	—	—	—
2004	223.9	140.3	83.6	—	—	—
2005	229.4	143.7	85.7	—	—	—
Low alternative projections						
1995	175.1	110.3	64.8	187.0	117.8	69.2
1996	179.8	113.6	66.2	201.5	127.3	74.2
1997	184.1	115.7	68.4	217.1	136.4	80.6
1998	189.7	119.2	70.5	235.3	147.9	87.4
1999	194.9	122.4	72.5	254.6	160.0	94.7
2000	200.2	125.8	74.4	—	—	—
2001	205.5	129.2	76.3	—	—	—
2002	210.7	132.5	78.2	—	—	—
2003	215.8	135.7	80.1	—	—	—
2004	220.9	138.8	82.1	—	—	—
2005	226.3	142.2	84.1	—	—	—
High alternative projections						
1995	176.7	110.4	66.3	186.6	116.5	70.0
1996	183.3	115.0	68.4	199.2	124.9	74.3
1997	188.8	118.1	70.7	210.9	131.9	79.0
1998	194.5	121.7	72.8	223.6	139.9	83.7
1999	200.0	125.1	74.9	237.1	148.3	88.8
2000	205.7	128.8	76.9	—	—	—
2001	211.4	132.5	78.9	—	—	—
2002	216.8	135.9	80.9	—	—	—
2003	222.1	139.3	82.8	—	—	—
2004	227.3	142.5	84.8	—	—	—
2005	233.0	146.1	87.0	—	—	—

SOURCE: U.S. Department of Education, National Center for Education Statistics, "Financial Statistics of Institutions of Higher Education" and "Fall Enrollment in Colleges and Universities" surveys. (Table was prepared September 1994.)
NOTE: Projections in current dollars are not shown after 1999 due to the uncertain behavior over the long term.
1. Based on the Consumer Price Index for all urban consumers (from Bureau of Labor Statistics, U.S. Department of Labor).
2. Projected.

on spending patterns and how these spending patterns affected student learning and degree completion. Cost pressures affecting col-

TABLE 1.11 Current-Fund Expenditures and Current-Fund Expenditures per Full-Time-Equivalent (FTE) Student of Public Four-Year Institutions, With Alternative Projections: 50 States and Washington, D.C., 1979-1980 to 2004-2005

Year ending	Full-time-equivalent enrollment (in thousands)	Constant 1992–93 dollars [1]		Current dollars	
		Total (in billions)	Per student in FTE	Total (in billions)	Per student in FTE
1980	4,059	$56.9	$14,019	$31.0	$7,632
1981	4,158	57.1	13,726	34.7	8,339
1982	4,209	57.4	13,634	37.9	9,003
1983	4,221	59.0	13,975	40.6	9,623
1984	4,266	61.0	14,310	43.6	10,218
1985	4,238	64.7	15,269	48.0	11,330
1986	4,240	68.3	16,119	52.2	12,309
1987	4,295	71.7	16,700	56.0	13,038
1988	4,396	74.0	16,826	60.1	13,681
1989	4,506	76.8	17,054	65.3	14,503
1990	4,620	79.5	17,217	70.9	15,339
1991	4,740	81.6	17,218	76.7	16,186
1992	4,796	83.9	17,492	81.4	16,965
1993 [2]	4,800	86.1	17,938	86.1	17,938
1994 [2]	4,935	88.9	18,011	91.3	18,494
		Middle alternative projections			
1995	4,942	91.4	18,494	96.8	19,596
1996	5,044	94.5	18,741	103.6	20,539
1997	4,942	96.6	19,555	109.6	22,168
1998	4,962	99.4	20,039	116.8	23,536
1999	5,006	102.2	20,416	124.4	24,854
2000	5,077	105.2	20,714	—	—
2001	5,158	108.1	20,967	—	—
2002	5,230	111.1	21,235	—	—
2003	5,294	113.9	21,518	—	—
2004	5,326	116.6	21,902	—	—
2005	5,390	119.7	22,199	—	—
		Low alternative projections			
1995	4,942	91.4	18,491	97.6	19,749
1996	5,044	94.2	18,678	105.6	20,935
1997	4,942	96.1	19,447	113.3	22,925
1998	4,962	98.9	19,928	122.7	24,722
1999	5,006	101.6	20,300	132.8	26,522
2000	5,077	104.5	20,586	—	—
2001	5,158	107.4	20,831	—	—
2002	5,230	110.3	21,098	—	—
2003	5,294	113.2	21,380	—	—
2004	5,326	115.9	21,763	—	—
2005	5,390	118.9	22,057	—	—
		High alternative projections			
1995	4,942	91.4	18,498	96.5	19,535
1996	5,044	94.9	18,815	103.1	20,445
1997	4,942	97.3	19,686	108.7	21,988
1998	4,962	100.1	20,177	115.1	23,199
1999	5,006	103.0	20,567	122.0	24,378
2000	5,077	106.0	20,878	—	—
2001	5,158	109.1	21,147	—	—
2002	5,230	112.0	21,423	—	—
2003	5,294	115.0	21,716	—	—
2004	5,326	117.7	22,108	—	—
2005	5,390	120.8	22,418	—	—

SOURCE: U.S. Department of Education, National Center for Education Statistics, "Financial Statistics of Institutions of Higher Education" and "Fall Enrollment in Colleges and Universities" surveys. (Table was prepared September 1994.)
NOTE: Projections in current dollars are not shown after 1999 due to the uncertain behavior over the long term.
1. Based on the Consumer Price Index for all urban consumers (from Bureau of Labor Statistics, U.S. Department of Labor).
2. Projected.

leges and universities were students shifting into higher-cost majors, the impact of new technology, socially mandated programs, and the

TABLE 1.12   Current-Fund Expenditures and Current-Fund Expenditures per Full-Time-Equivalent (FTE) Student of Public Two-Year Institutions, With Alternative Projections: 50 States and Washington, D.C., 1979-1980 to 2004-2005

Year ending	Full-time-equivalent enrollment (in thousands)	Current-fund expenditures			
		Constant 1992-93 dollars [1]		Current dollars	
		Total (in billions)	Per student in FTE	Total (in billions)	Per student in FTE
1980	2,333	$12.5	$5,345	$6.8	$2,910
1981	2,484	12.5	5,037	7.6	3,061
1982	2,573	12.6	4,903	8.3	3,238
1983	2,630	13.0	4,946	9.0	3,406
1984	2,616	13.3	5,086	9.5	3,631
1985	2,447	13.9	5,672	10.3	4,209
1986	2,428	14.4	5,938	11.0	4,534
1987	2,483	14.9	6,012	11.7	4,693
1988	2,542	15.4	6,050	12.5	4,919
1989	2,591	16.0	6,170	13.6	5,247
1990	2,752	16.7	6,080	14.9	5,417
1991	2,818	17.3	6,130	16.2	5,763
1992	3,067	18.0	5,878	17.5	5,700
1993 [2]	3,116	18.4	5,892	18.4	5,892
1994 [2]	3,057	18.4	6,028	18.9	6,189
Middle alternative projections					
1995	3,083	18.9	6,138	20.1	6,504
1996	3,139	19.7	6,279	21.6	6,882
1997	3,116	20.2	6,469	22.9	7,334
1998	3,144	20.9	6,641	24.5	7,800
1999	3,172	21.4	6,750	26.1	8,217
2000	3,212	22.0	6,846	—	—
2001	3,255	22.5	6,912	—	—
2002	3,285	22.9	6,975	—	—
2003	3,315	23.3	7,024	—	—
2004	3,321	23.6	7,113	—	—
2005	3,349	24.1	7,188	—	—
Low alternative projections					
1995	3,083	18.9	6,133	20.2	6,551
1996	3,139	19.4	6,178	21.7	6,924
1997	3,116	19.6	6,296	23.1	7,422
1998	3,144	20.3	6,462	25.2	8,017
1999	3,172	20.8	6,564	27.2	8,576
2000	3,212	21.3	6,640	—	—
2001	3,255	21.8	6,695	—	—
2002	3,285	22.2	6,755	—	—
2003	3,315	22.6	6,803	—	—
2004	3,321	22.9	6,891	—	—
2005	3,349	23.3	6,960	—	—
High alternative projections					
1995	3,083	18.9	6,144	20.0	6,489
1996	3,139	20.1	6,397	21.8	6,951
1997	3,116	20.8	6,679	23.2	7,460
1998	3,144	21.6	6,862	24.8	7,890
1999	3,172	22.2	6,992	26.3	8,288
2000	3,212	22.8	7,109	—	—
2001	3,255	23.4	7,201	—	—
2002	3,285	23.9	7,277	—	—
2003	3,315	24.3	7,341	—	—
2004	3,321	24.7	7,443	—	—
2005	3,349	25.3	7,540	—	—

SOURCE: U.S. Department of Education, National Center for Education Statistics, "Financial Statistics of Institutions of Higher Education" and "Fall Enrollment in Colleges and Universities" surveys. (Table was prepared September 1994.)
NOTE: Projections in current dollars are not shown after 1999 due to the uncertain behavior over the long term.
1. Based on the Consumer Price Index for all urban consumers (from Bureau of Labor Statistics, U.S. Department of Labor).
2. Projected.

cost of borrowing to purchase land, buildings, and equipment. Colleges and universities responded to these cost pressures in an envi-

TABLE 1.13 Current-Fund Expenditures and Current-Fund Expenditures per Full-Time-Equivalent (FTE) Student of Private Four-Year Institutions, With Alternative Projections: 50 States and Washington, D.C., 1979-1980 to 2004-2005

Year ending	Full-time-equivalent enrollment (in thousands)	Current-fund expenditures			
		Constant 1992–93 dollars [1]		Current dollars	
		Total (in billions)	Per student in FTE	Total (in billions)	Per student in FTE
1980	1.957	$33.3	$17,009	$18.7	$9,547
1981	2.003	33.8	16,865	21.2	10,565
1982	2.041	34.4	16,867	23.4	11,485
1983	2.028	36.1	17,793	25.6	12,633
1984	2.059	38.2	18,527	28.1	13,641
1985	2.055	40.2	19,542	30.7	14,952
1986	2.055	42.4	20,630	33.4	16,244
1987	2.065	45.9	22,250	37.0	17,910
1988	2.091	47.7	22,824	40.0	19,134
1989	2.158	49.9	23,138	43.8	20,289
1990	2.194	51.9	23,676	47.7	21,749
1991	2.228	53.5	24,021	51.9	23,282
1992	2.286	56.0	24,518	56.0	24,518
1993 [2]	2.332	58.2	24,974	60.0	25,751
1994 [2]	2.377	60.5	25,451	64.1	26,946
Middle alternative projections					
1995	2.383	62.4	26,174	68.1	28,597
1996	2.431	64.1	26,361	72.4	29,788
1997	2.382	66.3	27,840	77.5	32,542
1998	2.390	68.3	28,575	82.7	34,605
1999	2.408	70.3	29,191	88.2	36,643
2000	2.439	72.2	29,601	—	—
2001	2.474	74.1	29,940	—	—
2002	2.504	75.9	30,304	—	—
2003	2.533	77.7	30,692	—	—
2004	2.546	79.7	31,294	—	—
2005	2.577	81.6	31,675	—	—
Low alternative projections					
1995	2.383	61.5	25,829	67.8	28,444
1996	2.431	62.9	25,858	72.6	29,883
1997	2.382	65.0	27,293	79.0	33,175
1998	2.390	67.0	28,030	85.7	35,854
1999	2.408	68.9	28,619	92.8	38,553
2000	2.439	70.8	29,016	—	—
2001	2.474	72.6	29,339	—	—
2002	2.504	74.4	29,707	—	—
2003	2.533	76.2	30,100	—	—
2004	2.546	78.2	30,700	—	—
2005	2.577	80.1	31,076	—	—
High alternative projections					
1995	2.383	63.0	26,428	68.6	28,779
1996	2.431	64.9	26,716	72.8	29,933
1997	2.382	67.2	28,231	77.4	32,514
1998	2.390	69.3	28,984	82.1	34,360
1999	2.408	71.3	29,596	87.1	36,173
2000	2.439	73.2	30,017	—	—
2001	2.474	75.1	30,365	—	—
2002	2.504	77.0	30,748	—	—
2003	2.533	78.9	31,133	—	—
2004	2.546	80.8	31,753	—	—
2005	2.577	82.9	32,158	—	—

SOURCE: U.S. Department of Education, National Center for Education Statistics, "Financial Statistics of Institutions of Higher Education" and "Fall Enrollment in Colleges and Universities" surveys. (Table was prepared September 1994.)
NOTE: Projections in current dollars are not shown after 1999 due to the uncertain behavior over the long term.
1. Based on the Consumer Price Index for all urban consumers (from Bureau of Labor Statistics, U.S. Department of Labor).
2. Projected.

ronment of limited resources by freezing the number of faculty members, allowing the faculty to shrink through attrition, imposing tighter

TABLE 1.14 Percentage of Undergraduates Receiving Aid, by Aid
Source and Selected Student Characteristics: 1992-1993

	Any	Federal	Institution	State
Total	41.4	32.1	12.1	10.4
Dependency and income level				
Dep: Less than $10,000	78.5	76.0	18.9	26.0
Dep: $10K-19,999	72.1	67.1	20.4	24.1
Dep: $20K-29,999	61.0	54.4	21.7	21.4
Dep: $30K-39,999	46.4	35.7	18.2	14.2
Dep: $40K-49,999	33.2	23.2	15.4	8.1
Dep: $50K-59,999	32.3	18.6	16.7	6.9
Dep: $60K-69,999	30.0	15.9	17.6	5.2
Dep: $70K-79,999	32.6	18.2	18.9	3.7
Dep: $80K-99,999	29.2	14.2	16.4	3.9
Dep:$100K or more	19.8	6.4	12.6	2.6
Ind: Less than $5,000	78.0	73.8	15.8	21.8
Ind: $5,000-9,999	71.6	66.9	11.6	22.4
Ind: $10K-19,000	44.7	38.0	8.0	10.0
Ind: $20K-29,999	31.0	21.6	6.1	6.2
Ind: $30K-49,999	22.0	11.4	4.1	3.0
Ind: $50K or more	18.6	5.8	3.4	1.3
Institutional type				
Public, < 2-yr	22.2	18.3	0.9	3.3
Public, 2-yr	27.1	19.6	4.7	6.7
Public, 4-yr	45.6	35.1	13.6	13.1
Public, 4-yr, no PhD	45.2	36.6	10.9	15.2
Public, 4-yr, PhD	46.0	34.1	15.6	11.6
Private, nfp, < 4-yr	54.4	43.2	17.7	13.8
Private, nfp, 4-yr	60.6	45.0	36.6	18.9
Private, nfp, 4-yr, no PhD	63.4	49.0	34.6	21.6
Private, nfp, 4-yr, PhD	56.5	39.1	39.6	14.9
Private, for-profit	71.8	67.7	4.4	5.6
Private, for-profit, < 2-yr	74.5	70.6	4.4	3.4
Private, for-profit, 2-yr+	68.1	63.6	4.3	8.5
Attendance pattern				
Full-time/full-year	57.9	45.6	23.4	17.9
Full-time/part-year	55.9	48.7	11.0	12.2
Part-time/full-year	32.3	23.1	7.0	7.4
Part-time/part-year	22.6	15.5	4.2	3.5

SOURCE: National Center for Education Statistics, *NPSAS: '93 Undergraduate Students*, 3/17/95.
NOTE: "Any" aid also includes other sources of financial aid, such as employers, not shown
separately.

budget controls at all levels of the institution, delaying or deferring
renovations of facilities and capital maintenance projects, eliminating
marginal programs, and adjusting course offerings each semester.

Odden and Massy (1992) identified four categories of the cost/pro-
ductivity/resource allocation debate:

1. The *cost disease* is associated with any activity that is labor intensive. As costs or salaries rise, the cost of the activity also rises. This assumes that faculty salaries must increase to keep education competitive. The cost "disease" also assumes that the way institutions provide services is fixed and does not take advantage of new technology to increase productivity.
2. The *growth force* is the idea that quality costs and that any activity, such as education, has to grow over time to increase quality.
3. The *administrative lattice* is the phenomenon of middle managers and staff increasing at a rate faster than front-line service providers—in this case, faculty.
4. The *academic ratchet* is the evolution of teaching norms that, over time, produces smaller class sizes and teaching loads and more support staff for functions that professors performed in the past, changes that require more resources.

Applying these concepts to higher education provides insight into resource allocation decisions made by colleges and universities in the early 1990s.

Application of the cost disease to higher education was simple. Odden and Massy noted,

> Higher education is labor intensive. Assuming that teaching is provided by professors and that the student-faculty ratio does not increase over time, it follows that teaching costs will at least rise by an amount equal to the general rise in wages for the economy as a whole, which is usually a combination of both inflation and increases in general productivity. Professors' salaries would need to rise by an amount equal to the inflation rate plus the increase in productivity, in order for higher education to remain competitive. Absent internal efficiency improvements, annual cost increases for colleges and universities, then, would be higher than inflation on the basis of the cost disease alone. (p. 13)

This was the exact behavior that colleges and universities engaged in during the 1980s.

Higher education institutions continually try to expose students to new ideas. As Waggaman (1991) noted, new knowledge, coupled in some cases with the quest for increased academic prestige and stature, led to a need for increased technology, more classes, and the addition of new fields of study while at the same time maintaining traditional paths of study. In an attempt to continually improve quality, the growth force caused a "constant layering of new ideas, methods and programs on top of old ones, resulting in a constant pressure to add courses, faculty, technology, and facilities to keep pace with expanding knowledge" (Odden & Massy, 1992, p. 13). The construction or renovation of recreational, cultural, and housing facilities on many campuses contributed to criticism that colleges spend too much money on frivolous items not central to the institution's educational mission. Much of this activity took place, however, to maintain a "quality" edge (see also Hauptman, 1993; Waggaman, 1991).

Growth in revenues in the 1980s led to an increase in administrative staffs on many campuses, referred to as the administrative lattice. Hauptman (1993) noted, "In the 1970s and throughout the 1980s, administrative costs were one of the fastest growing components of higher education expenditures, and administrative staffs grew much faster than the number of faculty" (p. 19). Administrative staffs grew an average of 60% between 1975 and 1985, whereas faculty increased an average of less than 6% in the same period (Odden & Massy, 1992). Higher education leaders defended this growth in administrative staffs by arguing that regulatory burdens resulting from the enactment of environmental, health care, disability, campus crime, and other legislation created a greater demand for staff. Higher administrative costs were also associated with greater staff professionalism and the delivery of better services to students.

Faculty salaries overall increased in real terms in the 1980s, attributed to the catch-up from the 1970s when faculty salaries lagged behind the rate of inflation. Faculty priorities over the past several decades have changed, a phenomenon known as output creep and the academic ratchet. By the early 1990s, faculty no longer devoted the majority of their time to teaching and related activities such as academic advising and mentoring; instead, their primary focus increasingly was research, scholarship, and professional service. Faculty spent more time on research and scholarship because curriculum changes and increases in support staff or faculty/student ratios allowed this flexibility. Colleges and universities paid additional staff to provide advising and counseling services, once the responsibility of faculty. Institutions attempted to improve productivity by substituting lower-paid individuals for those with higher levels of expertise. Odden and Massy (1992) stated,

> In academic departments, this means hiring graduate teaching and research assistants, administrative assistants, secretaries, and technicians to take over certain faculty functions. Using less costly individuals frees up faculty to devote more time to research and other professional activities. But even less costly individuals require more resources. In most cases, therefore, leveraging faculty time drives up the overall costs of higher education. (p. 16)

"Enacted norms," shared beliefs about the faculty relationship with the environment, and curriculum restructuring also had resource allocation implications for colleges and universities. Faculty developed certain "property rights" they felt were inherent in their position, such as student/faculty ratios, number of courses taught per term, the division of teaching between upper and lower division courses, and ideal class size. Property rights had implications for students in terms of when classes were taught, the number of sections taught, and class size. Additionally, colleges and universities moved away from a structured curriculum to one that provided a large menu of courses, unconstrained by traditional sequence requirements. For students, this lack of structure often meant taking courses unnecessary for degree requirements.

By the early 1990s, competition for a declining pool of undergraduate students had resource allocation implications for colleges and universities. Institutions began spending more money on recruitment activities and expanding facilities and services such as recreational and cultural facilities, student unions, and grounds to make their campuses more attractive to prospective students. Institutions that experienced rising enrollments did not experience a concurrent growth in resources for faculty and facilities. The number and size of course sections taught did not meet student demand and was often restricted by limited classroom space and the number of faculty available to teach.

Resource limitations in the 1990s meant that colleges and universities could not do as much as they had in the past. Where institutions chose to spend these limited funds had implications for time-to-degree rates.

Summary

The higher education environment in the 1990s differed significantly from the environment of previous decades. Continued growth, changing student demographics, and diminished revenue sources coupled with increased concern over accountability for monitoring the relationship between performance and finance presented new challenges for postsecondary education. Outcome measurements assumed a new importance with the growing public demand for accountability. Traditional outcome measurements, such as graduation rates, student employability upon graduation, persistence and retention rates, and economic and social returns of the education process, gained greater importance in assessing the effectiveness of colleges and universities.

References

Alexander, K. (1993). The value of an education. In D. W. Breneman, L. L. Leslie, & R. E. Anderson (Eds.), *ASHE reader on finance in higher education*. Washington, DC: Association for the Study of Higher Education.

Becker, W. E., & Lewis, D. R. (Eds.). (1992). *The economics of American higher education*. Boston: Kluwer Academic.

Caffrey, J., & Isaacs, H. H. (1971). *Estimating the economic impact of a college or university on the local economy*. Washington, DC: American Council on Education.

Cohn, E., & Geske, T. G. (1990). *The economics of education* (3rd ed.). New York: Pergamon.

Garcia, P. (1994). *Graduation and time-to-degree: A research note from the California State University*. (Eric Document Reproduction Services No. 373 643)

Goldstein, H. A. (1990). Estimating the regional economic impact of universities: An application of input-output analysis. *Planning for Higher Education, 18*, 53.

Hauptman, A. M. (1993). *Higher education finance issues in the early 1990s*. New Brunswick, NJ: Consortium for Policy Research in Education.

Hodgkinson, H. L. (1990, November/December). Hard numbers, tough choices. *AGB Reports*, 12.

Leslie, L. L., & Brinkman, P. T. (1988). *The economic value of higher education*. New York: American Council on Education/Macmillan.

Levine, A. (1990). Defying demographics. *CASE Currents, 16*, 26.

O'Connor, P. J. (1994). The needs of adult university students: A case study. *College and University, 69,* 84.

Odden, A., & Massy, W. (1992). *Funding schools and universities: Improving productivity and equity.* New Brunswick, NJ: Consortium for Policy Research in Education.

Renner, K. E. (1993). On race and gender in higher education: Illusions of change. *Educational Record, 74,* 44.

Tinto, V. (1993). *Leaving college: Rethinking the causes and cures of student attrition.* Chicago: University of Chicago Press.

Waggaman, J. S. (1991). *Strategies and consequences: Managing the cost in higher education.* Washington, DC: ERIC Clearinghouse on Higher Education.

TWO

The Value of Investments in Higher Education
CAPTURING THE FULL RETURNS

TERRY G. GESKE

Several economists, including Adam Smith, Henrich Von Thünen, and Alfred Marshall, alluded to the benefits of education and the notion of human capital during the 1800s and early 1900s, but these topics only recently received much attention from the academic community. During the early 1960s, major publications by Theodore W. Schultz (1963) and Gary S. Becker (1964) focused considerable attention on the importance of the economics of education. The scholarly works by these two economists in the United States, both of whom would later receive Nobel prizes, were among the first to theorize the importance of the relationships among investment in education, hu-

AUTHOR'S NOTE: This chapter was first published in *Zeitschrift für Internationale Erziehungs- und Sozialwissenschaftliche Forschung* [Journal for International Education and Social Science Research, Germany], Vol. 12, No. 1 (1995), pp. 121-139. It is reprinted here with permission.

man capital formation, and the economic development and well-being of nations.

From an economic perspective, investments in human capital, such as formal education and on-the-job training, can be evaluated based on their ability to generate future returns in terms of additional lifetime income and greater personal satisfactions. Thus, when formal education is viewed as a form of capital, governmental and family allocation decisions with respect to schooling are treated as investment decisions. Investment decisions about education are influenced by some of the same factors that guide other investment decisions. In short, investment in education is encouraged if the return from investing a given amount of education equals or exceeds the return available from alternative sources (e.g., real estate, stocks, bonds, or savings certificates).

This chapter begins with a brief overview of the benefit-cost framework and techniques used to estimate the economic returns to investment in higher education. Next, the different types of costs and benefits associated with attending college are described, and a few of the difficult methodological problems involved when applying these benefit-cost techniques are demonstrated. Finally, a general survey is provided of selected research studies that have estimated the economic benefits of higher education in the United States. This survey focuses on those private monetary and nonmonetary benefits that individuals can capture that substantially contribute to the quality of one's life.

The survey first examines the magnitude of the monetary returns (i.e., increased lifetime earnings) that one can expect to obtain from an investment in a college education. The survey then delineates the range and diversity of the private nonmonetary benefits (i.e., increased productivity in activities outside the labor market) that also flow from this education. The nonmonetary benefits derived from education can significantly affect many important aspects of one's life such as health, family life, consumption behavior, asset management, and migration. It should be pointed out that this survey is not exhaustive and that considerable selectivity has been exercised. Moreover, the emphasis throughout this chapter is placed on the overall conclusions of the research surveyed. The difficult research design questions, methodological problems, and measurement issues involved in this type of research are not addressed.

Benefit-Cost Framework

In economic analysis, decision makers (governments and individuals) are assumed to maximize their own social welfare or well-being. Thus, in benefit-cost analysis, the "maximum social gain" principle dictates that prospective benefits must exceed anticipated costs, and more important, the excess of benefits over costs must be maximized. The end product of any benefit-cost analysis is the calculation of a ratio that represents the "present value" of the total benefits of the program to the total cost of the undertaking. The values specified in the benefit-cost ratio are economic benefits and costs expressed or measured in terms of dollars.

Over the years, the net present value (NPV) and internal rate of return (IRR) techniques, and more recently, the earnings differential (ED) approach, have been used to evaluate investment decisions with regard to higher education. The NPV criterion states that a project is profitable if the sum of its *discounted* benefits is at least as great as the sum of its *discounted* costs. For education projects, the implication is that the lifetime earnings differentials due to education, properly discounted, exceed the sum of the discounted costs. The IRR criterion states that a project is profitable if the calculated IRR exceeds the "appropriate" rate of discount i. To calculate the IRR, the value of the discounted rate that would make NPV = 0 is determined. If IRR > i, then the project is said to be worthwhile. The ED approach is used to calculate the difference or the ratio of average (mean or median) annual earnings of the cohort receiving a higher level of education (college graduates) and the cohort receiving a lower level of education (high school graduates). As the ratio increases, the returns to investment in the higher-education level become larger.[1]

Many analysts prefer the IRR over the NPV because it is unnecessary to determine in advance an "appropriate" discount rate. Although there are valid reasons for preferring the IRR, this criterion itself is subject to many problems (Cohn, 1972a, 1972b). In contrast, the ED approach provides a straightforward and elementary method for comparing earnings between groups but, in the process, simply ignores important methodological issues such as discounting or the timing and probability of the earnings.

Costs of Higher Education

Students enrolled in institutions of higher education in the United States sustain a variety of costs, including tuition and fees, room and board, and books and supplies. The largest cost sustained by students is related to the economist's notion of opportunity costs. Students who spend time in school (or in preparation for school) incur costs known as forgone earnings, to the extent that they could have been employed during this time. In other words, opportunity costs or forgone earnings represent the income that the average student could have earned had he or she been employed. This total of forgone earnings is an important consideration for college students who may give up substantial income while attending school but is far less important for high school students and of no consequence for the lower grade levels (because employment is not available to these students).

Because students (and their parents) are typically charged only a fraction of the total educational costs (because of subsidies provided by governments and philanthropies), there are considerable differences between the costs of education assumed by the student (the "private" cost) and the total costs of education assumed by society (the "social" cost). Measurement of private and social costs is an easier task than measuring the benefits of education, but the task is not simple. Calculation of earnings that students forgo while in school, for example, is highly problematic, and estimates of earnings forgone are, at best, reasonable approximations.

Benefits of Higher Education

Several scholars, including Schultz (1963) and more recently Bowen (1978), have provided taxonomies of educational benefits. These taxonomies include the benefits the economy obtains from educational research, the cultivation and discovery of (potential) talent, the increased ability of educated individuals to adapt to new job opportunities and rapidly changing technology, and the provision of manpower for sustained economic growth (Schultz, 1963). In addition, schooling provides for better citizenship, the ability to appreciate and recognize a wider range of cultural and other services, and the chance to give the next generation better education and therefore a better future.

For analytical purposes, educational benefits can be conveniently partitioned into "consumption" and "investment" categories, and also into "private" and "social" categories. With regard to the first classification, a product (or service) is placed in the consumption category if it yields satisfaction (or utility) in a single period only or is placed in the investment category if it is expected to yield satisfaction in future periods only. There are, of course, goods for which it is difficult to draw a sharp distinction between the consumption and investment aspects—that is, goods that yield satisfaction now and are also expected to yield satisfaction in the future. Education is a product that is best characterized by the "in between" classification.

Private benefits are those that accrue to the individual being educated. Social benefits include private benefits as well as benefits that accrue to other members of society. There are basically two types of benefits that belong in the social but not the private domain: tax payments associated with the educational benefit (that is, income taxes paid out of one's lifetime income stream) and "external" benefits, which are due to the educational investment but that the individual cannot capture.

Although the measurement of private benefits has improved over the years, the measurement of social benefits or externalities (with the exception of tax payments) remains problematic. Only limited research, for example, has addressed those external benefits of education that might further justify social investment, such as the effect of education on crime prevention or on political participation. Similarly, there is substantial evidence that education also significantly affects a country's research and development activities and its economic growth, but these types of educational effects are very difficult to estimate. Because external benefits are so difficult to calculate, they are almost always ignored in benefit-cost analyses of investments to higher education.

At the same time, empirical studies of educational benefits do not consider those benefits that may accrue a generation later. Studies show that persons are more likely to complete a given level of education if their parents are (or were) more highly educated. The intergenerational effect is the increment in a person's education that can be ascribed to the incremental education of the parent. Thus, some of the higher expected earnings of the children could be traced back to their origin in the increased educational investment by their parents. Therefore, if our investigation of the benefits of education is confined to the parents only, some (perhaps serious) underestimation of benefits would result.

Methodological Problems

A number of conceptual and methodological problems must be confronted when using census and other survey data to estimate the returns to education. These methodological issues include necessary adjustments for innate ability and other nonschool variables, the choice of an appropriate discount rate, selectivity bias, cross-sectional data versus life cycle data, annual earnings versus hourly wages, and the like. The relevant research issues have been explored in detail elsewhere (Cohn & Geske, 1990, chap. 3), but a few of them are mentioned here to illustrate the complexity of this type of research.

To begin with, what proportion of the observed education-income relationship is strictly due to education? In other words, what portion of the earnings differentials is due to differences in individual characteristics, such as ability and motivation, and other nonschool factors—all of which happen to correlate with years of school completed? Although recent research has been based on the earnings function, which includes controls for work experience, socioeconomic status, and other nonschool variables, the controls may be insufficient (as argued by Taubman, 1976), or too many control variables may be included that correlate with education (such as occupation, as argued by Becker, 1964). In the former case, the implication is that the education-earnings relation is biased upward; in the latter case, the opposite may be true.

Another problem involves the choice of a discount rate for use in determining NPVs. Cohn and Geske (1986) have clearly demonstrated the sensitivity of present value calculations to changes in discount rates. They calculate NPVs using different discount rates for male and female college graduates compared to high school graduates based on 1979 Bureau of Census lifetime earnings. For male college graduates, the estimated NPV earnings difference ranged from

$60,000 at a 5% discount rate to $329,000 at no discount rate, whereas for female college graduates, the NPV earnings difference ranged from $44,000 to $142,000.

Cohn and Geske then subtracted the present value of costs ($37,000), also discounted at 5%, from the low estimates for the present value of benefits ($60,000 for males and $44,000 for females) to obtain the NPV of college investment ($23,000 and $7,000, respectively). The results indicated that a dollar of investment in four years of college yields, on average, $1.62 and $1.19 in benefits for males and females, respectively. Obviously, these benefit-cost ratios would increase dramatically if the high estimates of the present value of earnings were used in these calculations. Additional lifetime income for any educational level becomes successively smaller as a higher rate of discount is applied.

The identification and conceptualization of educational costs and benefits is but the first step in the complex calculus to estimate the returns to investments in higher education. At the same time, the very nature of these costs and benefits suggests that their measurement will be a very difficult task and that placing a monetary value on their worth will be an even more difficult job. Although an extensive taxonomy of educational benefits has been developed over the years, benefit-cost studies have focused almost exclusively on the direct monetary returns, that is, on increased lifetime income. Moreover, even though these studies adopted a very narrow focus, examining only the effects of education on lifetime income, they still confronted several severe methodological problems.

Monetary Returns

During the past 40 years, numerous studies have investigated the private and social rates of returns to investment in higher education in the United States.[2] These studies applied benefit-cost techniques to measure the effects of education on lifetime income, using different methods involving the shape of age-earning profiles, earning differentials, and the discounted present value of lifetime income differentials. In general, the findings of the selected studies reviewed here are based on the internal rate of return technique.

Returns to College Education

Historically, estimates of the private rates of return to four years of college education have typically ranged from 10% to 15% (Becker, 1964; Hanoch, 1967; Hansen, 1963; Mincer, 1974). Estimates of the social rates of return are somewhat less, yielding approximately 11% to 13% (Carnoy & Marenback, 1975; Hansen, 1963). Although the internal rate of return to college appears to have remained fairly stable over the years, there was an apparent reduction in the IRR during the early 1970s. Freeman's (1976, 1977, 1980) findings indicated a relatively sharp decline in the returns to college education during the 5-year period from 1968 to 1973, when the private IRR dropped from 11% in 1968 to 7.5% in 1973.

A lively debate ensued during the late 1970s and early 1980s with regard to the diminishing rates of return reported by Freeman. Much of the debate focused on whether the observed decline in the economic value of college education would be a temporary or a permanent phenomenon. Freeman, for example, speculated on the effects of cohort size (the vintage effect) and on the effects of business cycles on earnings. Smith and Welch (1978) and Welch (1979) examined the effects of economic recessions and large cohort sizes on the earnings of recent entrants into the labor market.

More recently, Murphy and Welch (1989) examined the historical record of the monetary returns to higher education. The work by these economists documents that the returns to college education have increased in recent years. They found that the ratio of the average wages of persons completing 16 years of schooling to the average wages of those completing only 12 years of schooling was 1.33 during the period from 1975 to 1980, compared to 1.54 during the period 1981 to 1986. These ratios of 1.33 and 1.54 approximated private rates of return of 8.3% and 13.5%, respectively. Similar results were obtained for population subgroups (men, women, blacks, and whites) and also for groups with different labor market experience. Similarly, Cohn and Hughes (in press), who provide updated estimates of the IRRs to college education for the period 1965-1985, also reported a considerable increase in the returns during the early 1980s. Murphy and Welch concluded that much of the decline in the college wage premium during the early and mid-1970s could be attributed to an oversupply of college graduates during this period.

If the estimates of the returns to education in the United States during the 1970s suggested that Americans were "overinvesting" in education, the more recent estimates during the 1980s revealed a marked change in the payoff to education. Becker (1992) reported that this fairly dramatic upturn in the returns to college education apparently peaked in 1986, but then remained relatively stable at least through 1990. Becker pointed out that the average college graduate, after several years of work experience, ". . . now earns some 50 to 70 percent more than a high school graduate. College graduates, on average, receive $500,000 to $1,000,000 more than high school graduates over their lifetimes" (1992, p. 100). Why the rapid rise in the earnings ratio between college and high school graduates? Becker suggested that one possible explanation may be that a college education has not become worth more, but that a high school diploma has become worth less because of changing job prospects during the 1980s for high school graduates in the United States.

In a comprehensive study, McMahon and Wagner (1982) examined the considerable variation in monetary returns across major fields (and their related occupations), and across types of public and private institutions (i.e., research universities, comprehensive four-year colleges, and liberal arts colleges). Students who intended to become engineers, for example, expected a private rate of return (25.5%) twice as large as those who intended to become school teachers (12.3%). In addition, expected private rates of return for students planning to earn only a bachelor's degree were low at private liberal arts colleges (8.7%) when compared to rates of return at public and private four-year comprehensive colleges (21.0% and 18.5%, respectively). Similarly, after examining private returns to specific college majors, Berger (1992) found that individuals who received a bachelor's degree in engineering or in the natural sciences, and sometimes in business, received an earnings premium.

Returns to Graduate Education

The economic returns to graduate programs are generally much lower than for bachelor degree programs. Although the returns to graduate education are characterized by considerable variation, the private payoff, for the most part, has ranged from 2% to 10% (Hanoch,

1967; Mincer, 1974; Tomaske, 1974). In contrast, several studies have reported very low, even negative, returns to graduate education (Bailey & Schotta, 1972; Maxwell, 1970; Rogers, 1969). At the same time, there are some exceptions, such as the IRR for a three-year doctoral program calculated by Ashenfelter and Mooney (1968) as 10.5%; the higher IRRs for doctoral economists employed in business, estimated by Siegfried (1971) as high as 23.6%; and the average IRRs calculated by Weiss (1971) at over 12%.

McMahon and Wagner (1982) also documented the considerable variation that characterizes the returns to various graduate programs. They found that expected private rates of return to graduate education varied from −0.7% to +9.6% for the master's degree and from −1.8% to +19.3% for the doctoral or professional degrees, depending on the type of institution attended. The rates also varied from −0.8% to +12.7% for the master's degree and from −0.1% to +16.4% for the doctoral or professional degrees, depending on the intended occupation (e.g., medical doctor, lawyer, engineer, accountant, natural scientist, school teacher).

Although the costs of graduate education were highest for students at public and private research universities, the private rates of return for students who planned to pursue master's and doctoral degrees were highest there as well. The social rates of return were also highest at these types of institutions for students pursuing advanced degrees. With regard to major fields of graduate study, the expected private rates of return were highest in medicine, law, engineering, and business, ranging from 12% to 16.4%. The expected private rates were lowest for advanced training in teaching, natural science, and social science, ranging from −0.8% to +8.9%. Again, the differences in these private rates of return were also reflected in the differences in social rates of return for the various occupational fields.

Returns to Different Groups

For the most part, the results discussed previously have been "average returns," combining the returns to education for numerous disparate race-sex-ability groups. Considerable evidence, however, suggests that the returns to education differ significantly among various groups in society. For example, the economic returns to African Americans and females have increased in relative terms, as efforts toward integration, affirmative action, and other programs on behalf of minorities have become more effective (Jud & Walker, 1982; Link, Ratledge, & Lewis, 1976, 1980; Welch, 1973, 1980).

Hoffman (1984) examined black-white differences in returns to higher education for the 1970s and found that the earnings differential between the college-educated and the high-school-educated decreased for young white males but increased for blacks. Hoffman's findings suggested that the black-white earnings gap had narrowed to the point that predicted earnings (based on 1977 data) were equal for black-white college graduates. Becker (1992) also pointed out that the increased earnings for college graduates throughout the 1980s appear to have benefited minorities more than their white counterparts. These studies and others (Darity, 1982; Kiker & Heath, 1985) suggest that education is a much more important determinant of earnings for blacks than for whites.

Some evidence suggests that differential returns to education by sex (Christian & Stroup, 1981; Hines, Tweeten, & Redfern, 1970) may be due to various attributes of the male-female groups under consideration, such as labor market experience, commitment to full-time participation in the labor force, continuity in employment, or types of skills and professions for which individuals are qualified. Daymont and Andrisani (1984) argued that a substantial portion of the gender differential in hourly earnings among recent college graduates can be attributed to differences between men and women in preference for occupations and in preparation (college major) for these occupations. Similarly, Ferber and McMahon (1979) suggested that increased education and a shift to "male" occupations may result in higher rates of return to women.

The overall level of returns to investment in higher education indicates that, in general, such an investment is profitable both for the individual and for society. It must be recognized, however, that college education is not universally profitable, with rates of return varying considerably by major fields and types of institution. If certain college and university programs yield very low and even negative returns, why do individuals continue to enroll in such programs? One response to this question is that college education (and education in general) bestows not only labor market benefits but also various types of nonlabor market benefits, including private nonmonetary benefits.

Nonmonetary Benefits[3]

A major problem in estimating the full or true returns to education has to do with our inability to quantify and to value the nonmonetary benefits associated with education. As Michael (1982) pointed out, there are three basic categories of nonmonetary benefits of education. First, schooling affects the nonwage dimensions of labor market re-muneration (e.g., fringe benefits, working conditions, and earning stability). Second, schooling has pure consumption effects (e.g., the enjoyment of learning and discovery). Third, schooling affects pro-ductivity in activities outside the labor market (e.g., in household production and in capital markets). The survey of studies presented in this section focuses on the third category, and more specifically on the beneficial effects of education on health, family life, consumption behavior, asset management, and migration.

Education and Health

Extensive research has documented the positive correlation be-tween increased schooling and good health. Grossman (1976) found that schooling positively affects health, and as past health is con-trolled for in his model, he argues that the evidence supports a causal relationship that runs from schooling to current health. Grossman's findings indicate that a one-year increase in schooling is associated with a 3.5% increase in health capital when only age is held constant. This increase in health capital declines to 1.2% when all relevant variables are held constant (e.g., age, background characteristics, ability levels, wage rates, job satisfaction).

Given an assumed demand function for health, Grossman sug-gested that "schooling raises productivity in the production of health by 2.4% at a minimum" (p. 179). Grossman compared this nonmarket productivity effect of schooling on health to the market productivity effect of 5.5% in the hourly wage rate for his sample. "Although the nonmarket productivity effect of schooling may appear to be small in an absolute sense, it is approximately 40 percent [2.4 ÷ 5.5] as large as the market productivity effect" (p. 179).

Other researchers have also documented the relationship between schooling and health. Edwards and Grossman (1981) found that parental schooling levels (after controlling for differences in earnings) are positively correlated with the health status of their children. Lefocowitz (1973) argued that there is a causal relationship between levels of education and individual health status and that the observed correlation between income and medical deprivation appears to be a consequence of education's relationship with both variables. Orcutt, Franklin, Mendelsohn, and Smith (1977) disclosed that increased schooling (and higher relative income) are correlated with lower mortality rates for given age brackets. Finally, Sander (1995) pointed out the positive effect of schooling on health behavior by documenting that schooling reduces the odds that people smoke. He found that "men and women with more schooling are less likely to smoke and more likely to quit smoking" (p. 23). This finding was particularly true for college graduates.

Education and Family Life

Considerable empirical work has focused on the effects of education on family life, including marriage, family planning, and the rearing of children (Becker, 1981; Schultz, 1974). With regard to marriage, Michael (1982) argued that education facilitates a more productive sorting of men and women in the marriage market. In turn, this marital sorting may lead to subsequent benefits such as more stable marriages (Becker, Landes, & Michael, 1977) and also positive assortative mating by intelligence, which increases the probability of parenting "bright" children (Michael, 1982).

In terms of family planning, Michael (1975b) argued that education directly affects family size and fertility behavior through the efficiency with which parents process information about contraceptive products and techniques. Michael's analyses disclosed that couples who are more educated tend to adopt contraceptive practices more readily and at an earlier stage in marriage than do less educated couples and are also better informed about and more receptive to new contraceptive techniques and thus engage in more effective fertility control.

Education also affects the quality and quantity of time that parents devote to their children. Hill and Stafford (1974, 1980) found that women who are more educated spend substantially more time with preschool children than do less educated women—between 2.5 and 3.5 times as much per child. Moreover, Leibowitz (1975) found that although women with more education generally spend more time in the labor market than other women they are also less likely to work when they have preschool- or school-aged children in the home. Also, although aggregate time devoted to home production is about the same for the different education levels, women with more education spend less time in home maintenance activities and considerably more time in child care activities.

Leibowitz (1974; see also Rosenzweig & Wolpin, 1994) argued that this home production, primarily through parental time inputs, increases preschool and childhood stocks of human capital. She found that the mother's education is significantly related to the child's IQ and that preschool home investments strengthened this relationship beyond the genetic endowment factor. Murnane (1981) also documented a significant relationship between mother's education and children's cognitive skills and concluded that this relationship reflects, at least in part, the positive influence of home environment, including the quality of child care.

Education and Consumption Behavior

Michael (1972, 1975a) compared the effect of education on consumer behavior in the home or nonmarket sector with the effect of education on earnings in the labor market. He used a household production model to examine how education affects consumer expenditure patterns. He argued that if persons who are more educated are more productive in nonmarket activities, then families with more education should produce a higher level of output (commodities) for a given quantity of inputs (time and money). Accordingly, Michael reasoned that those more educated households will have more real wealth (in terms of commodities) and will, in effect, behave as if they have more real income (the equivalent of greater money income).

Michael labeled this effect of schooling on real income through nonmarket productivity the "consumption income effect." To verify and estimate this consumption income effect, Michael structured an empirical test to determine if differences in education levels influence consumer behavior in the same manner that they influence money income. Michael concluded that education produces a positive effect on the efficiency of consumption and estimated that the effect of schooling is approximately 60% as great in nonmarket activities as in the labor market. In addition to Michael's work, other studies (Hettich, 1972) have provided substantial evidence that individuals with more education seek out, and are better informed about, consumer goods markets.

Education and Asset Management

Solmon (1975) analyzed the relationship between education and savings behavior. He hypothesized that individuals with more education will save a higher proportion of income and will tend to exercise different savings alternatives. Overall, his various analyses supported the basic proposition that these individuals have a higher propensity to save and are more efficient at managing their savings portfolios. Solmon also examined the relationships between schooling and individuals' attitudes with respect to portfolio management, savings objectives, and risk preference and concluded that "at least with respect to inflation, the more educated are more sophisticated (or efficient) investors" (pp. 279-280). He inferred from these findings that the more highly educated are more likely to accept risk, to be more informed and rational in investment decision making, and to plan ahead with a longer time horizon.

Education and Migration

Research on the determinants of migration has documented that persons with more education are much more likely to be involved in long-distance moves than are less educated persons (Greenwood, 1975; Schwartz, 1971). DaVanzo (1983) reported that educational attainment is a critical variable for repeat migrants who move after a brief one-year interval, stating that "the more educated the migrant, the less likely he is to return, compared with both the alternative of not moving again and that of moving onward" (p. 566). DaVanzo concluded that "the less educated are the likeliest to return quickly," whereas "the most highly educated are the likeliest to move quickly onward" (p. 558). In an attempt to interpret this education effect, DaVanzo speculated that "the less educated may base their initial moves on more limited information, lowering the success rate of their moves and hence increasing the likelihood of 'corrective' return moves" (p. 556).

Initial attempts to quantify and value these private nonmonetary benefits suggest that estimates of the returns to schooling may be considerably understated. After surveying and describing various nonmarket effects of schooling such as those just discussed, Haveman and Wolfe (1984) attempted to place an appropriate value on them. They speculated that benefit-cost studies that have focused exclusively on increased earnings may have captured only about 50% of the total value of an additional year of schooling.

Summary

Although significant advances in research on human capital formation have occurred in recent years that permit more accurate estimates of the full or true returns to investments in higher education, several caveats are in order. Much knowledge about the relationship between education and income has been gained over the years, but the precise contribution of schooling to earnings is unknown. The studies reviewed in this chapter, for example, have all concentrated on the quantity of schooling (years completed), rather than on the quality of schooling (expenditure levels), although both dimensions are clearly important. Also, even though analyses have become much more sophisticated, there is considerable room for improvement in the quality of the data base.

A basic shortcoming of benefit-cost calculations of investments in higher education has been related to our inability to include the nonmonetary benefits of schooling. Considerable attention has been focused on some of these elusive educational benefits in the past two decades, and progress has been made in conceptualizing and even measuring some of them. As the survey of private nonmonetary benefits clearly shows, these types of benefits can significantly enhance people's lives. The difficult task of incorporating such benefits into the benefit-cost calculus, even in some judgmental ways, must be pursued. At the same time, some economists have argued that substantial external benefits are associated with education, even though it may be impossible to empirically verify them.

Although there will always be disagreement over the magnitude of nonmonetary and external benefits, and although the inclusion of these types of benefits in the benefit-cost calculus promises to remain highly problematic, additional knowledge about the effects of these important benefits will have to be obtained before the full or true returns to higher education can be estimated with greater precision. But just as research designs, methodological approaches, and measurement techniques have improved over the past two decades to enable more accurate estimations of the effects of schooling on earnings, research investigating the effects of schooling on the nonmonetary and external benefits of education might also improve substantially in the future.

Notes

1. For a discussion of the NPV and IRR techniques, including the involved mathematical equations, and an explanation of present value analysis, see Cohn and Geske (1990, chap. 5). For a discussion of the ED approach, see Becker (1992).

2. For a review of similar studies that have estimated the rates of return to investment in higher education in about 50 other countries, see Cohn and Geske (1990, chap. 5).

3. This section draws heavily from Cohn and Geske (1992).

References

Ashenfelter, O., & Mooney, J. D. (1968). Graduate education, ability and earnings. *Review of Economics and Statistics, 50,* 78-86.

Bailey, D., & Schotta, C. (1972). Private and social rates of return to education of academicians. *American Economic Review, 62,* 19-31.

Becker, G. S. (1964). *Human capital.* New York: Columbia University Press (for National Bureau of Economic Research).

Becker, G. S. (1981). *A treatise on the family.* Cambridge, MA: Harvard University Press.

Becker, G. S., Landes, E. M., & Michael, R. T. (1977). Economics of marital instability. *Journal of Political Economy, 86,* 1141-1187.

Becker, W. E. (1992). Why go to college? The value of an investment in higher education. In W. E. Becker & D. R. Lewis (Eds.), *The economics of American higher education* (pp. 91-120). Boston: Kluwer Academic.

Berger, M. C. (1992). Private returns to specific college majors. In W. E. Becker & D. R. Lewis (Eds.), *The economics of American higher education* (pp. 141-195). Boston: Kluwer Academic.

Bowen, H. R. (1978). *Investment in learning: The individual and social value of American higher education.* San Francisco: Jossey-Bass.

Carnoy, M., & Marenback, D. (1975). The return to schooling in the United States, 1939-69. *Journal of Human Resources, 10,* 312-331.

Christian, V. L., Jr., & Stroup, R. H. (1981). The effect of education on relative earnings of black and white women. *Economics of Education Review, 1,* 113-122.

Cohn, E. (1972a). On the net present value rule for educational investments. *Journal of Political Economy, 80,* 418-420.

Cohn, E. (1972b). Investment criteria and the ranking of educational investments. *Public Finance, 27,* 355-360.

Cohn, E., & Geske, T. G. (1986). Benefit-cost analysis of investment in higher education. In M. P. McKeown & K. Alexander (Eds.), *Values in conflict: Funding priorities for higher education* (pp. 183-215). Cambridge, MA: Ballinger.

Cohn, E., & Geske, T. G. (1990). *The economics of education* (3rd ed.). Oxford, UK: Pergamon.

Cohn, E., & Geske, T. G. (1992). Private nonmonetary returns to investment in higher education. In W. E. Becker & D. R. Lewis (Eds.), *The economics of American higher education* (pp. 173-195). Boston: Kluwer Academic.

Cohn, E., & Hughes, W. W., Jr. (in press). A benefit-cost analysis of investment in college education in the United States: 1969-1985. *Economics of Education Review, 13*(2).

Darity, W. A., Jr. (1982). The human capital approach to Black-White earnings inequality: Some unsettled questions. *Journal of Human Resources, 14,* 72-93.

DaVanzo, J. (1983). Repeat migration in the United States: Who moves back and who moves on? *Review of Economics and Statistics, 65,* 552-559.

Daymont, T. N., & Andrisani, P. J. (1984). Job preferences, college major, and the gender gap in earnings. *Journal of Human Resources, 19,* 408-428.

Edwards, L. N., & Grossman, M. (1981). Children's health and the family. In R. M. Scheffler (Ed.), *Advances in health economics and health services research* (Vol. 2). Greenwich, CT: JAI.

Ferber, M. A., & McMahon, W. W. (1979). Women's expected earnings and their investment in higher education. *Journal of Human Resources, 14,* 405-420.

Freeman, R. B. (1976). *The over-educated American.* New York: Academic Press.

Freeman, R. B. (1977). The decline in the economic rewards to college education. *Review of Economics and Statistics, 59,* 18-29.

Freeman, R. B. (1980). The facts about the declining economic value of college. *Journal of Human Resources, 15,* 124-142.

Greenwood, M. J. (1975). Research on internal migration in the United States: A survey. *Journal of Economic Literature, 13,* 397-433.

Grossman, M. (1976). The correlation between health and schooling. In N. E. Terleckyj (Ed.), *Household production and consumption* (pp. 147-211). New York: Columbia University Press.

Hanoch, G. (1967). An economic analysis of earnings and schooling. *Journal of Human Resources, 2,* 310-329.

Hansen, W. L. (1963). Total and private rates of return to investment in schooling. *Journal of Political Economy, 71,* 128-140.

Haveman, R. H., & Wolfe, B. L. (1984). Schooling and economic well-being: The role of nonmarket effects. *Journal of Human Resources, 19,* 377-407.

Hettich, W. (1972). Consumption benefits from education. In S. Ostrey (Ed.), *Canadian higher education in the seventies.* Ottawa: Economic Council of Canada.

Hill, C. R., & Stafford, F. P. (1974). Allocation of time to preschool children and educational opportunity. *Journal of Human Resources, 9,* 323-341.

Hill, C. R., & Stafford, F. P. (1980). Parental care of children: Time diary estimates of quantity, predictability, and variety. *Journal of Human Resources, 15,* 219-239.

Hines, F., Tweeten, L., & Redfern, M. (1970). Social and private rates of return to investment in schooling, by race-sex groups and regions. *Journal of Human Resources, 5,* 318-340.

Hoffman, S. D. (1984). Black-white differences in returns to higher education: Evidence from the 1970s. *Economics of Education Review, 3*(1), 21-31.

Jud, G. D., & Walker, J. W. (1982). Racial differences in the returns to schooling and experience among prime-age males: 1967-1975. *Journal of Human Resources, 17,* 623-632.

Kiker, B. F., & Heath, J. A. (1985). The effect of socioeconomic background on earnings: A comparison by race. *Economics of Education Review, 4*(1), 45-55.

Lefocowitz, M. J. (1973, March). Poverty and health: A reexamination. *Inquiry,* pp. 3-13.

Leibowitz, A. (1974). Education and home producion. *American Economic Review, 64,* 243-250.

Leibowitz, A. (1975). Education and the allocation of women's time. In F. T. Juster (Ed.), *Education, income and human behavior* (pp. 171-198). New York: McGraw-Hill.

Link, C., Ratledge, E., & Lewis, K. (1976). Black-white differences in returns to schooling: Some new evidence. *American Economic Review, 66,* 221-223.

Link, C., Ratledge, E., & Lewis, K. (1980). The quality of education and cohort variation in black-white earnings differentials: Reply. *American Economic Review, 70,* 196-203.

Maxwell, L. (1970). Some evidence on negative returns to graduate education. *Western Economic Journal, 8,* 186-189.

McMahon, W. W., & Wagner, A. P. (1982). The monetary returns to education as partial social efficiency criteria. In W. W. McMahon & T. G. Geske (Eds.), *Financing education: Overcoming inefficiency and inequity* (pp. 150-187). Urbana: University of Illinois Press.

Michael, R. T. (1972). *The effect of education on efficiency in consumption.* New York: Columbia University Press (for National Bureau of Economic Research).

Michael, R. T. (1975a). Education and consumption. In F. T. Juster (Ed.), *Education, income and human behavior* (pp. 235-252). New York: McGraw-Hill.

Michael, R. T. (1975b). Education and fertility. In F. T. Juster (Ed.), *Education, income and human behavior* (pp. 339-364). New York: McGraw-Hill.

Michael, R. T. (1982). Measuring non-monetary benefits of education: A survey. In W. W. McMahon & T. G. Geske (Eds.), *Financing education: Overcoming inefficiency and inequity* (pp. 119-149). Urbana: University of Illinois Press.

Mincer, J. (1974). *Schooling, experience and earnings*. New York: Columbia University Press.

Murnane, R. J. (1981). New evidence on the relationship between mother's education and children's cognitive skills. *Economics of Education Review, 1*(2), 245-252.

Murphy, K., & Welch, F. (1989). Wage premiums for college graduates: Recent growth and possible explanations. *Educational Researcher, 18*(4), 17-26.

Orcutt, G. H., Franklin, S. D., Mendelsohn, R., & Smith, J. D. (1977). Does your probability of death depend on your environment? A microanalytic study. *American Economic Review, 67*, 260-264.

Rogers, D. C. (1969). Private rates of return to education in the U.S.: A case study. *Yale Economics Essays, 9*, 89-134.

Rosenzweig, M. R., & Wolpin, K. I. (1994). Are there increasing returns to the intergenerational production of human capital? *Journal of Human Resources, 29*(2), 670-693.

Sander, W. (1995). Schooling and smoking. *Economics of Education Review, 14*(1), 23-33.

Schultz, T. W. (1963). *The economic value of education*. New York: Columbia University Press.

Schultz, T. W. (Ed.). (1974). *Economics of the family: Marriage, children and human capital*. Chicago: University of Chicago Press (for National Bureau of Economic Research).

Schwartz, A. (1971). On efficiency of migration. *Journal of Human Resources, 6*, 193-205.

Siegfried, J. J. (1971). Rate of return to the Ph.D. in economics. *Industrial and Labor Relations Review, 24*, 420-431.

Smith, J. P., & Welch, F. R. (1978). *The overeducated American? A review article*. Santa Monica, CA: RAND.

Solmon, L. C. (1975). The relation between schooling and savings behavior: An example of the indirect effects of education. In F. T. Juster (Ed.), *Education, income and human behavior* (pp. 253-294). New York: McGraw-Hill.

Taubman, P. J. (1976). Earnings, education, genetics, and environment. *Journal of Human Resources, 11*, 447-461.

Tomaske, J. A. (1974). Private and social rates of return to education of academicians: Note. *American Economic Review, 64*, 220-224.

Weiss, Y. (1971). Investment in graduate education. *American Economic Review, 67*, 833-852.

Welch, F. (1973). Black-white differences in returns to schooling. *American Economic Review, 67*, 893-907.

Welch, F. (1979). Effects of cohort size on earnings: The baby boom babies' financial bust. *Journal of Political Economy, 87*, S65-S98.

Welch, F. (1980). The quality of education and cohort variations in black-white earnings differentials: Reply. *American Economic Review, 70*, 192-195.

THREE

State Funding Formulas
PROMISE FULFILLED?

MARY P. McKEOWN

The use of state funding formulas or guidelines for public higher education will reach the half-century mark in the 1990s. Despite the long history of use, controversy has surrounded state funding formulas for higher education since their inception. It is likely that the only point on which experts would agree is that there is no perfect formula. In fact, one observer has noted that "formula budgeting, in the abstract, is neither good or bad, but there are good formulas and bad formulas" (Caruthers, 1989). Twenty years ago, some experts even were questioning whether formula usage was dead (Moss & Gaither, 1976). Like Mark Twain, reports of its death were a little premature. Funding formula usage for public four-year institutions may not be dead; however, the question remains: Have these funding formulas fulfilled their promise of identifying an adequate and predictable resource base and distributing those resources equitably?

The capacity of funding formulas to distribute adequate state funds to public colleges and universities in an equitable manner has prompted many debates among those concerned with the public funding of

49

higher education. Increasing competition from other parts of state government (notably health services and prisons), renewed demands for expanded accountability, and the need for the economic, efficient, and wise use of scarce state resources all prompt the debate.

Originally envisioned as simply a means to distribute public funds in a rational and equitable manner, funding formulas have evolved over time into complicated methodologies for allocating public funds. Although funding formulas provide some rationale and continuity in allocating state funds for higher education, formulas are designed and used for many purposes, including measurement of productivity. Even though the genesis of funding formulas may lie in rational public policy formulation, the outcome may not. Formulas are products of political processes, which implies that formulas result from compromise.

Formulas are used in almost every state in the allocation of state funds to elementary and secondary school districts. The stated public policy goal has been to attain equity in the distribution of funds through improvements in funding formulas. Federal and state courts have presented many decisions on the equity and adequacy of elementary and secondary funding formulas, and relatively sophisticated analyses of elementary-secondary education funding formulas have been completed.

In contrast, the goal of equality of educational opportunity through equalized funding has not been accepted in higher education, and treatments of higher education formulas are largely descriptive in nature. Issues of student and taxpayer equity are not addressed often in the literature of higher education finance and certainly are not driving forces in state funding formulas despite the federal government's intervention by litigation in several states (McKeown, 1989). All but one of the states against which the Office of Civil Rights has filed suit in higher education are (or were) formula states; some have argued that, in these states, funding formulas may serve to perpetuate past inequities that existed among previously segregated institutions of higher education (McKeown, 1986).

The use of funding formulas or guidelines in the resource allocation or budgeting process varies from state to state. In some states, the higher education coordinating or governing board may use formulas as a means of recommending to the legislature and governor the resources for each campus. In other states, the legislative or executive budget offices may use formulas to make their recommendations on funding (McKeown & Layzell, 1994). Some states use formulas to determine the allocation of resources to each campus, given available funding. Although this latter use has been defined by some to be the only "true" formula funding, for purposes of this chapter, states will be counted as using formulas if a formula or guideline is used at any point in the resource allocation process.

Development of an optimal, or best, formula is complex because there are differences in institutional missions and in the capacities of institutions to perform their missions. These differences do not negate the value of formulas but suggest that formulas can be used to provide a fiscal base to which (or from which) funding can be added (or subtracted), if justified. Formulas typically are considered enrollment driven because they are based on credit hours, students, or faculty members, which makes it relatively easy to evaluate change. If additional funds are justified, then formulas can provide the basis to target supplemental funding. Because formulas may be enrollment driven, when enrollments are steady or decline, funding may decrease. This aspect of formula use brought formulas under attack in several states when several institutions experienced declines in enrollment.

Debates over formulas because of declining enrollments and over the equitable distribution of resources to public institutions of higher education caused several states to examine critically the methods used to recommend or distribute funding to public colleges and universities. When enrollments decline or remain constant, methods are sought that provide additional resources. Development of new programs and services to meet the varied needs of a changing clientele may require different configurations of resources in addition to different programs. The student of the 21st century likely will have not only different noninstructional needs but also different preferences for instructional programs.

The student in the new century may be taught by alternative instructional delivery methods, which require a shift in the paradigm on funding. The trend in this direction is developing as more and more universities offer courses through telecommunication technology. In December 1995, the Western Governors' Conference announced a joint "virtual university," whose funding (and delivery of courses by telecommunication technology) would be shared by the western states (Bass, 1995). Because the primary user states for the virtual university are formula states, funding for this university will require at least a shift in formulas that perhaps will lead to the development of new methods of funding.

To accomplish the purpose of providing an equitable distribution of available state resources, a majority of states have used funding formulas in budget development or in resource allocation to public higher education institutions. A formula is a mathematical representation of the amount of resources or expenditures for an institution as a whole or for a program at the institution (Boutwell, 1973). Programs in this context refer to those categories into which expenditures are placed, as defined by the National Association of College and University Business Officers (NACUBO). The "programs," "functional categories," or "budget areas" commonly used are the following (NACUBO, 1988):

Instruction	Institutional Support
Research	Operation and Maintenance of Plant
Public Service	Scholarships and Fellowships
Academic Support	Auxiliary Enterprises
Student Services	Hospitals
Mandatory Transfers	

Many states provide funding for higher education based on these functional or budget programs, with the exception of auxiliary enterprises, hospitals, and mandatory transfers. These three areas usually are not funded by the state, and hospitals and auxiliary enterprises are not included in what are called educational and general (E&G) expenditures, which result from expenditures for the three basic missions of colleges and universities: instruction, research, and public service. Funding for the remaining categories may be based on formulas in the determination of the total resource allocation to the institution.

In most states, however, total institutional needs are not determined by a formula mechanism. Additions are made to the formula amounts to recognize special needs or special missions. Similarly, given political structures and competition for funds from other state agencies, the amount determined by a formula calculation may be reduced to conform to total funds available.

Formula Development

Formulas have been considered the offspring of necessity (Gross, 1979). The development of an objective, systematic method of dealing with the funding of many diverse institutions that served differing constituencies prompted many states to investigate and subsequently to begin using formulas (Miller, 1964). Prior to 1946, institutions of higher education served a limited and fairly homogeneous clientele. After World War II, enrollments jumped, and each state had a variety of liberal arts colleges, land-grant colleges, teacher training colleges, and technical schools to meet the needs of its citizens.

As the scope and mission of the campuses increased and changed (i.e., teachers colleges becoming regional universities), so did the complexity of distributing resources equitably among competing campuses. Unfortunately, state resources did not keep pace with expanding enrollments and the competition for state funds became greater. Because no two campuses are ever alike, methods were sought to allocate available funds in an objective manner, to provide sufficient justification for additional resources to satisfy state legislators, and to facilitate interinstitutional comparisons.

The desire for equity was a prime factor in the development of funding formulas, but other factors served as catalysts: the desire to determine an "adequate" level of funding; institutional needs to gain stability and predictability in funding levels; and increased professionalism among college and university business officers (Miller, 1964). The objective of equity in the distribution of state resources is to provide state appropriations to each of the campuses according to its needs. To achieve an equitable distribution of funds required a distribution formula that recognized differences in size, clients, location, and the mission of the college (Millett, 1974).

The concept of "adequacy" is more difficult to operationalize in the distribution of resources. What might be considered to be adequate for the basic operation of one campus would be considered inadequate for a campus offering similar programs but having a different client base. Indeed, the concept of adequacy has created operational problems in the distribution of funds to elementary and secondary education, where the definition of "need" is much more refined.

Texas was the first state to use funding formulas for higher education. By 1950, California, Indiana, and Oklahoma also were using funding formulas or cost analysis procedures in the budgeting or resource allocations process (Gross, 1979). In 1964, 16 states (Alabama, California, Colorado, Florida, Georgia, Indiana, Kentucky, Mississippi, New Mexico, New York, North Carolina, Ohio, Oregon, Tennessee, Washington, and Wisconsin) were identified as using formulas at some point in the allocation process (Miller, 1964). By 1973, the number had increased to 25 states (Gross, 1973) and to 33 by 1992 (McKeown & Layzell, 1994).

Formulas evolved over a long period of time and contributed to a series of compromises between institutions, state coordinating agencies, and state budget officials. For example, institutions sought autonomy while state coordinating or governing boards and budget officials sought adequate information to enable control over resources. The development of the Texas formulas is an example of the trade-offs and compromises that must be made between accountability and autonomy.

When sudden enrollment increases following World War II caused confusion in the amounts to be appropriated to Texas public colleges, each institution lobbied the legislature for additional funds. Texas legislators felt that the institutional requests were excessive and that the division of resources among institutions was inequitable. Consequently, the legislature asked for some rational mechanism to distribute funds. In 1951, a teaching salary formula based on workload factors was developed; this formula did not recognize differences among the campuses in roles and missions. By 1957, a series of budget formulas developed by institutional representatives, citizens, and the new Commission on Higher Education was presented to the legislature. These formulas were developed only after completion of a major study of the role and scope of the institutions. The study included an inventory of program offerings and attempted to measure costs by program. After 1958, a cost study committee was established that recommended adoption of five formulas for teaching salaries, general administration, library, building maintenance, and custodial services.

In 1961, two formulas for organized research and departmental operating costs were added (Miller, 1964).

In 1996, Texas used 13 separate formula calculations that were developed through complex cost studies of each of the program offerings at the campuses. Texas continues to use advisory committees to revise and improve its formulas to encompass two broad objectives: provide for an equitable distribution of funds among institutions and assist in determining the funding needed for a first-class system of higher education (Ashworth, 1994). At each stage of formula development, compromises were reached between the desire for additional data for increased accuracy and for differentiating among the institutions and the cost of providing the data.

The trend in formula development in many other states parallels the experience of Texas: refinement of procedures, greater detail and reliability in the collection and analysis of information, and improvement in the differentiation between programs and activities. Some states appear to have used different methods to develop formulas. For example, Alabama adapted the formulas used by Texas to the particular circumstances of Alabama and continues to modify the formulas to reflect circumstances specific to Alabama, and to incorporate judicial interventions. Adaptation rather than development of a new formula appears to be the preferred method because of the time and cost required to do a good cost study. Accounting procedures are not refined enough in some states to permit the calculation of costs differentiated by academic discipline and level of student and to separate professorial time into the multiple work products generated by carrying out the university's three main missions: teaching, research, and service. States continue to adapt formulas from other states because methods that work in one state may work equally well in another at considerable savings of time and resources.

Many formulas have been based on simple least squares regression analysis or the determination of an "average cost" for providing a particular type of service. Others have been based on staffing ratios and external determinations of "standard costs." The key to the process seems to be the isolation or identification of variables or factors that are directly related to actual program costs (Anderes, 1985). Isolation of variables that are detailed, reliable, not susceptible to manipulation by a campus, and sufficiently differentiated to recognize differences in role and missions requires collection of myriad amounts of data. Data must be collected and analyzed in an unbiased manner that does not raise questions of preferential treatment for one campus or sector. For this reason, statewide boards or other state agencies have been given responsibility for formula development.

For a formula to be effective, several criteria should be met (Miller, 1964):

- Formula development should be flexible.
- Formulas should be used for budget development, not budget control.
- Formulas should be related to quantifiable factors.
- Data should be consistent among institutions.
- Normative data should reflect local and national trends.
- The formula should be useful to institutions, boards, other state agencies, and the legislature.

Formula Advantages and Disadvantages

States use funding formulas for a variety of reasons, including these advantages among the reasons for use:

- Formulas provide an objective method to determine institutional needs equitably.
- Formulas reduce political competition and lobbying by the institutions.
- Formulas provide state officials with a reasonably simple and understandable basis for measuring expenditures and revenue needs of campuses and determining the adequacy of support.
- Formulas enable institutions to project needs on a timely basis.
- Formulas represent a reasonable compromise between public accountability and institutional autonomy (Millett, 1974).
- Formulas ease comparisons between institutions.
- Formulas permit policy makers to focus on basic policy questions.

Formulas promote efficiency in institutional operation.

State funding formulas also can provide for equity among institutions depending on how the formulas are constructed. Two types of equity are achieved through formula use: horizontal and vertical.

Horizontal equity is defined as the equal treatment of equals, and vertical equity is defined as the unequal treatment of unequals. An example of a horizontal equity element is a formula that provides a fixed dollar amount for one credit hour of lower division English instruction, no matter where the class is taught. Texas and Alabama use this in their instruction-funding formulas. An example of a vertical equity element in a formula is the allowance of $2.80 per gross square foot (GSF) of space for maintenance of a frame building but $3.20 per GSF for maintenance of a brick building.

However, formulas do have shortcomings, and there have been many heated debates over whether the advantages of formulas outweigh the downside of use. Some disadvantages of funding formulas are the following:

- Formulas may be used to reduce all academic programs to a common level of mediocrity by funding each one the same because quantitative measures cannot assess the quality of a program.
- Formulas may reduce incentives for institutions to seek outside funding.
- Formulas may perpetuate inequities in funding that existed before the advent of the formula because formulas may rely on historical cost data (Millett, 1974).
- Enrollment-driven formulas may be inadequate to meet the needs of changing client bases or new program initiatives.
- Formulas cannot serve as substitutes for public policy decisions (Miller, 1964).
- Formulas are only as accurate as the data on which the formula is based.
- Formulas may not provide adequate differentiation among institutions.
- Formulas are linear in nature and may not account for sudden shifts in enrollments and costs (Boutwell, 1973).

Formula Approaches

Formulas reflect one of two computational approaches: all-inclusive, where the total entitlement or allocation for the program area is determined by one calculation, or itemized, where more than one calculation or formula is used in each budget area. Most states use the latter.

Computational Methods

Three computational methods have been identified under which every formula calculation can be classified: rate-per-base factor unit (RPBF), percentage-of-base factor (PBF), and base factor–position ratio with salary rates (BF-PR/SR) (Moss & Gaither, 1976). The rate-per-base factor method starts with an estimate of a given base, such as credit hours or full-time-equivalent (FTE) students, and then multiplies that base by a specific unit rate. Unit rates generally have been determined previously by cost studies and can be differentiated by discipline, level, and type of institution.

The PBF assumes there is a specific relationship between a certain base factor like faculty salaries and other areas like departmental support services. The PBF method can be differentiated by applying a varying percentage to levels of instruction or type of institution (Miller, 1964), but this is unusual. Reportedly, the PBF was developed because of the perception that all support services are related to the primary mission of a college or university—instruction (Boling, 1961).

The BF-PR/SR is based on a predetermined optimum ratio between a base factor and the number of personnel; for example, ratios such as student/faculty and credit hours per faculty member are used. The resulting number of faculty positions determined at each salary level then is multiplied by the salary rate for that level and the amounts summed to give a total budget requirement. The BF-PR/SR also is used commonly in plant maintenance and is the most complex of the computational methods.

Base Factors

Base factors used in most formulas can be classified into five categories: head count, number of positions, square footage or acreage, FTE students, and credit hours. Square footage or acreage is used most often in the operation and maintenance of the plant, whereas credit hours, FTE students, or positions are the most prevalent bases in the instruction, academic support, and institutional support areas. Head count is used as the base unit in student services and scholarships and fellowships.

Differentiation

Formulas may differentiate among academic disciplines (e.g., education, sciences, and architecture), levels of enrollment (freshman and sophomore—called lower division; junior and senior—called upper division; master's; and doctoral), and types of institutions (community colleges, baccalaureate institutions, and research universities). Recently, some states like Kentucky and Alabama have introduced differentiation for historically black institutions as an institutional type.

States have found it necessary to introduce factors that differentiate among institutions in funding formulas because each institution, if examined closely enough, is different and has a different mission and mix of program offerings. Differentiation is used to recognize that there are legitimate reasons for costs to vary; reasons include economies and diseconomies of scale, method of instruction, and class size. Differentiation became more prevalent and more complex as accounting and costing methods improved and reliable cost data became available.

Differentiation is especially commonplace in formulas used to calculate funding requirements for the instruction program area. All of the states using formulas for instruction differentiate by discipline, institutional type, or level of enrollment. Only a few formulas in other budget areas differentiate by these three types of factor.

Formula Use by the States

In 1996, 30 states reported using funding formulas in the budget or resource allocation process for four-year public institutions. Twenty states indicate that they are in the process of revising current formulas or adopting new formulas. The number of states employing formulas changes from year to year, as states continually adopt, modify, and drop formulas and because what one person may consider a formula may be called by another name by another person. For example, Louisiana typically is identified as a formula state, although the person responding to the survey used to collect data for this chapter indicated that Louisiana was not using formulas in 1996. States iden-

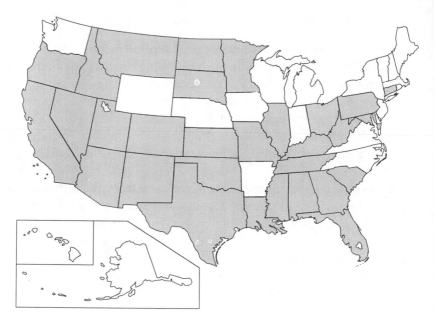

Figure 3.1. States Using Funding Formulas in 1996
NOTE: Shaded states use formulas.

tified as using funding formulas, peers, or quality/outcome measures
for four-year public higher education institutions in 1996 are listed in
Table 3.1 and shown in Figure 3.1.

Although all the southern states except North Carolina have used
funding formulas over the past 20 years and have been leaders in
formula development and innovation, that picture has changed somewhat since 1992. Virginia and Arkansas completely dropped the use
of formulas in the resource allocation or budgeting process, and most
of the other southern states have modified their formulas since 1992.
Of the 13 western states, all except Washington, Hawaii, Wyoming,
and Alaska used formulas, whereas 8 of the 13 midwestern states and
2 of the 10 northeastern states used formulas. California has a formula
but has suspended distribution of resources under it during the
current budgetary crisis.

Among the states, there is some variety in the type and number of
formulas and in the functional or budget areas for which formulas

are used. The number of formulas used by the states in each of eight NACUBO functional areas is displayed in Table 3.2. Of the 30 states identified as using formulas, only Kentucky, Maryland, and Mississippi have at least one formula in each functional area, but 12 states had at least six formulas. Kansas, Idaho, and Arizona have only one basic formula.

Of the states using formulas, 22 have only one formula for instruction. Oregon has four, one of each of the cost areas related to instruction. The majority of states applied formulas to all institutions but differentiate among types. Texas uses 13 formulas to compute budget requirements for E&G expenditures, and South Carolina uses 12. In 13 of the states, more than one computational formula is used to determine academic support needs. As most states have a separate formula for determining library needs, the academic support area, which includes libraries, academic computing support, and academic administration, usually will have expenditure needs computed by more than one formula. Academic support is an area for which the itemized approach generally is used.

These data reflect a watershed change in the use of funding formulas that is discussed in more detail in the concluding section of the chapter. Briefly, it appears that states are beginning to eliminate the use of formulas and substitute productivity or accountability methods to determine resource allocations. Other states that previously had used formulas now use incremental budgeting with base budgets that were computed by formula in prior years; this method implies a formula base. These are major shifts apparently away from equity and adequacy goals toward goals of accountability and efficiency.

Instruction Formulas

This category includes all expenditures for credit and noncredit courses; for academic, vocational, technical, and remedial instuction; and for regular, special, and extension sessions. Excluded are expenditures for academic administration when the primary assignment is admininstration, such as deans (NACUBO, 1988). Instruction is the most complex, and most expensive, component of an institution's expenditures. Because of its importance, identification of appropriate

TABLE 3.1   Comparison of Funding Formula Use Among the States: 1984, 1992, and 1996

State	Using Funding Formulas			Using Peers			Using Quality/ Outcome Factors		
	1984	1992	1996	1984	1992	1996	1984	1992	1996
Alabama	x	x	x		x	x			
Alaska		x							
Arizona	x	x	x		x	x			x
Arkansas	x	x			x	x			x
California	x	x	x		x	x			
Colorado	x	x	x						
Connecticut	x	x	x		x	x	x		x
Delaware									
Florida	x	x	x		x	x	x		x
Georgia	x	x	x		x	x	x		
Hawaii					x				
Idaho		x	x		x	x	x		
Illinois	x	x	x	x	x	x			x
Indiana					x	x			
Iowa					x	x			
Kansas	x	x	x		x	x			
Kentucky	x	x	x	x	x	x	x	x	
Louisiana	x	x	x		x	x	x		
Maine					x				x
Maryland	x	x	x				x		
Massachusetts	x							x	
Michigan	x								
Minnesota	x	x	x				x		x
Mississippi	x	x	x		x	x		x	x
Missouri	x	x	x		x		x	x	x
Montana	x	x	x		x	x			
Nebraska					x	x			
Nevada	x	x	x		x	x	x		
New Hampshire									

cost factors is critical to the validity of the formula development process. Summary information on the instruction formulas used by the states is displayed in Table 3.3.

TABLE 3.1 *Continued*

	Using Funding Formulas			Using Peers			Using Quality/ Outcome Factors		
State	*1984*	*1992*	*1996*	*1984*	*1992*	*1996*	*1984*	*1992*	*1996*
New Jersey	x						x	x	
New Mexico	x	x	x		x				
New York	x								
North Carolina					x	x		x	
North Dakota	x	x	x		x	x		x	
Ohio	x	x	x				x	x	x
Oklahoma	x	x	x		x	x			
Oregon	x	x	x		x	x			
Pennsylvania	x		x						
Rhode Island					x	x			x
South Carolina	x	x	x		x	x			
South Dakota	x	x	x						
Tennessee	x	x	x		x	x	x	x	x
Texas	x	x	x		x	x			
Vermont						x			x
Utah		x	x		x	x			
Virginia	x	x			x	x	x	x	x
Washington	x			x	x	x	x		
West Virginia	x	x	x		x	x			
Wisconsin	x				x	x			
Wyoming					x	x			
N	36	32	30	3	28	36	15	10	14

Because the instruction program is the major component of expenditures at institutions of higher education, formulas for this activity are quite complex. Each of the states using formulas explicitly or implicitly uses at least one formula for instruction. Each state provides differential funding for activities within the instruction program to recognize differences in costs by level of instruction and among academic disciplines. Over time, formulas for instruction have become more complex in part because improvements in cost accounting procedures have resulted in more accurate data.

TABLE 3.2 Number of Formulas Used by the States in 1996, by Functional Area

State	Public Instruction	Research	Service	Academic Support	Student Services	Institutional Support	Scholarships and Fellowships	Plant Operations
Alabama	1	1	1	2	1	1		1
Arizona	*			*	*	*		*
California	*	*	*	*		*		*
Colorado[a]								
Connecticut	1			3				5
Florida	2	*	*	3	1	1		3
Georgia	1	*		1	*	*		1
Idaho	*							
Illinois	*							
Kansas	*	*	*	*	*	*		*
Kentucky	1	1	1	5	1	1	1	1
Louisiana	*	*		*	*	*		*
Maryland	1	1	1	2	1	1	1	3
Minnesota	*			*	*	*		*
Mississippi	2	1	1	2	1	1	1	1
Missouri	1			2	1	1		1
Montana	2	*	*	*	*	*	1	
Nevada	2			2	1	1		2
New Mexico	1			1	1	1		1
North Dakota	1			2	*	*		2
Ohio	*			*	*	*		1
Oklahoma	*	*	*	*	*	*	*	*
Oregon	4	1		6	1	3		5
Pennsylvania	*	*	*	**	**	**		1
South Carolina	1	1	1	2	1	1		5
South Dakota	*	*		*	*	*		
Tennessee	1		1	2	1	1		1
Texas	2	1		2	2	1		5
Utah	*			*	*	*		*
West Virginia	*	1		*	*	*		*

NOTE: These formulas do not correspond to functional area analysis.
* or ** indicates that more than one functional area is combined in one formula.
a. Colorado distributes by formula funding for productivity, enrollment increases, and adult literacy.

States use both the all-inclusive approach and the itemized approach in the instruction area, but the majority use the itemized approach. In the formula(s) for instruction, the majority of the states recognize differences in institutional roles and missions, in the mix of classes by level and by academic discipline, and in teaching method; that is, all the states using instruction formulas differentiate. Explicitly, the states have attempted to distribute in an equitable manner state funds for the instructional operations of public institutions within the state by recognizing the equality of class credit hours by discipline and level and the differences in institutional roles and missions.

Because the formula allocations provide varying amounts based on enrollments by level and discipline, each institution in the state may receive differing amounts for instruction and different amounts per student from the formulas. Moreover, the recognition of the differences promotes achievement of vertical equity (i.e., the unequal treatment of unequals).

An example of a simplified formula for instruction follows. Student/faculty ratios by level by discipline vary in the formula.

Instruction funding = the sum of (the number of faculty positions per discipline × the average faculty salary for that discipline), where the number of faculty positions is determined by student/faculty ratios and the number of FTE students is determined by credit hours by level.

Research Formulas

This category includes expenditures for activities designed to produce research outcomes (NACUBO, 1988). Explicitly, or implicitly by inclusion with at least one other functional area, 17 states have a formula that provides funds for the research budget area (Table 3.4).

Florida's formula is complex and involves computations related to the magnitude of research activities engaged in at each institution. The number of research positions is calculated based on a ratio by specific department and is then multiplied by a specified salary rate. Kentucky uses a formula that calculates a level of support that recognizes differing roles and missions in research among institutions. A sample research formula follows.

(Text continued on p. 69)

TABLE 3.3 Instruction Funding Formulas

	Calculation Method			Base		Approach			Differentiation			Costs	
State	RPBF	PBF	BFPR/SR	All-Inclusive	Itemized	Credit Hours	Head Count	FTES/FTEF	Discipline	Level	Type of Institution	Fixed	Variable
Alabama	X				X	X			X	X	X		X
Arizona *			X		X	X		X	X	X	X		
California *			X		X	X		X	X	X	X	X	X
Connecticut			X		X	X		X	X	X	X		X
Florida	X				X	X		X	X	X	X		X
Georgia			X		X	X		X	X	X			X
Idaho *	X			X		X			X	X	X		X
Illinois *			X		X	X			X	X	X		X
Kansas *	X				X	X				X	X	X	X
Kentucky	X				X	X			X	X	X		X
Louisiana *	X				X	X			X	X	X		X
Maryland	X				X	X			X	X	X		X
Minnesota *	X				X	X			X	X	X		X
Mississippi		X	X		X	X			X	X	X		X
Missouri	X				X	X			X	X			X
Montana	X		X		X	X		X	X	X			X
Nevada			X		X	X		X		X			X
New Mexico	X		X		X	X			X	X	X		X
North Dakota	X		X		X	X			X	X	X		X
Ohio *	X				X	X		X	X	X	X	X	X

Oklahoma *	x			x	x		x			x	x			x
Oregon		x	x	x	x	x		x	x	x	x			x
Pennsylvania *		x	x	x	x	x		x	x	x		x	x	x
South Carolina		x	x	x	x	x		x	x	x	x			x
South Dakota *		x	x	x	x	x		x	x	x	x			x
Tennessee		x	x	x	x	x		x	x	x	x			x
Texas	x		x	x	x	x			x	x	x	x		x
Utah *		x	x	x	x	x		x	x	x	x		x	x
West Virginia *	x		x	x	x	x		x	x	x				x

* Indicates that more than one functional area is included in this formula.

67

TABLE 3.4 Research Formulas

State	Calculation Method			Approach		Base			Differentiation			Costs	
	RPBF	PBF	BFPR/SR	All-Inclusive	Itemized	Credit Hours	Sponsored Research	FTES/FTEF	Discipline	Level	Type of Institution	Fixed	Variable
Alabama		x		x		x			x	x			x
California *			x			x			x	x	x	x	x
Florida *			x		x	x			x	x	x		x
Georgia *			x		x	x		x	x	x			x
Kansas *	x				x	x				x	x	x	x
Kentucky		x		x			x						x
Louisiana	x				x	x			x	x	x		x
Maryland		x			x	x			x	x	x		x
Mississippi	x				x			x	x				x
Montana *	x		x		x	x		x	x	x			x
Oklahoma *	x				x	x		x	x	x	x		x
Oregon		x		x				x			x		x
Pennsylvania *			x		x	x		x		x		x	x
South Carolina		x		x			x						x
South Dakota *			x		x	x		x	x	x			x
Texas	x				x			x					x
West Virginia	x			x				x					x

* Indicates that more than one functional area is included in this formula.

Research amount = 5% of outside funding for research.

South Carolina allocates 25% of the prior year's sponsored and nongeneral fund research expenditures. Texas provides an amount equal to the number of FTE faculty times a dollar amount. Alabama's budget formula for research provides 2% of instruction and academic support allocations, plus 5% of sponsored research dollars expended in the last year for which data were available.

Most of these formulas incorporate horizontal and/or vertical equity features. Features that provide a set amount per position (Texas) or matching funds for each dollar of sponsored research (Alabama and South Carolina) provide horizontal equity, or the equal treatment of equals. Formulas that provide research support based on institutional type like Kentucky's or Oklahoma's meet the goal of providing vertical equity.

Public Service Formulas

This category includes funds expended for activities that primarily provide noninstructional services to individuals and groups external to the institution (NACUBO, 1988). Alabama, Kentucky, Maryland, Mississippi, Tennessee, and South Carolina are the only states that use an explicit formula approach for the funding of public service activities (Table 3.5). In Florida, public service positions are generated based on ratios specific to disciplines and then multiplied by a salary amount per position. South Carolina provides 25% of prior year sponsored and nongeneral fund public service expenditures; Alabama's funding formula is 2% of the combined allocations for instruction and academic support. A sample of a public service formula is shown below.

Public service allocation = .02 (instruction + academic support).

Academic Support Formulas

Table 3.6 displays summary information on the academic support formulas used by the states. The category academic support includes

TABLE 3.5 Public Service Formulas

State	Calculation Method			Approach		Base				Differentiation			Costs	
	RPBF	PBF	BFPR/SR	All-Inclusive	Itemized	Credit Hours	Expenditure Mission	Mission	FTES/FTEF	Discipline	Level	Type of Institution	Fixed	Variable
Alabama		×		×		×				×	×			×
California *			×		×	×				×	×	×	×	×
Florida *			×		×	×					×	×		×
Kansas *	×				×	×				×	×	×	×	×
Kentucky	×				×	×				×	×	×	×	×
Maryland		×			×	×				×	×	×		×
Mississippi	×			×				×				×		×
Montana *	×		×		×	×			×	×	×			×
Oklahoma *	×				×	×			×	×	×	×		×
Pennsylvania *			×		×	×			×		×			×
South Carolina		×		×				×						×
Tennessee		×			×	×				×	×	×	×	×

* Indicates that more than one functional area is included in this formula.

funds expended to provide support services for the institution's primary missions of instruction, research, and public service. The area includes expenditures for libraries, museums, and galleries; demonstration schools; media and technology, including computing support; academic administation, including deans; and separately budgeted course and curriculum development (NACUBO, 1988). However, costs associated with the office of the chief academic officer of the campus are included in the institutional support category.

To fund the library component of the academic support category, Alabama, Connecticut, Florida, Georgia, Kentucky, Maryland, Mississippi, Missouri, Nevada, Oregon, South Carolina, Tennessee, and Texas have at least one formula. Texas allocates an amount per credit hour differentiated by level of instruction.

Standards on the size of library collections, number of support personnel, and other factors have been developed by the American Library Association (ALA) and the Association of College Research Libraries (ACRL). Formulas to apply these standards, like the Voight formula and the Clapp-Jordan formula, have been developed so that institutions may determine if their library holdings meet the minimum requirements established by professional librarians. Only three states use a library formula that would permit meeting the ACRL criteria; however, no formula or standard currently in use accounts for the changes in resource requirements necessitated by increasing use of technology. In fact, the ALA and ACRL standards on size of collection do not consider the use of the "virtual library" found on the Internet, where the text of some "books" may be accessed on the computer networks. These technological changes in media availability certainly will have profound impacts on funding of libraries, but such changes have not yet been reflected in the funding formulas. An example of an academic support formula is shown below.

Academic support funding = .05 (instruction funding).

Florida, Kentucky, Missouri, South Carolina, and Texas each have at least one formula for other components of the academic support category. South Carolina calculates an amount based on a percentage of instructional costs. Because the instructional cost allocation includes vertical equity components, academic support calculations

TABLE 3.6 Academic Support Formulas

State	Calculation Method			Approach		Base			Differentiation			Costs	
	RPBF	PBF	BFPR /SR	All- Inclusive	Itemized	Credit Hours	Head Count	FTES/ FTEF	Discipline	Level	Type of Institution	Fixed	Variable
Alabama	x	x			x	x			x	x			x
Arizona *			x		x	x		x		x			x
California *			x		x	x			x	a	x	x	x
Connecticut	x		x		x	x	a	x		a	x	x	x
Florida	x		x		x	x	x	x	x	x	x		x
Georgia *		x			x	x			x	x			x
Kansas *	x				x	x				x	x	x	x
Kentucky	x	x			x	x	x			x	x	x	x
Louisiana *	x				x	x			x	x	x		x
Maryland	x	x			x						x		x
Minnesota *	x				x			x	x	x	x		x
Mississippi		x			x	x		x	x	x	x		x
Missouri	x				x	x			x	x			x
Montana *	x			x									x
Nevada	x	x			x	x		x		x		x	x
New Mexico	x	x			x	x				a	x		x
North Dakota	x				x			x		x			x
Ohio	x				x	x		x	x	x	x	x	x
Oklahoma *	x			x			a	x	x	x	x		x
Oregon	x	x			x	x	a	x	x	a	x	x	x

	1	2	3	4	5	6	7	8	9
Pennsylvania *	x	x	x			x		x	x
South Carolina		x	x		x	x			x
South Dakota *		x	x	x	x	x			x
Tennessee	x	x	x				x		x
Texas	x	x	x		x	x		x	x
Utah *	x	x	x	x	x	x	x		x
West Virginia *	x	x	x	x	x		x		x

* Indicates that more than one functional area is included in this formula.
a. Indicates that the state uses the Association of College Research Libraries formula.

73

based on instruction implicitly also include vertical equity components to provide an unequal amount for unequals.

Student Services Formulas

This expenditure category includes funds expended to contribute to a student's emotional and physical well-being and intellectual, social, and cultural development outside the formal instruction process. This category includes expenditures for student activites, student organizations, counseling, the registrar's and admissions offices, and student financial aid administration (NACUBO, 1988) (see Table 3.7).

The student services formulas used by Alabama, Kentucky, South Carolina, and Texas provide a different amount per head count or FTE students. As the size of the institution increases, the rate per student decreases to recognize economies of scale. The formula implicitly does this by adding an amount per weighted credit hour to a base. Such a calculation inherently recognizes economies of scale. Each of these formulas attempts to provide vertical equity in the distribution of resources by allocating unequal amounts to institutions of unequal size. A sample student services formula follows.

Student services funding = $395 per student for the first 4,000 headcount + $295 per student for the next 4,000 headcount + $265 per student for all students over 8,000 headcount.

Institutional Support Formulas

This category includes expenditures for the central executive level management of a campus, fiscal operations, administrative data processing, employee personnel services, and support services (NACUBO, 1988). Table 3.8 displays information on the institutional support formulas used by the states. Alabama, Mississippi, South Carolina, and Tennessee multiply a specified percentage by all other E&G expenditures to calculate institutional support needs. Kentucky includes some differentiation and a base amount to recognize economies of scale and complexity of operation, Texas multiplies a specified

TABLE 3.7 Student Services Formulas

State	RPBF	PBF	BFPR/SR	All-Inclusive	Itemized	Credit Hours	Head Count	FTES/FTEF	Discipline	Level	Type of Institution	Fixed	Variable
Alabama	x				x		x					x	x
Arizona *			x		x	x		x		x			x
Florida	x				x		x	x		x	x		x
Georgia *		x			x	x			x				x
Kansas *	x				x	x				x	x		x
Kentucky	x				x		x			x		x	x
Louisiana *	x				x	x			x	x	x	x	x
Maryland	x			x									x
Minnesota *	x				x			x	x	x	x		x
Mississippi	x				x	x		x	x			x	x
Missouri	x				x	x			x	x			x
Montana *	x		x		x	x		x	x	x			x
Nevada			x		x		x	x			x	x	x
New Mexico			x		x		x					x	x
North Dakota *	x				x		x			x		x	x
Ohio *	x				x	x		x	x	x		x	x
Oklahoma *	x				x	x		x	x	x	x		x
Oregon	x				x		x					x	x
Pennsylvania *	x				x	x		x				x	x
South Carolina	x				x	x	x			x		x	x
South Dakota *			x		x	x		x	x				x
Tennessee	x				x	x	x	x	x		x		x
Texas	x				x		x					x	x
Utah *			x		x	x			x	x	x		x
West Virginia *	x				x			x			x		x

* Indicates that more than one functional area is included in this formula.

rate by a measure of enrollment to determine institutional support amounts. All of these methods achieve vertical equity given that unequals are treated unequally. An example of an institutional support formula is shown below.

Institutional support = base amount + $150 per headcount student.

Scholarships and Fellowships Formulas

This category encompasses all expenditures for scholarships and fellowships, including prizes, awards, federal grants, tuition and fee waivers, and other aid awarded to students for which services to the institution are not required (NACUBO, 1988). Only Kentucky, Maryland, Mississippi, Montana, and Oklahoma calculate an allocation for scholarships and fellowships (Table 3.9). In each case except Oklahoma, which calculates the amount as a dollar value times the number of FTE students, the formula amount is equal to a percentage of tuition revenues. These approaches all provide horizontal equity but fail to provide vertical equity in that neither the cost to the student nor the institution nor the student's ability to pay is considered in the formula.

Operation and Maintenance of Plant Formulas

Table 3.10 displays information on the plant formulas used by the states. The plant category contains all expenditures for current operations and maintenance of the physical plant, including building maintenance, custodial services, utilities, landscape and grounds, and building repairs. Not included are expenditures made from plant fund accounts, or expenditures for hospitals, auxiliary enterprises, or independent operations (NACUBO, 1988).

Connecticut, Oregon, South Carolina, and Texas use five forumulas to calculate detailed plant needs. These complicated methods differentiate among types of building construction, usage of space, and size of institution. Horizontal equity is achieved in that equal dollars are provided for equal components of the physical plant. Moreover, differences among buildings are recognized and the unequal costs of maintaining, cooling, heating, and lighting each building are built into the formulas, resulting in vertical equity. An example of a simple plant formula is given below.

Plant funding = $6.50 per gross square foot of frame buildings + $3.75 per gross square foot of brick or masonry buildings.

Trends in the Use of Funding Formulas

As was mentioned earlier, there appears to have been a watershed in the use of funding formulas in the budgeting and resource allocation process for higher education institutions. On the one hand, formulas are becoming more complex; on the other hand, states that have used formulas for nearly a quarter of a century are abandoning their use. In the place of formulas, productivity measures and other accountability techniques are being used to measure institutional performance and allocate resources. Also, as state support for higher education stagnates, institutions are attempting to protect their base budgets by using an incremental approach to funding over the base formula-developed budget.

Formulas are becoming more sophisticated or complex. One of the major ways the complexity is shown is in the increase in the number of formulas within a budget area (e.g., instruction) and the differentiation within the formulas. The added complexity appears to be a recognition of differences in roles and missions and in costs among academic programs. From a technical or public policy standpoint, the increased complexity can be perceived as good. Formulas that more closely model reality, or that which is considered reality, always are preferable to more simplistic models. However, legislators, governors, and other state policy makers, who are the ultimate "consumers" of formulas, generally prefer one that is simple to understand.

Institutions appear to be protecting their base budgets by going to incremental budgeting in place of formula budgeting. Several states that had used funding formulas for at least a decade now use the incremental budgeting method. The base budget, however, was com-

(text continued on p. 81)

TABLE 3.8 Institutional Support Formulas

State	Calculation Method			Approach		Base				Differentiation			Costs	
	RPBF	PBF	BFPR /SR	All- Inclusive	Itemized	Credit Hours	Head Count	Other	FTES/ FTEF	Discipline	Level	Type of Institution	Fixed	Variable
Alabama		x		x		x				x	x			x
Arizona *			x		x	x			x		x			x
California *		x	x		x	x			x	x	x	x		x
Florida		x			x	x							x	x
Georgia *		x		x		x				x				x
Kansas *	x				x	x					x	x	x	x
Kentucky		x			x	x	x			x	x	x	x	x
Louisiana *	x				x	x				x	x	x		x
Maryland	x				x			x						x
Minnesota *	x				x				x	x	x	x		x
Mississippi		x			x	x				x	x			x
Missouri	x				x	x				x	x			x
Montana *	x			x										x
Nevada		x		x				x					x	x
New Mexico		x	x		x			x					x	x
North Dakota *	x			x			x						x	x
Ohio *	x				x	x	x		x	x	x	x	x	x
Oklahoma *	x				x	x			x	x	x	x		x
Oregon	x	x				x		x					x	x
Pennsylvania *	x				x	x			x				x	x

78

State										
South Carolina			x		x		x		x	x
South Dakota *	x		x		x		x	x	x	x
Tennessee	x	x	x			x			x	x
Texas	x			x	x				x	x
Utah *		x	x	x		x	x	x	x	x
West Virginia *	x		x	x		x	x	x	x	x

* Indicates that more than one functional area is included in this formula.

79

TABLE 3.9. Scholarships and Fellowships Formulas

State	Calculation Method			Approach		Base			Differentiation			Costs	
	RPBF	PBF	BFPR /SR	All- Inclusive	Itemized	Credit Hours	Head Count	Tuition Revenue	Discipline	Level	Type of Institution	Fixed	Variable
Kentucky		x		x				x					x
Maryland		x		x				x				x	
Mississippi		x		x				x					x
Montana		x		x				x				x	
Oklahoma*		x			x	x	x			x	x	x	x

* Indicates that more than one functional area is included in this formula.

puted by formula, so several of these states consider themselves "formula states." As state funding for higher education becomes more scarce, institutions understandably are concerned with maintaining the funding they have with minimal restrictions from the state. Formulas are, in effect, a zero-based budgeting method under which each institution justifies its request for state funds each year. Maintenance of the base can become the primary goal when enrollment declines or shifts into less expensive course offerings.

Many states adopted formula usage to provide and/or achieve equity in the distribution of resources. In the southern states, the provision of equity through a formula appears to be directly related to desegregation orders filed by the federal government. (It also is possible that these equity features are spillovers from state concerns with equity in K-12 funding formulas.) However, no attempt is made to determine whether a formula is "more" or "less" equitable in the distribution of state resources to institutions. Evaluations of formulas, and their impacts, like those done for elementary and secondary education using range ratios, gini coefficients, or other equity measures, are not used yet in higher education, except in a few federal court cases.

Now that states appear to be dropping formula use for four-year higher education, is this a shift away from the commitment to achieve goals of adequacy and equity in the distribution of resources toward a commitment to goals of efficiency and accountability? Clearly, the higher education "industry" has fallen on "hard times" in many states (Harman, 1995). Many institutions have suffered from absolute cuts in state funding during the 1990s. Tuition and fees have risen dramatically, and enrollments in some states have declined or shifted among institutions. Perhaps the switch away from funding formulas is merely a reflection of the hard times that necessitate a protection of the base budget rather than a movement away from equity and adequacy.

Yet maintenance of the base may not be possible when the general public seems to no longer be a willing participant in its love affair with higher education. Hardly a week goes by when the popular media does not have a story pointing out the indiscretions of higher education. Legislators have been calling for reform and accountability fueled by stories of how industries have been restructuring their budgets, rethinking their strategic plans, reorganizing, and reengi-

TABLE 3.10 Plant Formulas

State	Calculation Method			Approach		Base					Differentiation		Costs	
	RPBF	PBF	BFPR/SR	All-Inclusive	Itemized	NSF/GSF	Replacement Cost	Acres	Credit Hours	FTES/FTEF	Type of Building	Level	Fixed	Variable
Alabama	x				x	x					x	x		x
Arizona*			x		x				x	x	x	x		x
California*			x		x				x			x	x	x
Connecticut	x	x	x		x	x	x				x			x
Florida	x				x	x					x			x
Georgia	x				x	x								x
Kansas	x		x		x	x								x
Kentucky	x	x			x	x					x			x
Louisiana*	x				x	x								x
Maryland	x	x			x	x	x							x
Minnesota*	x				x					x		x		x
Mississippi	x				x	x					x			x
Missouri	x				x	x					x	x		x
Nevada		x	x		x	x	x	x						x
New Mexico	x		x		x	x					x			x
North Dakota	x				x		x	x		x	x	x		x
Ohio	x				x	x				x	x	x		x
Oklahoma*	x				x	x				x		x		x
Oregon	x	x	x		x	x		x			x			x
Pennsylvania	x				x	x	x					x	x	x

South Carolina	x		x	x	x			x		x
South Dakota *	x	x			x	x		x		x
Tennessee	x		x	x	x	x			x	x
Texas	x		x	x	x	x	x	x	x	x
Utah *	x		x	x		x		x		x
West Virginia *	x		x		x	x	x		x	x

* Indicates that more than one functional area is included in this formula.

neering the corporation to be more efficient and produce higher quality. Corporate leaders, long-time supporters of higher education, have called on institutions to reinvent themselves, to rethink their missions (and return to teaching as the primary mission), and to adopt continuous quality improvements (Harman, 1995) just as industry has done. The movement to accountability and performance measures suggests that a watershed may have been reached in the way in which higher education is funded. Perhaps it is time for a new paradigm.

And perhaps the new paradigm is the movement to "productivity" formulas. Tennessee has included productivity measures as a formula component for more than a decade. Colorado now distributes some funds based on productivity measures, and Florida begins its productivity component for four-year institutions in 1997. Arizona, Kentucky, Minnesota, Missouri, Ohio, and Oklahoma already have or are developing productivity components to the funding process. In total, 14 states indicate that they are using productivity components in funding, up from 8 reported in 1995 (Caruthers & Layzell, 1995). Arkansas, a long-time user of funding formulas, abandoned its formulas to go to productivity funding. This appears to be a significant change.

Some observers (Odden & Clune, 1995) call for a restructuring or reinventing of education finance to address the issue of productivity or accountability. They assert that changing state school finance structures and restructuring teacher compensation systems will result in increased student achievement and productivity. Perhaps a new paradigm for higher education funding would lead to increased productivity and student achievement. The challenge to higher education finance researchers and analysts is to develop that new paradigm.

Formulas never will solve the resource allocation problems in higher education. Formulas cannot recognize the full range of objective and subjective differences among institutions, nor can they anticipate changes in the missions of institutions, such as those changes that will come about with the advent of "virtual" universities. Formulas do provide an objective allocation mechanism that can provide more equity than independent funding of each institution with the power plays and patronage that inevitably characterize such allocation decisions. Determining the method for funding higher education will continue to be part of a political process that involves the art of compromise. Compromise will be necessary to preserve and improve the quality of public higher education and to accommodate the changing condition of education in the new millenium. Perhaps the promise will never be fulfilled, not because the goals were unworthy but because the goals have changed. Or, has the promise changed?

References

Anderes, T. (1985). Formula budgeting in higher education. *NACUBO Business Officer, 19*, 33-36.

Ashworth, K. H. (1994). *Formula recommendations for funding Texas institutions of higher education.* Austin: Texas Higher Education Coordinating Board.

Bass, D. D. (1995, December 1). High-tech sharing of campuses forecasted. *Las Vegas Sun*, p. 2B.

Boling, E. (1961). *Methods of objectifying the allocation of tax funds to Tennessee state colleges.* Unpublished doctoral dissertation, George Peabody College, TN.

Boutwell, W. K. (1973). Formula budgeting on the down side. In G. Kaludis (Ed.), *Strategies in budgeting* (pp. 41-50). San Francisco: Jossey-Bass.

Caruthers, J. K. (1989, November). *The impact of formula budgeting on state colleges and universities.* Paper presented at the meeting of the American Association of State Colleges and Universities, San Francisco.

Caruthers, J. K., & Layzell, D. T. (1995, March). *Performance funding for higher education at the state level.* Paper presented at the annual meeting of the American Education Finance Association, Savannah, GA.

Gross, F. M. (1973). *A comparative analysis of the existing budget formulas used for justifying budget requests or allocating funds for the operating expenses of state supported colleges and universities.* Unpublished doctoral dissertation, University of Tennessee.

Gross, F. M. (1979). Formula budgeting and the financing of public higher education: Panacea or nemesis for the 1980s? *AIR Professional File, 3.*

Harman, S. (1995, November/December). A widening rift. *Trusteeship*, p. 36.

McKeown, M. P. (1986). Funding formulas. In M. P. McKeown & S. K. Alexander (Eds.), *Values in conflict: Funding priorities for higher education.* Cambridge, MA: Ballinger.

McKeown, M. P. (1989). State funding formulas for public institutions of higher education. *Journal of Education Finance, 15*, 101-112.

McKeown, M. P., & Layzell, D. T. (1994). State funding formulas for higher education: Trends and issues. *Journal of Education Finance, 19*, 319-346.

Miller, J. L., Jr. (1964). *State budgeting for higher education: The use of formulas and cost analysis.* Ann Arbor: University of Michigan.

Millett, J. D. (1974). *The budget formula as the basis for state appropriations in support of higher education.* Indianapolis, IN: Academy for Educational Development.

Moss, C. E., & Gaither, G. H. (1976). Formula budgeting: Requiem or renaissance? *Journal of Higher Education, 47*, 550-576.

National Association of College and University Business Officers (NACUBO). (1988). *Management reporting and accounting for colleges.* Washington, DC: Author.

Odden, A., & Clune, W. (1995). Improving educational productivity and school finance. *Educational Researcher, 24*(9), 6-10.

FOUR

Accountability and Quality Evaluation in Higher Education[1]

JOHN V. LOMBARDI

ELIZABETH D. CAPALDI

In this era of constant competition for scarce resources, universities enjoy no immunity from the obligation to measure their performance and account for it to those who support the institution. Although general accountability for university quality and productivity has a long tradition, the new pressure focuses on linking measures of productivity to annual institutional budgets. This poses a major challenge for universities because they produce complex products whose value may not appear for years or whose quality may not be visible on an annual basis that fits the annual budget cycle. Research products from university laboratories, publications, or creative activities may have no commercial value in the year produced but generate tremendous economic advantage 10, 15, or 20 years after the original investment. Instructional products, delivered primarily as degrees or courses, often generate a value unmeasurable except over 5- to 10-year periods, well beyond any budgeted point of delivery. Universities find it especially difficult to measure the undeniable benefits that society receives from higher education that flow from the generally higher standard of living experienced by college graduates or that come from the greatly enhanced economic opportunity for all members of society that results from the deployment of the research products and individual talents that create industries, jobs, and substantial economic value.

Given the almost universal recognition that university education and research produce a high return on the aggregate investment society makes in them, we should accept the proposition that the individuals and political units and subunits that pay for higher education receive a high return on their private or public investment. This conclusion reflects the multiple economic analyses that demonstrate this high rate of return to society from university education and research. Other analyses clearly demonstrate that the economic development of states and regions depends at the first level of competitiveness on the educational level of its population and at the second level on the ability of society to translate that education into a highly motivated workforce. Economists may argue about the multipliers that translate a dollar invested in higher education into many dollars returned to individuals, industries, and society at large, but no one doubts the high rate of return. Although this general proposition may be above challenge, we find it much more difficult to link this high rate of return directly to university budgets because of the complexity and time delays that characterize the delivery of university value to the economy. If we can agree on the general value of higher education, however, then the critical issues for the universities' constituencies relate less to the general return on investment, which is clearly high, and more to the specific performance of universities in delivering their two main missions of teaching and research. Modern universities often provide a wide range of additional services to their many constituencies, but most of these services simply extend or translate either teaching or research products into alternative areas, for alternative purposes, through alternative delivery systems or for special subgroups within the general population interested in higher education.

The complexity of the university's products and the greatly varied time frame for determining their total economic value make the general business profit-and-loss mechanisms difficult to adapt for university management. At the same time, most universities have accounting structures oriented toward the integrity of fund management rather than toward the analysis of costs and the evaluation of benefits. To improve the quality and productivity of our programs without the normal private enterprise tools of profit-and-loss analysis that support the delivery of stockholder profit, we have chosen instead to use benchmarking strategies that evaluate our programs within the context of the best institutions in our competitive marketplace. This strategy prompted the university to invent an ongoing program called the Florida Quality Evaluation Project as the internal planning and evaluation mechanism at the University of Florida (Lombardi & Capaldi, 1992).[2]

This accountability project has as its major product an accounting mechanism that records university expenditures and incomes along with a range of productivity and quality indicators in an annual report format. This document (FQEP) attempts to translate the fund accounting information, the quality evaluation information, and the productivity information collected in various formats by the university into a consistent and comparable report on the performance of departments, colleges, and the divisions of the institution. This report then can serve legislators, faculty, students, staff, administrators, and other interested observers specific and consistent data reflecting the university's effectiveness. The FQEP data demonstrate the relative effectiveness of the various colleges and programs in generating funds collected for teaching, research, and service and illustrate how the university spends these funds. The Florida Quality Evaluation Project requires that the document include all revenue, whether from state, federal, private, fees for service, contract, or tuition sources. The project also enables the University of Florida to benchmark the quality, effectiveness, and productivity of its programs against a reference group chosen from the membership of the Association of American Universities (AAU) public universities. In the end, FQEP data ensure that the University of Florida remains accountable to its many constituents, from the university's Board of Regents, to the political authorities of legislature or cabinet or governor, to donors, citizens, students, foundations, and others who care about and contribute to the success of the university.

The FQEP data come in two major sections: Part I of the FQEP reports the standard data for each unit of the university for the academic and fiscal year (see Table 4.1). Organized in terms of the units, colleges, and academic support units on campus, Part I captures sources of funds (resources), uses of funds (expenditures), and a variety of productivity measures. The evaluation of productivity requires a consideration of both the resources available relative to other units and the uses made of these resources. These data offer a measure of the contribution of each unit to the three missions of the university: teaching (graduate and undergraduate), research, and service.

Key to understanding productivity is the concept of effort. In the universe recognized in the FQEP, every full-time faculty member of the university appears as 100% effort. We do not measure the actual effort (e.g., hours) but, instead, start from the assumption that all FTE faculty work 100% for the University of Florida and when the university allocates resources to a faculty member in terms of salary or support, it is in exchange for 100% effort. Then, we distribute portions of that faculty member's effort among the university's various functions, principally research or teaching but also including academic administration, service, and other activities. We then have a mechanism to allocate cost to the effort of the faculty and to distribute the cost of other support functions to the primary functions of teaching and research. Although there is an element of arbitrariness in this model, it has the virtue of focusing our attention on what our faculty do and how they allocate their talents and abilities, and it also avoids the endless arguments and irrelevant discussions about time spent on a particular task. The effort of each faculty member is a formally designated assignment derived from an agreement between the faculty member and the department. Consequently, faculty effort devoted to any particular university purpose, expressed as a percentage of total faculty effort, becomes an excellent unit for analyzing cost and determining productivity.

In Part I of the FQEP, we also have the ability, using the effort model, to distinguish between the effort and its associated productivity funded by Florida resources and the effort funded by other, nonstate resources such as grants, contracts, clinical fees, and tuition. The FQEP

(text continued on p. 95)

TABLE 4.1 Florida Quality Evaluation Project: Report Format Generalized

SOURCES AND USES OF FUNDS

			Resources				
	State	Tuition and Fees	Sponsored Research: Indirect Cost Generated	Sponsored Research: Indirect Cost Allocated	Sponsored Research: Direct Cost	Private	Auxiliaries	Total
Academic Units							
College A							
College B							
etc.							
Support Units							
President's Office							
Academic Affairs							
etc.							

			Expenditures			
	Salaries	Temporary Personnel	Expense	Equipment	Electronic Data Processing	Other	Total
Academic Units						
College A						
College B						
etc.						
Support Unit						
President's Office						
Academic Affairs						
etc.						

continued

PRODUCTIVITY DATA

Effort

	Instruction	Academic Advising	Research	Public Service	Academic Administration	Other
Academic Units						
College A						
College B						
etc.						
Support Units						
President's Office						
Academic Affairs						
etc.						

Credit Hours

	Lower	Upper	Graduate	Thesis/Dissertation
Academic Units				
College A				
College B				
etc.				
Support Units				
President's Office				
Academic Affairs				
etc.				

Sections Taught by Rank

	Professor	Associate Professor	Assistant Professor	Instructor and Other Faculty	Adjunct	Other	
College A							
College B							
etc.							
Support Units							
President's Office							
Academic Affairs							
etc.							

Sections Taught by Level / Section Size

	Lower	Upper	Graduate	1-30	31-60	61-120	> 120
College A							
College B							
etc.							
Support Units							
President's Office							
Academic Affairs							
etc.							

continued

Degrees Awarded

	Bachelor's	Master's	Doctoral	First Professorship	Other	Total
College A						
College B						
etc.						
Support Units						
President's Office						
Academic Affairs						
etc.						

data include all funds generated and spent by the University of Florida in the fiscal year and represent a complete accountability report. The following is a summary of the sections of Part I of the Florida Quality Improvement Project report with a comment on the usefulness of these data:

1. Resources include all sources of funds, state and nonstate (sponsored research, private, miscellaneous gifts and grants, auxiliary services, and for the Health Center private practice plan), organized by colleges or academic support units. These tables illustrate the significant differences in the funding generated from external grant money, private funds, tuition and fees, and state dollars.

2. Expenditures distribute costs by category, including salaries, temporary personnel, operating expenses, minor equipment, data processing expenses, debt service, and a variety of special categories. These categories, defined by state and Regents rules, provide a rough guide to the expenditure patterns of each unit and permit a comparison of management across units. These differences also produce widely differing distribution of effort within and among units. The university uses these data to help maximize the effectiveness of each unit in the use of total faculty effort funded from different sources. So, in colleges with high external funding for research, we expect to find high total effort on research, relatively low effort on research funded by state sources, and relatively high effort for teaching funded on the state accounts. In units with lower external funding per faculty member, the state support of teaching effort remains high, but also the state's support of research effort likely is high. In these cases, we look at the productivity from the investment of state resources in research and teaching to determine whether the institution is using its funds effectively to gain the maximum benefit from the various sources of revenue. A special category of local funds captures expenditures from locally generated revenues such as housing, student activities, and athletics. These locally generated funds come from enterprises that, by definition, must earn the revenue to meet their expenses and are operated as cost and revenue centers, independent from the general university funds.

3. Faculty productivity and other productivity effort tables summarize the effort allocation to state-funded activities. The FQEP reports state-funded effort for ranked faculty separately from other

state-funded effort—for example, these might be unranked faculty or other teaching personnel or nonranked research personnel. These tables show the effort and then resources spent on instruction, advising, research, public service, academic administration, governance, and other. The same elements appear for the faculty and other personnel effort funded from sponsored research as well as other sources such as private funds. These tables capture the complete effort of the faculty and staff that produce the work of the university, and the data make clear the different functions supported with state and nonstate funds in the key areas of teaching and research.

4. Teaching productivity tables addresses a clear and focused interest of state legislators, parents, and citizens everywhere, including the state of Florida. In developing these tables we use a statistical artifact to represent the faculty effort. Called *personyears*, this label refers to a faculty member employed full-time for 12 months. Because many faculty have 9- or 10-month appointments, a faculty personyear represents a statistical artifact useful for data but not an accurate representation of an individual faculty member. Using this metric, the tables show the number of faculty personyears funded from state resources, sponsored research revenues, or other sources for each unit. We then view the productivity numbers in terms of the number of faculty personyears available to each unit and gain considerable insight into the following teaching-related productivity measures for each unit:

- Credit hours taught at each level (lower division undergraduate through doctoral dissertation)
- Course sections taught by faculty in each rank (professor, associate professor, assistant professor, instructor and other faculty, graduate assistant, adjunct faculty, and other)
- Course sections taught at each level (freshmen and sophomore level, junior and senior level, graduate classroom, and thesis/dissertation)
- Course sections taught by size of class (number of students in class)
- Degrees awarded, including undergraduate, graduate, and professional

Part II of the FQEP provides benchmarking data that each unit provides on a three-year cycle. This benchmarking requires each unit to compare itself to the comparable unit at three large, high-quality, comprehensive, land-grant research universities: Ohio State University, University of Minnesota, and University of Illinois. These three universities have the size and academic scope most comparable to the University of Florida among the AAU public institutions, and they have the excellent quality and productivity against which we compete. Besides these core comparators, each unit adds seven others from among the AAU public institutions that also have exemplary programs. This method gives both a standard benchmark for all units and a range of program- or discipline-specific benchmarks for particular competitive programs.

Because the scientific fields, the arts and humanities, and social sciences measure quality of research differently, each unit picks its own quality indicators and provides data to validate the appropriateness of these indicators. Principal among these validation criteria is the existence of national comparative data for these indicators that include the University of Florida and our specific benchmarked institutions.

In presenting these benchmarking data, we use the university's aggregate measures as the reference for the public and the legislature. This reflects the need to present relatively straightforward data without the endless detail required to inform college-level or departmental-level decisions. In the case of the legislature, the state focuses primarily on the university's performance in using the state's resources to support teaching and research. Florida must also contend with the rapid and continuing growth of student demand for access to higher education associated with the state's population growth. In responding to this demand over the past few years, the University of Florida has admitted more students, offered more courses, and expanded its degree programs. At the same time, state support for higher education continues to drift downward in terms of dollars per student, and tuition and fee revenue remain constrained by legislative limits. This pressure on resources and institutional capabilities, driven by the public's recognition that a college education has become a requirement for reasonable employment opportunities, has forced all of Florida's state universities to reexamine their curricula, reorganize their operations, and seek economies that permit them to maintain quality in the face of rising demand and stagnant resources. The University of Florida has been deeply involved in this activity.

Although we organize the university and recruit and retain faculty within a holistic notion of university education that joins undergraduate instruction, graduate education, research productivity and service in a mutually reinforcing structure, efficiencies in operation require that we examine each component of our institution's productivity separately to determine how we can best maintain quality under current conditions. We focused considerable attention in this effort on undergraduate instruction, reflecting its importance in our institution's mission and the intense public and legislative interest in it.

Undergraduate Instruction

In response to the challenges of declining resources and growing enrollment, the University of Florida developed a number of programs to improve the efficiency and accountability of undergraduate education. These efforts have as their goal the enhancement of a student-centered undergraduate program in the university. Rather than focusing on the efficiency of undergraduate education from the perspective of the college, department, or faculty member, we have reconsidered our system from the perspective of the student and the student's progress through our curriculum toward the successful completion of a degree.

The key analysis in this effort compared the number of credit hours required for a degree to the number of credit hours attempted for the degree (Lombardi, 1994a). By studying the complete college records of all the undergraduate degree recipients in one year, this analysis demonstrated that the average University of Florida student took about 24 credit hours beyond those required for the degree. Subsequent analysis replicated this result with a second graduating class at the University of Florida and demonstrated that the average for the 9-campus state university system of Florida also centered at 24 excess hours. As we reviewed the data for the spring 1994 University of Florida graduating class, we discovered that students acquire some excess credit hours because they cannot get seats in a few basic required courses in the semester they need those courses. Students who cannot obtain the classes they need often register for classes they do not need in order to keep their financial aid or their eligibility for other benefits accorded full-time students. Having identified this bottleneck, the university received help from the legislature to increase the sections in these courses, and for example, added just under 3,000 new seats in required English classes in the 1995-1996 academic year.

We cannot manage all of the difference between the ideal and the actual number of hours. About 9% (2 credit hours) of the extra credit hours resulted from students changing their majors once during their college career. About 83% of graduating students never changed majors or changed majors only once if we consider "undecided" a first major, so changing majors does not account for the bulk of the excess credit hours students acquire. A more important cause of excess credit hours comes from students who drop, repeat, or fail courses. We may reduce this somewhat through better advising, but probably excess hours from this source will always remain. About 25% of the credit hours unused for the degree were taken outside the University of Florida and did not fulfill any of the requirements for the degree. Students took the remainder of the excess credit hours at the University of Florida, and these simply did not contribute toward their degree. Sometimes, students took a minor and used extra credit hours for that, or students simply acquired courses to improve their skills or pursue interests unrelated to their degrees. Some students clearly took additional courses to enhance their marketability after leaving the university. Some also took courses to maintain their standing as they sought to gain entrance into high-demand programs with very high entrance requirements such as physical therapy or veterinary medicine. Many of these causes of excess credit hours offer opportunities for better management to ensure that the student's progress through the university toward the degree flows smoothly, effectively, and efficiently.

Tracking

In response to this analysis, the university began developing a tracking pilot program that would guide students throughout their undergraduate academic careers and provide a clear path through requirements to the achievement of a degree (Lombardi, 1994b). The tracking program experiment received support from the legislature and the university piloted a trial program with a small number of community colleges and entering university students. In Florida, the large community college system (28 campuses) and the strong commitment to smooth articulation between community college and university programs (known as the 2+2 system) requires that any effort to improve efficiency and quality at the university must accommodate and include the community college students who will become university students in the junior and senior year. The pilot program experiment led to a number of improvements, and a full program called universal tracking began for all undergraduate students at the University of Florida in fall 1996 (Lombardi, 1996b).

Under universal tracking, the university provides each undergraduate student with an optimum individual path through the curriculum that leads them to their degree objective. This track is easy to modify to reflect a different degree goal as students explore and discover their talents and interests. The tracking audit lists the courses required and electives possible as defined by the student's chosen degree program in a semester by semester sequence. The catalog also reflects these tracks for each degree, beginning with the 1996 catalog. The tracking audit informs students which requirements they have fulfilled by courses already taken, requirements yet to be fulfilled, and the total credit hours attempted. Students are on track if every course taken fulfills a requirement or counts as an elective in their required degree program. If students change their majors or degrees, the university's universal tracking system generates a new audit that outlines the optimal path through the curriculum toward the new major or degree. The university mails the audit to the student's local address each semester and students can also access the audit on-line.

Degree Funding

Besides providing the critical element in a student-centered undergraduate system, universal tracking creates the infrastructure for the successful implementation of the University of Florida's degree funding (Lombardi & Capaldi, 1996).

Degree funding creates the link between the productivity of the university in helping students earn degrees over a period of years and the annual budget cycle of state funding. In degree funding, each university is funded for each student's degree requirements plus a 10% margin for changes and adjustments. Once the university and the student have used up this degree funding, the state reallocates the funds to support a new student. If the student has not graduated within the degree requirements plus 10%, then the university and the student must support the costs of the rest of the student's undergraduate instruction. The student pays a surcharge, and the university pays for the instruction without state support. This mechanism of charging the student and the university for hours beyond those required plus 10% provides an incentive for both the university and the students to reduce excess hours, increasing instructional efficiency. The state uses the dollars saved by not paying for hours over those required plus 10% to purchase access for new students. Thus, the state increases access to the University of Florida without an increase in funding but, rather, through an increase in instructional efficiency. This system extends to graduate education once the equivalent analysis of credit hours for graduate degrees has been completed.

Research

If instruction represents one of the state's principal interests in university activity, research represents one of the university's most important products. The faculty, staff, and students of a major university participate in the process of discovery throughout their careers at the institution. Undergraduate students receive the immediate benefit of research in the classroom as faculty transfer the results of their scholarship into relentlessly updated information and interpretation. Undergraduates also participate in the research process directly through laboratory and other research assistant assignments, and many undergraduates do independent research under the direction of a senior professor. Graduate students also participate directly in research as part of their program of education, working independently or in group projects with senior professors. However, the principal benefit of research is the advancement of knowledge that has and continues to lead inexorably to improvements in the quality of life and the vitality of our state and national economy. Research is the lifeblood of prosperity in our highly technology driven society. The solutions to our most pressing problems and the capture of our most promising opportunities require research for success.

Florida supports two major types of research. The first takes place through the Institute for Food and Agricultural Science (IFAS) as part of the University of Florida's mission as a land-grant institution. The IFAS pursues research with the direct purpose of enhancing the effectiveness and commercial viability of agriculture in Florida and is funded directly and explicitly by the state legislature. This investment has, over the years, produced a substantial return to the citizens of the state by permitting the development of a wide range of Florida agricultural industries that would have been impossible without the IFAS's research base. Estimates vary, but over 80% of the agricultural industry in Florida exists because of IFAS research, and 92% of all crops grown in Florida are varieties developed by the IFAS.

The second category of research takes place in all the other colleges of the university including the Health Sciences Center. This research varies from explorations at the outer edges of knowledge with not a glimmer of immediate practical benefit, as in the development of quantum theory that was necessary to develop lasers, to the most practical research on the strength of materials used in building roads, bridges, and schools. Although the products of this research vary dramatically from the art exhibit to the specifications for concrete, we can find a variety of indexes to the productivity and quality of the research we do. We should first recognize that the teaching mission of the university requires that our faculty engage in research scholarship to maintain the currency of the expertise that underlies their instruction. This effort represents 10% of the total faculty effort and 4% of the state general revenue and lottery expenditures on research at the University of Florida (Lombardi & Capaldi, 1995a, 1995b). Scholarship of this variety does not necessarily produce publications, and faculty who engage in the research that supports teaching do not have an obligation to publish because the product of this research appears in the enhanced quality of their teaching and we evaluate this work through the quality evaluation of teaching.

For the rest of the research effort in this second category, however, we require publication. Publication takes many forms. It can involve an article in a journal, an exhibit in a gallery, a book for popular audiences, the award of a patent, or the appearance of a poem in a magazine. Whatever the form, publication represents the product of the research effort, and without a product there can be no contribution to our store of knowledge. A promising idea that never sees the light of day cannot be criticized and tested and cannot contribute to the national and international conversation that moves our understanding forward. Science, for example, that remains an unexpressed idea contributes nothing to the combination of ideas, experiments, and theories out of which come the cumulative improvements in our lives. So we demand that research, to be considered research, must in a reasonable period of time be recorded in a publication or the results publicly expressed that can be reviewed and understood by others.

Because research requires an investment of resources, we expect every faculty member engaged in research to seek outside sources of funds to support their research. In some fields, few sources exist for research support; in others, we find research dollars more available. In almost every field, our faculty compete against the best in the world to get these outside dollars, and so the amount of dollars earned serves as a rough approximation of the aggregate quality of the university's research enterprise. This is the measure used almost universally on a national scale to evaluate the research productivity of institutions.

Florida invests a substantial number of state dollars in general research, and the best indicator of the university's effectiveness in using these dollars comes from the ratio of the state dollars invested directly in the university's general research to the outside dollars earned by university research. At the University of Florida we expect that in the aggregate this ratio will reach at least 3 to 1 for non-IFAS research—that is, 3 outside dollars earned for every 1 state dollar invested directly in general university research. This rough measure serves as a quick and effective reference for the university's aggregate research productivity, although it does not serve as an effective management tool to distinguish research productivity among departments and colleges.

Within the university we use more defined if less easily aggregated measures. Here we attempt to measure research by discipline, college, and field to benchmark our productivity to the competition, as described above for Part II of the FQEP.

Faculty Productivity

In determining our success, it is the faculty who provide the critical elements of talent, expertise, inspiration, and productivity. To succeed, we must focus considerable attention on the issue of faculty evaluation and reward. Effective evaluation produces the material for adequate reward, and universities require these mechanisms as much as any private sector enterprise.

Within the University of Florida, each department uses measures of quality performance to determine merit pay increases and to make merit pay decisions. In the case of research, we have nationally defined, well-specified measures because the national and international market for research establishes these measures through competition. However, measures of quality and productivity for teaching have no national definitions, nor do they have clearly defined local measures at the University of Florida. In response to this challenge, the university established a teaching improvement committee in 1992 that developed a protocol for defining and rewarding quality and productivity in teaching. This led to a proposal to the legislature and the funding of what we call the Teaching Improvement Program (TIP). The legislature adapted the TIP program and funded it for the entire state university system in 1993, and the universities conferred the first awards in December 1993, consisting of $5,000 base salary increases for 168 faculty at the University of Florida.

The TIP essentially established an internal market for faculty productivity and quality in teaching. To participate in this marketplace, faculty members had to satisfy a minimum productivity standard and then compete on quality to receive a TIP award. The productivity measure required that the faculty must be above the median in their department or college in either student credit hours (the number of students taught) or contact hours (the number of hours spent in class) during the three years previous to the competition. Then, the quality measure required the faculty to present evidence of the quality of their teaching in portfolios. For the first year of the program, only under-

graduate teaching was considered; in subsequent years, both graduate and undergraduate teaching were included (for more information
on this program, see Ross, Barfield, Campbell, Capaldi, & Lombardi,
1995). In the three years since the TIP program began, sections taught
per faculty personyear have increased 4.6%, and total credit hours per
faculty personyear have increased 8.3%. Also, the focus on defining
quality classroom performance and quality instructional materials
has led to a considerable interest in peer review of teaching, peer
review of teaching materials, and a variety of teaching improvement
programs sponsored by the various colleges.

Conclusion

These efforts to reformulate the budget to reflect income and expenses, to identify the elements of productivity and quality, to benchmark them to the best of the competition, and to identify and reward
quality and productivity for individual faculty members represent
but the first element in the Florida Quality Evaluation Project. We
currently are at work defining a performance-based budgeting model
that will draw on the degree funding and the elements of research
productivity to design an annual budgeting mechanism for the state
that can be indexed to performance (Lombardi, 1996a). No one who
observes higher education today can doubt that success requires
measures of this kind, and every university with a commitment to
success finds itself engaged in similar projects. We have just begun
and there is much yet to do, but the progress to date indicates that the
effort is worth the commitment.

Notes

1. Reprints may be obtained from John V. Lombardi, President, University of Florida,
Gainesville, FL 32611.

2. Copies of the Florida Quality Evaluation Project data and any of the University
of Florida reports mentioned in this chapter can be obtained from the Office of
Institutional Research, P.O. Box 118140, Gainesville, FL 32161, or by e-mail to
ufdata@nervm.nerdc.ufl.edu.

References

Lombardi, J. V. (1994a). *Undergraduate degrees, credit hours, and cost of degrees at the University of Florida: A preliminary project report.* Unpublished manuscript, University of Florida, Gainesville.

Lombardi, J. V. (1994b). *Undergraduate student academic tracking system: A pilot project in engineering, political science and architecture.* Unpublished manuscript, University of Florida, Gainesville.

Lombardi, J. V. (1996a). *Performance based budgeting considerations: A simple example.* Unpublished manuscript, University of Florida, Gainesville.

Lombardi, J. V. (1996b). *Universal tracking program.* Unpublished manuscript, University of Florida, Gainesville, FL.

Lombardi, J. V., & Capaldi, E. D. (1992). *University mission, quality, and performance: The Florida quality evaluation project.* President's Office, University of Florida, Gainesville.

Lombardi, J. V., & Capaldi, E. D. (1995a). *Measuring university performance: Research (Vol. 1).* Unpublished manuscript, Office of Institutional Research, University of Florida, Gainesville.

Lombardi, J. V., & Capaldi, E. D. (1995b). Measuring university performance: Research benefits (Vol. 2). Unpublished manuscript, Office of Institutional Research, University of Florida, Gainesville.

Lombardi, J. V., & Capaldi, E. D. (1996). *A proposal for degree funding.* Unpublished manuscript, Office of Institutional Research, University of Florida, Gainesville.

Ross, D. D., Barfield, C. S., Campbell, E. S., Capaldi, E. D., & Lombardi, J. V. L. (1995). Teaching as a priority: A promising program at the University of Florida. *College Teaching, 43,* 134-139.

Benefit and Retirement Issues in Higher Education

JAY L. CHRONISTER

The 1990s have been, and will continue to be, a decade of change for higher education. Among the volatile issues that institutions have been forced to address are age and cost factors directly related to faculty and staff. This chapter addresses major retirement and benefit trends and issues that colleges and universities are currently facing. Also, many of the same problems are applicable to other professional staff and nonprofessional staff of the institutions. However, before discussing these issues, it is important to place them in a historical context.

In the 1960s, higher education grew at a significant rate to accommodate the post World War II baby boom. The burgeoning college age population and a social policy that placed emphasis on providing access to postsecondary education led to major increases in the number and size of colleges and universities. According to the National Center for Education Statistics (NCES; 1994a), between 1960 and 1970, enrollments increased from 3.6 million to 8.6 million students (p. 174), and the number of institutions increased from 2,004 to 2,556 (p. 242).

One result of this growth in the number of students and institutions was that the number of full-time faculty increased from about 154,000 in 1960 to approximately 369,000 in 1970 (NCES, 1979, p. 104). By 1992-1993, there were 885,796 faculty in higher education, of whom 593,941 were full-time (NCES, 1994c, pp. 9-10).

Aging of the Faculty

The faculty hired during the growth years of the 1960s were a significant portion of the faculty with which higher education entered the decade of the 1990s. In 1977-1978, nearly 17% of the professoriate was age 55 or older, with 2% age 65 or older (National Education Association, 1979, p. 7). By 1987-1988, the percentage of full-time faculty age 55 and older had increased to 25%, with 4% age 65 or older (NCES, 1990, p. 9). Data from the 1993 National Study of Postsecondary Faculty indicate that 26% of the faculty was age 55 or older that year, with 4% age 65 or older, including about 1% age 70 or older (NCES, 1993).

Table 5.1 provides a comparison of the distribution of the ages of full-time faculty and staff between 1987-1988 and 1992-1993. The data in this table reflect the aging trend that has gained increased attention from higher education policy makers. Key points in the table are the decline of faculty under age 35 and between ages 35 and 44 and the increases in the percentage of those over age 45.

The combination of the aging professoriate, constrained financial resources, and the passage of the 1986 amendments to the Age Discrimination in Employment Act (ADEA), which abolished mandatory retirement by reason of age, raised several questions for higher education. Although there was an exemption in the legislation that permitted institutions to retain a mandatory retirement age for tenured faculty until January 1, 1994, there was a concern that without a mandatory retirement age, many faculty would remain with institutions well beyond their productive years and create both academic and financial problems. A 1991 report from the National Research Council concluded that at most institutions few tenured faculty would work beyond age 70, with the possible exception of research universities that had a large proportion of faculty working up to the manda-

TABLE 5.1 Age Distribution of Full-Time Instructional Faculty and Staff: Fall 1987 and Fall 1992 (in percentages)

Age	Fall 1987	Fall 1992
Under 35	10.2	7.9
35-44	31.6	28.8
45-54	34.1	37.1
55-59	11.7	13.1
60-64	8.6	8.7
65-69	3.3	3.4
70 and older	0.5	1.0

SOURCE: U.S. Department of Education, National Center for Education Statistics, "1988 National Study of Postsecondary Faculty" and "1993 National Study of Postsecondary Faculty."

tory retirement age prior to passage of the 1986 amendments to the ADEA (Hammond & Morgan, 1991, p. 2).

Recent reports appear to confirm the conclusions reached by the National Research Council study. *Campus Trends, 1995* (El-Khawas, 1995, p. 47) reports that between 1993-1994 and 1994-1995, 19% of all institutions reported a net gain in faculty age 65 and over, 65% reported no change, and 16% cited a net loss. When queried as to changes in faculty age 70 and over, 11% cited net gains, 80% indicated no change, and 9% stated they had a net loss. It is the disaggregation of data by type and control of institution where important distinctions arise. Whereas 7% of public institutions reported a net gain in faculty over 70, 18% of all independent institutions reported a net gain. Distinctions are also evident by type of institution in that 41% of independent research/doctoral universities cited a net gain in faculty age 70 or older, whereas only 16% of the public research/doctoral institutions reported such a gain.

Emphasis on the total number of faculty and the age distribution of those faculty should not obscure the fact that many of the issues for institutions that relate to faculty age, retirement actions, and benefit costs may also be attributable to other professional staff and nonprofessional personnel. Faculty account for about 50% of the professional staff on college and university campuses and about 33% of the total staff. For example, colleges and universities employed approximately 2.6 million individuals in the fall 1991, of whom 1.6 million (62.7%)

were professional staff and 950,000 (37.3%) were nonprofessional. Full-time and part-time faculty made up 826,000 (51.6%) of the professional staff (NCES, 1994a, p. 228).

Aging of the professoriate has important implications for higher education for a variety of reasons. An aging faculty is an expensive faculty in terms of salary and total compensation. Using academic rank as a general proxy for age, data from 1993-1994 provide insight into the implications of age/rank for salaries. In 1993-1994, the average salaries for full-time faculty on 9-month appointments were as follows: professors, $60,649; associate professors, $45,278; assistant professors, $37,630; instructors, $28,828; and lecturers, $32,729 (NCES, 1994b). Data derived from the 1993 National Study of Postsecondary Faculty indicate that full-time faculty were distributed across ranks as follows: professors, 30.6%; associate professors, 23.5%; assistant professors, 23.4%; instructors, 13.9%; lecturers, 2.2%; and other, 6.4%. Of all full-time faculty, 26% were age 55 and older, including 48% of the professors and 21% of the associate professors, and nearly 80% of those age 55 and older were tenured (NCES, 1993). It is evident from these data that senior faculty, in terms of age, rank, and tenure status, account for a sizable portion of faculty compensation expenditures and reduce the financial flexibility of institutions as increasing proportions of the faculty reach the higher age classification.

Fringe Benefits

Fringe benefits are an important part of institutional budgets and a significant part of the compensation package for faculty and staff. Most benefit packages provide financial protection for faculty and staff during employment years and address financial concerns of the retirement years. For example, health insurance plans substitute known and regular payments to cover unknown and potentially significant expenses that may arise from medical problems, whereas life insurance and disability insurance provide financial security during employment years. Social Security, pension plans, and, at some institutions, subsidized health insurance coverage provide financial security during the retirement years. Benefit plans provided to faculty and staff vary considerably by type and control of institution and by employee status within institutions (Chronister, 1995).

There are three general classifications of benefits: statutory, voluntary, and support. Statutory benefits are required by law and include Worker's Compensation, Unemployment Compensation, and Social Security. Voluntary benefits are those the institution chooses to offer, or that may be specified in a collective bargaining contract, and include such items as pension plans, health insurance, life insurance, and disability insurance. Support benefits may include such items as housing, parking, tuition repayment programs, and free or reduced costs for cultural and athletic events (Chronister & Kepple, 1987). Table 5.2 provides information on the types of benefits provided to full-time faculty in 1987-1988 and the percentage of institutions offering the benefit.

Approximately 98% of institutions of postsecondary education offered some type of pension plan to full-time faculty and staff in 1987-1988, with 100% of two-year public and four-year public and private institutions providing this benefit. Nearly 100% of all institutions also offered medical insurance coverage for full-time employees. As discussed and analyzed later, pension plans and health insurance programs are two of the most expensive benefits for institutions of higher education to provide, with health insurance costs being the most volatile in recent years.

The institutions vary significantly in terms of the other benefits offered. Life insurance is the third most prevalent benefit, followed by disability insurance, with private institutions more likely than their public sector counterparts to provide the latter. Tuition benefits are more likely to be available for children and spouses at private institutions than at public institutions; however, the public institutions are more likely to provide dental insurance.

Costs of Benefits

The cost of benefits can be viewed from a number of perspectives. First, they can be analyzed on a per-full-time-employee basis, with these figures traced over time to ascertain the magnitude of change

TABLE 5.2 Colleges and Universities Providing Benefits to Full-Time Faculty, Fall 1987 (in percentages)

Type and Control of Institution	Pension	Medical Insurance or Care	Life Insurance	Disability Insurance	Tuition Benefit: Children	Tuition Benefit: Spouse	Dental Insurance or Care	Paid Maternity Leave	Wellness Program	Housing	Meals	Paid Paternity Leave	Child Care
All institutions[a]	98	99	88	79	65	63	59	49	31	11	11	10	4
Four-year public	100	98	90	76	47	53	62	54	40	5	1	14	7
Four-year private	100	99	88	94	99	94	44	60	39	25	16	5	2
Two-year public	100	97	85	70	41	46	73	44	31	0	0	17	4
Other	92	100	89	75	69	55	55	40	15	24	23	4	7

SOURCE: National Center for Education Statistics, 1990, p. 44.
a. All accredited, nonproprietary U.S. postsecondary institutions that grant a two-year (A.A.) or higher degree and whose accreditation is recognized by the U.S. Department of Education.

TABLE 5.3 Average Salary, Average Benefit Costs, and Benefit Costs as a Percentage of Average Salary for Faculty on 9 to 10- Month Contracts, by Type of Institution: 1989-1990 to 1993-1994

Type of Institution	1989-1990	1990-1991	1991-1992	1992-1993	1993-1994	% Change 1989-1990 to 1993-1994
Associate of Arts						
Salary	33,171	34,717	35,798	36,713	38,412	15.8
Benefits	8,376	9,077	9,630	10,236	10,236	25.1
Benefits % of salary	25.3	26.1	26.9	27.9	27.3	2.0
Bachelor of Arts						
Salary	33,580	35,861	37,446	38,635	39,783	18.5
Benefits	7,862	8,867	9,384	9,762	10,485	33.4
Benefits % of salary	23.4	24.7	25.1	25.3	26.4	3.2
Bachelor of Arts+						
Salary	37,147	38,592	40,410	41,515	43,222	16.4
Benefits	9,032	9,767	10,247	10,843	11,352	25.7
Benefits % of salary	24.3	25.1	25.4	26.1	26.3	2.0
Doctoral						
Salary	45,386	47,954	49,415	50,766	52,199	15.0
Benefits	10,144	10,853	11,550	12,023	12,608	24.3
Benefits % of salary	22.4	22.6	23.4	23.7	24.2	1.8
Average						
Salary	39,809	41,947	43,361	44,606	46,186	16.0
Benefits	9,303	10,040	10,649	11,162	11,721	26.0
Benefits % of salary	23.4	23.9	24.6	25.0	25.4	2.0

SOURCE: National Center for Education Statistics, *IPEDS Salary Survey, 1989-90 through 1993-94*.
NOTE: Based on 1,508 institutions reporting data in all years.

from year to year. A second type of assessment is the analysis of benefit costs as a percentage of salary on an annual basis and over a period of time.

The data in Table 5.3 show the average costs of providing benefits on a per-full-time-faculty basis for the years 1989-1990 through 1993-1994 and highlight several factors with which institutions have had to grapple over the past half decade. First, average benefit costs per faculty member have increased at a rate faster than the rate of average salary increases. Between 1989-1990 and 1993-1994, the average salary increased by 16%, and benefits increased 26%. Benefit costs as a percentage of salary increased from 23.4% to 25.4% over the same period. Important differences in these averages occur when analyzed by type of institution. It was among bachelor's-degree-type institutions that both the largest percentage increases in average salary and average benefit cost took place; doctoral institutions experienced the lowest increases. Average benefit costs as a percentage of salary were highest among two-year institutions each year, with doctoral institutions, on average, the lowest on that particular ratio.

It is assumed that increased dollars committed to fringe benefits are dollars that might have gone into faculty salaries if the benefit costs had not grown so significantly. Studies have shown that many institutions paid increased benefit costs during years when institutional revenues were reduced or did not grow at a rate commensurate with inflation (El-Khawas, 1991, p. 1).

The three components that serve as the major fringe benefit cost centers for institutions of higher education are retirement contributions, medical/dental plan costs, and Social Security expenditures, regardless of type and control of institution. Among public institutions, these three categories accounted for over 90% of costs in 1993-1994; at private institutions, they accounted for over 80% of expenditures.

Retirement contributions account for between 37.1% and 41.8% of average benefit costs at public institutions and between 24.4% and 34.9% percent at private institutions (Chronister, 1996). Nearly 100% of institutions provide either a defined benefit or defined contribution pension plan for full-time faculty and staff, although some institutions provide employees with a choice between the two (NCES, 1993).

Defined benefit plans provide the participant with a specific annuity at the time of retirement, usually determined by a formula that consists of a final year average salary (or X years of average highest salary), multiplied by years of service, times a percentage factor, such as 1.5% or 2%. The employer must accumulate the funds needed to pay the annuity, even though the employee may be required to contribute to the fund. The employer's cost in such plans will vary based on investment returns, personnel turnover, and mortality factors (TIAA-CREF, 1995b, p. 1). State pension plans are generally defined benefit plans and in 1987-1988 were made available by 89% of public four-year institutions and 95% of public two-year colleges

(NCES, 1990, p. 39). In recent years, there has been increasing concern that many defined benefit plans may be underfunded due to weak state economies that have restricted maintaining adequate contribution levels to fund accounts, "borrowing" from the retirement fund to meet other state needs, or poor investment decisions.

Defined contribution plans are characterized by the specified level of contribution that will be made into participants' individual pension accounts, as opposed to guaranteeing a specific formula-driven annuity at retirement. In these plans, the participant assumes the risk for the adequacy of the retirement annuity because the amount of the annuity is based on the contributions to the fund, the investment earnings on the contributions, and one's age at retirement. The risk for the participant is heavily affected by the financial performance of the investment vehicles in which funds are invested.

The Teachers Insurance Annuity Association and College Retirement Equities Fund (TIAA-CREF) is the most widely offered defined contribution pension plan in higher education. Nearly 60% of institutions offered TIAA-CREF, including 77% of public four-year and 84% of independent four-year institutions, but only 39% of public two-year institutions made it available. About 41% of institutions provide another 403b or 401k plan (NCES, 1990, p. 42). The 1993 National Study of Postsecondary Faculty indicated that 63% of institutions provide multiple pension plans from which personnel may choose the option in which they wish to participate (NCES, 1993).

Social Security, as an institutional expense, is driven by federal policy in terms of the maximum salary subject to tax and the rate of FICA tax and the Medicare tax that has no salary ceiling. This is a benefit item for which the institution must comply with federal requirements and tax rates, both in terms of the institutional contribution and the employee withholding. With the much publicized concern about the long-term viability of Social Security, both the FICA tax rate and the salary ceiling up to which the rate is applied have been increasing and will undoubtedly continue to increase in the near future. To encourage individuals to work longer and to relieve some of the pressure on the Social Security "trust" fund, the Social Security Amendments of 1983 (P.L. 98-21) revised the normal retirement age beginning in the year 2000. In that year, the normal retirement age will gradually increase to 66 for those reaching age 62 in 2005 and to 67 for those reaching age 62 in 2022 (TIAA-CREF, 1989, p. 3).

As the third major cost center, health benefits have received considerable attention in recent years. The average institutional costs for health coverage for 9- to 10-month faculty in 1993-1994 ranged from 26.0% to 33.4% of total benefit expenditures, depending on the type of public institution, compared with 21.4% to 25.2% at the private institutions, depending on type (Chronister, 1996). Health insurance benefits have been one of the fastest growing cost centers in benefit plans. Between 1977 and 1989, average health care benefits costs for institutions increased from 2.2% to 6.1% of payroll (TIAA-CREF, 1991a).

Health insurance costs have been the focus of a significant number of institutional efforts to control costs. In an attempt to control the increases in the costs of indemnity insurance plans, an increasing number of colleges and universities have been turning to managed health care plans provided by health maintenance organizations or by preferred provider organizations (Hewitt Associates, 1992, p. 7). In attempting to control these costs, it is also common for institutions of higher education to adopt health benefit plans that require faculty and staff to assume a larger share of costs of health care through higher premiums, higher copayments, and larger deductibles.

It is evident from the above that benefit costs have grown faster than faculty (and staff) salaries over the past decade. The problem has been exacerbated by the fact that with constrained financial resources the increases in benefit costs have been achieved at the expense of salary growth and support for other desirable institutional programs. As an example, in 1990-1991, 45% of surveyed institutions reported mid-year budget cuts, and 79% were required to increase spending for health insurance for the year (El-Khawas, 1991, p. 1).

Rising costs of benefits in relation to anticipated financial constraint during the remainder of the current decade will remain a serious fiscal challenge for colleges and universities. Uncertainty at the federal level about how best to address national health care issues and how to resolve the problem of adequate funding for the Social Security system adds to institutional uncertainty for the long term. Many of the cost issues are directly related to the retirement issues addressed in the next section.

Retirement Trends and Issues

A discussion of retirement trends and issues must take into account past retirement patterns and changing social, economic, health, and professional variables that affect the retirement decision. It must also be recognized that there are at least two dimensions to the discussion, one being the individual perspective and the other the institutional.

Recent years have been witness to a number of competing and at times diametrically opposed factors affecting retirement decision making on the part of individuals. Among the factors analyzed in this section are increased longevity for individuals, the economic variables that affect the retirement decision, the nature of incentive retirement plans offered by institutions to encourage retirement, and differences between faculty and staff in terms of retirement.

Longevity

At the midpoint of the decade of the 1990s, higher education faces a longevity challenge similar to that of the rest of society. Longevity is highlighted by the fact that the life expectancy of 65-year-old men and women in America has increased by about two years since 1970 (TIAA-CREF, 1995a, p. 3). The implications of increased longevity are severalfold. Improved health in later years brought about by better health care and advances in medical science provides individuals the opportunity for a longer professional career or a greater number of years of retirement.

Age of Retirement

What are faculty and staff likely to do with this freedom of choice about retirement in the face of increased longevity, better health, and the absence of a mandatory retirement age? Will the choice or decision differ to any degree between faculty and staff or by variables such as discipline, gender, and race/ethnicity? As a basis for attempting to determine whether different cohorts of employees within institutions of higher education differ on the age at which they may retire, some insights can be gained from the results of a study undertaken in spring 1990. Data on the retirement ages of several occupational groups from among 19,126 faculty and staff from a cross section of 130 institutions shows different retirement age patterns by group (Table 5.4). Faculty tend to retire at later ages than do members of the other occupational classifications. Whereas from 52% to 58% of the support staff and professional and management personnel had retired prior to age 65, only 43% of the faculty had retired by that age. Conversely, a much larger proportion of the faculty (28%) had retired after age 65 and into their 70s than had the other occupational groups (13% to 17%) (TIAA-CREF, 1991b).

Two important questions arise from the data in Table 5.4. First, in the absence of a mandatory retirement age, can it be expected that this occupationally differentiated distribution of retirement ages will continue in the future? Second, will retirements continue to cluster at or below age 65? Analysis of actual retirement ages of faculty, other professionals, and nonprofessional staff over the next several years will be necessary to answer the first question. Limited data available from institutions that had abolished mandatory retirement for tenured faculty prior to the January 1, 1994 effective date mandated in the federal legislation indicated that although a few faculty members remained employed there was no great proportion staying on beyond age 70 (Hammond & Morgan, 1991, pp. 27-28). Comparable data are not available on the recent retiree behavior of nonfaculty personnel on college and university campuses.

An interesting perspective on factors that may affect the decision about when to retire or the likelihood of continued employment is presented in "Longevity's Gift: A Second Middle Age" (TIAA-CREF, 1995c), where it is suggested that increased and healthy longevity has created a second middle age between the ages of 50 and 75 that provides individuals the opportunity for a long career. Besides the studies, there is growing evidence that college faculty are using this longer career potential in current retirement planning. Data from the 1993 National Study of Postsecondary Faculty indicate that 17.2% of full-time faculty expect to work to age 70, and an additional 8.6% anticipate working beyond that age. Although 75% of the full-time faculty who were age 70 in fall 1992 expected to retire in the next three years, only 33% of those *over* 70 expected to retire in three years

TABLE 5.4 Distribution of Respondents, by Retirement Age and Former Occupation (in percentages)

Age at Retirement	Total Respondent	Faculty	Administration or Management	Professional or Technical Staff	Administration Support Staff	Maintenance Support Staff
Under 65	49	43	57	56	58	52
65	24	24	21	23	22	26
66 to 69	15	20	13	13	13	10
70 and over	5	8	4	3	3	3
No response	6	4	5	5	4	9
All ages combined[a]	100	100	100	100	100	100

SOURCE: "The NACUBO/TIAA-CREF Survey of College and University Retirees," *Research Dialogues*, No. 31, October 1991, p. 2.
a. Some percentages may not add to 100 because of rounding.

(Chronister & Baldwin, in press). These faculty members may indeed be in their "second middle age" in terms of career fulfillment.

Factors Affecting the Retirement Decision

The variables that contribute to the decision to remain employed or to retire may be generally classified as either personal or professional or a combination of the two. Studies have shown that among the most influential factors affecting the decision about whether or not to retire are the availability of a satisfactory retirement income, the health of the individual or the health of a significant other, and the level of satisfaction with one's career and with one's job and place of employment (Gray, n.d.). The majority of factors beyond finances and health that affect the retirement decision of individuals can generally be classified as either push variables (job-related stresses that make the current employment situation unattractive), pull variables (expected postretirement activities that make retirement attractive), and status quo variables (factors that make the continuing employment attractive) (Daniels & Daniels, 1990, p. 70).

Among the variables that may differentiate between faculty and nonfaculty personnel in choosing when they will retire are such work environment variables as the socialization that faculty have received during their graduate study preparation, the latitude they have in how they fulfill their role on campus, and the opportunity for role fulfillment away from campus. This role identity and work context for faculty is significantly different from nonprofessional staff and some other campus professionals who have limited flexibility in role definition and fulfillment, limited resources for professional development, and limited institutional rewards and recognition. Where faculty may have numerous institutional "status quo" variables affecting their decision about retirement, nonfaculty may be directly affected by work environment and personal variables that serve to "pull" or "push" them toward retirement. The recognition of the variables that affect faculty retirement decisions is critical to institutions that are seeking ways to create faculty and staff turnover through incentive retirement plans or are attempting to discourage faculty and staff from working into their 70s and to take "regular" retirement.

For the "push" or "pull" variables to trigger the actual retirement decision, the need for adequate postretirement income must be satisfied. Concern for adequate income does not center only on immediate postretirement income but on the adequacy of income to offset the long term effects of inflation in the face of longevity. This inflation issue is highlighted in a recent TIAA-CREF publication (Biggs, 1995) about the implications of longevity for a retired couple: "Using our current mortality table, there is a two-thirds chance that one of the two 65-year olds will still be relying on the (retirement) income twenty-five years later at age 90" (p. 2).

Pension Issues

The adequacy of retirement income creates one of the challenges for which the landscape has changed for institutions and faculty in recent years. Over the past decade, colleges and universities have provided faculty and staff with increased numbers of retirement plan choices and increased investment opportunities within the majority of those plans. Placing this higher education change in a national context, a recent report states that between 1975 and 1987 the proportion of workers participating in defined contribution plans for their primary pension coverage increased from 13% to 32%, whereas the proportion of workers with primary coverage under defined benefit plans dropped from 87% to 68% (TIAA-CREF, 1995b).

With the increase in investment options to employees, institutions have a responsibility to provide educational experiences for employees that assist them in understanding the nature of the differences in investment opportunities so that educated investment decisions can be facilitated (VALIC, 1994). This responsibility does not assume that institutions will give investment advice, but it does assume the need to provide faculty and staff with educational programs that highlight they may need investment advice from a professional financial adviser. The fact that defined contribution retirement plans place the risk of attaining adequate retirement income on the investment decisions of the employee rather than on the institution heightens the need for investment education programs, especially in an environment that provides multiple investment options. The provision of such programs has not become widespread across campuses as yet and is a challenge that faces a growing number of institutions.

The joint responsibility of institutions and employees for effective planning for the achievement of adequate retirement income is highlighted in the following statement:

> The substantial growth of defined contribution plans since passage of ERISA in 1974 underscores an important point about them—individual participants are responsible for their own asset allocation decisions as they direct plan contributions to individual annuity accounts. Clear plan communication and financial educational materials are critical to the success of such participant-directed accounts. Participants also require good financial planning skills for building the personal savings they need to supplement pension and Social Security benefits for an adequate retirement income. (TIAA-CREF, 1995b, p. 1)

Medical Coverage Issues

Integral to retiree financial considerations are concerns about health insurance protection and the cost of such protection. As stated earlier, during employment, institutional health insurance plans provide a known and regular cost to the employee to cover unknown and potentially significant medical expenses. This concern with known and "affordable" health care coverage gains increased significance during the retirement years when medical needs are expected to be greater than during an individual's younger years. Retirees tend to be in a higher "health risk" group for coverage and therefore, if they do not continue in their institution's group plan or another group-based plan, individual expenses for health care coverage can become highly significant for persons on retirement income. Studies indicate that the availability of health insurance for retirees through an institution's group plan at institution, shared, or retiree cost is important in the decision about when to retire.

In an attempt to address concerns about the availability and cost of health insurance, some colleges and universities provide for retirees to continue participation in the institution's group plan at institutional expense. For example, the University of Michigan (1991) provides for retirees and eligible dependents to continue health and dental care coverage with the institution's contribution to the cost of the premium being no more than the university's contribution toward the cost of Blue Cross/Blue Shield (p. 3). This retirement benefit continues until death and is therefore a continuing financial obligation of the institution. That obligation for the University of Michigan currently amounts to about $8 million per year for about 4,000 retirees (Blackburn & Lawrence, 1995, pp. 340-341).

Other institutions address the health care cost concerns of potential retirees by including health benefits as incentives in early retirement plans. The University of Virginia (1995) has provided health benefits for phased retirement plan participants for the period of time the faculty member is phasing into retirement at institutional cost (as though the faculty member were fully employed). Plans such as that of the University of Virginia provide control of institutional costs by specifying the length of time of phased retirement, which is currently five years. Retirees may then continue in the institutional group plan but at their own expense.

With institutional attempts to control health care costs it can be expected that more institutions will use managed care plans and there will be a reduction in the use of indemnity plans. It is very likely that changes in the type of health care coverage provided for employees will also affect retirees in terms of higher-cost premiums and larger deductibles and copayments.

In the absence of the provision of subsidized or otherwise afford-able medical coverage, employees may continue employment solely for the purpose of maintaining such coverage. An added concern that has gained increased interest for retirement planning in recent years in relation to health care involves the high cost of long-term care.

Fringe Benefit Opportunities for Part-Time Faculty

Part-time faculty in American higher education have generally had no access, or minimum access, to fringe benefits on college and university campuses. With an expected increased reliance on part-time faculty in the near future, institutions can expect increased requests for benefits for these faculty members. The growth in the use of part-time faculty is highlighted in *Campus Trends, 1995,* which reported that 47% of institutions responding to a national survey have increased the number of part-time faculty, but only 27% have experienced decreases in recent years. These increases have been reported by both public and private institutions (El-Khawas, 1995).

A 1988 survey of colleges and universities found that only about 55% of institutions provided some benefits to regular part-time faculty. Whereas institutions expend the equivalent of about 25% of salary on benefits for full-time faculty, benefits for part-time faculty amounted to about 14% of salary (NCES, 1990, p. 41). About 43% of the institutions provided a pension plan for part-time faculty, and 31% of them subsidized the plan (NCES, 1990, p. 43). Although 31% of institutions offered subsidized pension plans for part-time faculty, only about 20% of all part-timers receive such a benefit (Gappa & Leslie, 1993, p. 162).

Health insurance benefits for part-time faculty members is a topic of intense interest on many college and university campuses, especially where a large proportion of the faculty consists of part-timers. A report based on the 1988 National Survey of Postsecondary Faculty stated that only 16.6% of part-time faculty received subsidized health/medical insurance (NCES, 1990). Gappa and Leslie (1993) found that subsidized medical insurance benefits for part-time faculty were most likely the result of collective bargaining and that there was often a minimum contracted work effort and minimum length of service requirement to establish eligibility.

With the national uncertainty surrounding the availability of adequate and affordable health insurance and health care, the provision of health insurance for part-time faculty who have no other access to subsidized coverage will continue to be an issue placed before institutional policy makers. The issue gains increased significance in that many institutions pay part-time faculty minimum salaries for teaching on a limited basis. Unless a part-time faculty member has another source of income to meet basic expenses and that source also provides health care coverage, the low salary exacerbates the financial condition for this large proportion of the professoriate.

Conclusion

Over the past decade, colleges and universities have been faced with the twin challenges of an aging faculty and significant increases in the costs of providing fringe benefits for its workforce. During this same period, constrained financial resources and a variety of external forces have combined to make these challenges more complex, and these factors will continue to affect institutions in the foreseeable future.

The abolition of the mandatory retirement age makes the decision about the age at which personnel will retire an entirely and highly personal decision. Indications are that for the next 10 to 15 years institutions will be required to adjust to a workforce that is older and may have different personal and professional needs and aspirations than does a faculty and staff that is, on average, younger. Affecting the decisions of faculty and staff about when they will retire are concerns about the adequacy of retirement income, the availability of affordable medical insurance or medical coverage of some kind, and opportunities to participate in postretirement activities that are fulfilling and meaningful. The expectation of a longer retirement period in one's life increases the importance of retirement planning, including special emphasis on retirement income. Research has shown that personnel who participate in meaningful retirement planning activities are more likely to be satisfied with retirement and to have more adequately planned for the transition in lifestyle that retirement creates. A significant part of that planning process begins early in the career and involves the financial planning related to pension plan choice and investment decisions geared to differing career stages. Retirement planning programs are a resource that the majority of institutions do not provide employees.

Control of the costs of providing fringe benefits will continue to be a challenge to colleges and universities in the foreseeable future. Not only will institutions need to control the cost of such items as health coverage for employees currently covered but they will need to address the needs of a growing number of part-time faculty, the majority of whom do not now have access to subsidized benefits as do their full-time colleagues. This accommodation will need to take place in an environment of constrained financial resources and competition for scarce resources from other institutional functions.

Finally, it is possible that, in view of an aging faculty, colleges and universities will need to develop and implement programs that assist faculty and staff in adapting to changing institutional needs and work role demands.

References

Biggs, J. (1995, August). Take a second look at the graded payment. *The Participant*, p. 2.

Blackburn, R., & Lawrence, J. (1995). *Faculty at work: Motivation, expectation, satisfaction.* Baltimore: Johns Hopkins University Press.

Chronister, J. L. (1995). Benefits and retirement, 1992-93. *NEA 1995 Almanac of Higher Education*, pp. 97-108.

Chronister, J. L. (1996). Fringe benefits and retirement: A changing environment. *NEA 1996 Almanac of Higher Education*, pp. 97-106.

Chronister, J. L., & Baldwin, R. G. (in press). *Faculty retirement and other separation plans.* Washington, DC: National Center for Education Statistics, U.S. Department of Education.

Chronister, J. L., & Kepple, T. R., Jr. (1987). *Incentive early retirement programs for faculty: Innovative responses to a changing environment* (ASHE-ERIC Higher Education Report No. 1). Washington, DC: Association for the Study of Higher Education.

Daniels, C. E., & Daniels, J. D. (1990). Voluntary retirement incentive options in higher education. *Benefits Quarterly, 6*(2), 68-78.

El-Khawas, E. (1991). *Campus trends, 1991.* Washington, DC: American Council on Education.

El-Khawas, E. (1995). *Campus trends, 1995.* Washington, DC: American Council on Education.

Gappa, J. M., & Leslie, D. W. (1993). *The invisible faculty.* San Francisco: Jossey-Bass.

Gray, K. (n.d.). *Retirement plans and expectations of TIAA-CREF policyholders.* New York: Teachers Insurance and Annuity Association–College Retirement Equity Funds.

Hammond, P. B., & Morgan, H. P. (1991). *Ending mandatory retirement for faculty: The consequences for higher education.* Washington, DC: National Academy Press.

Hewitt Associates. (1992). *College and university experience in managed care.* Lincolnshire, IL: Author.

National Center for Education Statistics (NCES). (1979). *Digest of education statistics, 1979.* Washington, DC: U.S. Department of Education.

National Center for Education Statistics (NCES). (1990, January). *Institutional policies and practices regarding faculty in higher education.* (NSOPP-88). Washington, DC: U.S. Department of Education.

National Center for Education Statistics (NCES). (1993). *1993 national study of postsecondary faculty data base.* Washington, DC: U.S. Department of Education.

National Center for Education Statistics (NCES). (1994a). *Digest of education statistics, 1994.* Washington, DC: U.S. Department of Education.

National Center for Education Statistics (NCES). (1994b). *Salaries, tenure, and fringe benefits, 1993-94.* Washington, DC: U.S. Department of Education.

National Center for Education Statistics (NCES). (1994c). *Faculty and instructional staff: Who are they and what do they do?* Washington, DC: U.S. Department of Education.

National Education Association. (1979). *Higher education faculty: Characteristics and opinions.* Washington, DC: Author.

Teachers Insurance and Annuity Association–College Retirement Equities Fund (TIAA-CREF). (1989). Social Security to increase delayed retirement credit. *The Participant.* New York: Author.

TIAA-CREF. (1991a). Trends in payments for employee benefits. *Research Dialogues,* No. 29.

TIAA-CREF. (1991b). The NACUBO/TIAA-CREF survey of college and university retirees. *Research Dialogues,* No. 31.

TIAA-CREF. (1995a). The retirement security of the baby boom generation. *Research Dialogues,* No. 43.

TIAA-CREF. (1995b). Planning for retirement–the age of individual responsibility. *Research Dialogues,* No. 44.

TIAA-CREF. (1995c). Longevity's gift: A second middle age. *Research Dialogues,* No. 45.

University of Michigan. (1991). Retirement. In *Standard practice guide.* Ann Arbor: Author.

University of Virginia. (1995). *Phased incentive retirement plan for faculty.* Charlottesville: Author.

VALIC. (1994). The employers education responsibility under 404(c). *Educated Choices, 3*(1).

Responsibility-Centered Management
AN APPROACH
TO DECENTRALIZED
FINANCIAL OPERATIONS[1]

EDWARD L. WHALEN

Institutions of higher education come in a wide variety of sizes and degrees of complexity, at least in the United States. Most of the more than 2,000 institutions of higher education are small; 91% of them are under 10,000 full-time-equivalent students in enrollment, and over 85% of the institutions of higher education have expenditures of less than $100 million (U.S. Department of Education, 1992). But the largest and most complex—the ones enrolling more than 10,000 students and expending more than $100 million annually account for over 48% of all enrollments and for 73% of higher education's annual expenditures. This chapter is directed to those 200 or so public institutions of higher education in that numerically small but nevertheless important group.

Despite differences in size and complexity, most institutions of higher education are governed and managed in much the same way. Generally, difficulties in effective management that come with increasing size and complexity are ignored. The system of personal relationships and collective awareness that works satisfactorily in a small liberal arts college or university breaks down in a "megaversity." Individuals no longer recognize or appreciate the consequences of their actions for the total institution. For individuals, including the heads of major operating units, the total costs and total revenues of their operations are unknown.

Total costs and benefits of all activities—research as well as teaching—are not clear to those engaged in them. For example, office and research space often are perceived as free goods. They appear free to the individuals, but they clearly are not free to the institution. As a result, individuals within an institution of higher education often are induced to behave in ways that are at variance with institutional objectives. Incentives, the reward structure, and signals in the form of information on the consequences and benefits of action at the operating unit level often do not promote behavior that accomplishes institutional objectives. A new management arrangement is needed to make large public institutions of higher education governable, manageable, and controllable.

The Changing Financial Environment

Changes in the financial environment for higher education—particularly for public higher education—provide an additional imperative for a new management arrangement. As evidence over the past decade shows (U.S. Department of Education, 1994, Table 333), no longer can state-supported colleges and universities count on a steadily increasing and substantial portion of their operating and capital resources coming from their respective state capitals in the form of tax-supported appropriations.

When a preponderance of institutional funding came from a single source—state appropriations—and when student fee rates were low and student fee income constituted a relatively small portion of total revenue, a system of centralized budgeting and distribution of resources among operating units by a central administration made sense. Garnering state appropriation was correctly viewed as a responsibility of the central administration. The head of an institution represented it in the state legislature and the governor's office. Centrally estimated enrollment projections and centrally determined tuition fee policies produced a budget for student tuition and fee income. With most of an institution's revenue produced as the result of centralized activities and initiatives, operating units became passive recipients of centralized resource allocation decisions.

Today, however, centralized methods of revenue generation and of resource allocation are less well suited to the financial environment. Increasingly, with state support declining relatively if not absolutely and with student fees reaching the limits of students' and their parents' ability to pay, public colleges and universities must look to new sources of revenue and expansion of sources that heretofore have been incidental to the financial health of the institution. Those new and emerging revenue sources, however, are less amenable to centralized management. They rely on initiatives taken by operating units. Such sources as indirect cost recovery on grants and contracts, continuing education fees, sales and service income, and gift income are generated in a myriad of ways by numerous operating units. Central administration does not play a key role in their generation.

Granting that the constraints on governmental sources of revenue are liable to continue, growth in the relative importance of institutional income is likely to continue. And institutionally generated income is very different than revenue obtained from governmental sources. Its generation is dependent on the initiative and effort of operating units and individuals within the organization, not on central direction. Costs are associated with the undertaking of initiative and effort directed toward revenue generation. Consequently, an arrangement in which revenue is ladled out to operating units without regard to their contribution to the pool of revenue no longer is appropriate. The established order of centralized resource distribution traditionally characterizing public institutions of higher education is subject to challenge.

The present and future financial environment for public universities bodes well for those institutions that encourage and stimulate decentralized revenue generating activities among their operating units. Increasingly, those institutions most sensitive to opportunities to be of service to those willing to pay for the cost of providing them will enjoy the benefits of revenue growth. However, institutions are not of themselves sensitive. It is the individuals within those institutions who must be sensitized to such opportunities. A change from traditional arrangements of centralized resource distribution is needed to promote incentives within large public institutions of higher education for responsive and responsible management not only of operating costs but also of revenue generating activities.

Responsibility-Centered Management

Responsibility-centered management (RCM) is proposed as the change agent that addresses the governance, management, and control needs of large and complex public institutions of higher education in the current financial environment. How does it do it? At the risk of oversimplification, it empowers deans (and other members of the senior management team). Under RCM, they get the same set of signals confronting university presidents. Their schools or colleges or divisions become financial management centers. Financial management centers become microcosms of the university. Like a university president, heads of RCM centers are charged with academic, service, and management missions. Like a university, their units retain the income they generate from their activities. Like a university, they pay for all the costs of their activities—indirect as well as direct. Like a university, they function as separate financial entities retaining their year end balances—positive or negative. Like university presidents, heads of centers are expected to manage the resources at their disposal to maximize the effectiveness of their performance.

RCM automatically transforms dean and division heads into a president's allies. Each member of the management team operates in an environment in which all the benefits and consequences—at least, all the revenues and all the costs—are recognized. A "megaversity" is broken up into more manageable parts that, although separate, nonetheless continue to operate as coordinated parts of a single institution.

Principles of RCM

How does RCM work? One of the positive things about RCM is that, when properly designed, it proceeds from a set of principles. The principles approach to developing the foundations for RCM was developed in the early 1980s by Jon Strauss, then Senior Vice President for Administration at the University of Southern California, and John R. Curry, Vice President for Budget and Planning at USC. During 1981, they hammered out their principles as they worked with a representative group of deans and key administrators in anticipation of a move to a new budgeting and management system.

Indiana University's move to RCM certainly profited from Strauss and Curry's path-breaking work. Building on the USC effort, the Indiana University experience led to the development of nine concepts or terms relating to behavior or a condition deemed reasonable and desirable. Three of the concepts relate to decision making, three to motivation, and three to coordination.

Concepts related to decision making:
  Proximity
  Proportionality
  Knowledge
Concepts related to motivation:
  Functionality
  Performance recognition
  Stability
Concepts related to coordination:
  Community
  Leverage
  Direction

1. Proximity

The closer the point of an operating decision is to the point of implementation the better the decision is likely to be. What do we mean by better? For a given amount of resources, decisions that maximize the effectiveness of an activity are better than those that do not. For a specific task, decisions that minimize the resources required for its accomplishment are better than those that do not. One message for central administration embodied in this principle is, Set objectives, but don't tell people how to accomplish them.

2. *Proportionality*

The degree of decentralization is positively related to an organization's size and its complexity as well as to the complexity of its environment. Not everything should be centralized; not everything should be decentralized in an organization. When too much is centralized, problems outside the immediate environs of the central office seem remote, do not seem important, do not receive attention, and do not get corrected. Opportunities are lost. Communication burdens become excessive. Decentralization can address those problems but imposes its own costs and hazards in the form of duplication of functions, coordination, and loss of control. An efficiency maximizing balance between the two extremes has to be recognized.

3. *Knowledge*

Correct decisions are more likely to occur in an information rich environment. Making correct decisions is not easy, and timely and accurate information does not guarantee they will be made, but the absence of such information substantially lowers the probability of their being made.

Whether decisions are centralized or decentralized, information is needed if decision makers are to arrive at directives that promote the objectives of the institution they serve. For decision making in a decentralized environment, local managers must know not only how those decisions affect their units but also how they affect the entire institution. Actions should be planned, undertaken, and evaluated in a context of full information on benefits and consequences.

4. *Functionality*

Authority and command over resources should be commensurate with responsibility for the task assigned and vice versa. The message here is, Couple responsibility with authority.

In a complex organization, one unit's performance may affect others in very important ways. Attempting to strike a balance by assigning responsibility to one and control over resources or authority to another may force communication between units but does not promote responsible behavior and effective performance.

5. Performance Recognition

To make operational the distribution of responsibility and authority, a clear set of rewards and sanctions is required. Managers should be able to operate in an environment characterized by straightforward and easily understood mechanisms designed to automatically recognize and reward effective performance. Specifically, the full costs and the full benefits have to be recognized and attributed to local managers to motivate decisions designed to promote an institution's objectives as well as those of a single operating unit.

6. Stability

Good planning and performance are facilitated by stable environments. If incentives are to motivate behavior effectively, assignment of responsibility, authority, and resources has to be stable, and the rules for performance evaluation and the consequences of alternative outcomes have to be known in advance. For those rules to be effective, people must expect that they will not change and that they will be enforced.

7. Community

Institutions of higher education are collective human endeavors. That the fate of individual units is bound up in the success of the entire institution has to be recognized in the structure and operating procedures of the organization. Just as the property value of a house is limited by the condition of the neighborhood in which it is located, so too is recognition of the national and international distinction of any one unit ultimately limited by the performance of the entire institution. The relationship of the parts to the whole and to one another has to be explicitly reflected in the assignment of responsibility and authority and in the allocation of resources.

8. Leverage

In a decentralized decision making and operating system, the legitimacy of both institutional and local responsibilities has to be recognized. Central management should retain sufficient academic and fiscal leverage to facilitate achievement of institutional goals, maintain an institutional balance among programs, and respond to initiatives and opportunities presented by the environment in which the institution operates.

Certain services are needed for the collective benefit of the academic community and are provided as public utilities. In those instances, the central management must determine the level of such services and the resources to be allocated to provide them in accordance with appropriate governance procedures.

9. Direction

The existence of a mutually supportive academic and administrative plan for the institution is assumed and is absolutely essential. A clear set of objectives for the short and long run must be defined, the trade-off between scope and quality identified, and priorities among programs established. A plan is needed to focus decision making. Only in the context of a plan can performance be evaluated

How do those nine concepts influence how an institution operates? They affect decision making, motivation, and coordination.

Decision Making

The first three concepts—proximity, proportionality, and knowledge—relate to decision making. In a large organization, closing the gap between the point of decision and the point of implementation requires that the definition of responsibility centers be configured to correspond with the institution's academic and administrative structure. Academic responsibility centers carry out the institution's primary missions in teaching, research, and public service. Support centers, grouped to reflect the administrative structure, provide services to the primary mission units in the form of academic support, student support, institutional support, and operations and maintenance of physical facilities.

Chances are that there will be some colleges or schools that are large and others that are small. Either you organize your structure to achieve balance in size and complexity among responsibility centers or violate the principles of proximity and proportionality and live with the consequences.

Whatever your choice, RCM creates a demand for decentralized, up-to-date information. Center managers can be responsible for their programs and accountable for the fiscal integrity of their enterprise only if they act upon accurate and timely information and are able to perform and monitor transactions easily. Moreover, the information available to them must be the same as that used by central administrators to monitor performance if evaluation and accountability are to be conducted according to a common standard.

To operate effectively, academic and support centers must have access to a flow of comprehensive, consistent, readily manipulated, and timely information. Within its sphere of influence, a center needs the same range of information available to central management. Although information should be designed to serve the needs of a unit, it has to be based on a common standard for comparability across all centers.

Motivation

The second set of three concepts—functionality, performance recognition, and stability—relate to motivation. Responsibility of a dean of a school or head of an academic unit for accreditation, recruitment, appointment, promotion, and tenure of faculty, determination of curriculum and degree requirements, the research program, and generation of outside support should be accompanied by authority to make decisions relating to those issues and by command over resources necessary to execute them. Who knows better than a dean the number of faculty needed to deliver the courses in his or her discipline? Where to recruit the best faculty? Their performance? The optimum trade-off between graduate student support and equipment expenditures? If someone else is better prepared to make those decisions, that person should be the dean. Adherence to the principle of functionality requires that if a dean has responsibility for those areas, he or she should have the authority to make the decisions regarding them.

As well-defined entities, centers enjoy the full benefit of their performance and bear the full consequences of their actions. All income and all costs accrue to the centers whose activities generate them. Center managers make their decisions and carry out their programs in the same context as that of an entire university. Although they promote the objectives of their individual units, they also serve to promote the objectives of the entire institution.

Academic units designated as financial management centers retain income directly attributable to their departments, programs, and activities. Student and other fee income generated from courses; other earned income; indirect cost recovery from external grants and contracts; designated fund income from continuing education and public service activities; restricted fund income from grants, contracts, and gifts; and income from auxiliary and service units are to be credited to the schools and other major primary mission units.

In addition, central administration will allocate a portion of a central pool of resources obtained from state-appropriated funds or through contributions from all academic units as part of the annual budgetary review process. At that review and through that allocation, each school's role in meeting university objectives can be assessed and adjusted.

Not only does an academic financial management center receive the income generated by its activities, but it also incurs all costs, both direct and indirect, associated with them. An academic unit's budget typically consists of planned expenditures for personnel compensation, office and classroom supplies, telephone charges, travel, departmental equipment, and miscellaneous general supplies and expenses. Under RCM, all costs associated with conducting teaching, research, and public service activities are recognized. Academic units are assessed or charged for academic support services, library and computing services, student services, general administration, space, and related physical plant costs.

Like academic financial management centers, major support units designated as financial management centers receive income attributable to their activities. Some of that income is generated from external sources. Much of it is received in the form of assessments and charges to academic units for academic support, student services, general administration, and facilities operation and maintenance. Like academic centers, support centers incur all costs associated with delivering their services.

Fiscal accountability extends beyond the general education fund and includes designated and restricted fund groups as well as auxiliary and service enterprises involved in carrying out a center's responsibilities. Just as a center's year-end balances are carried forward as funds available, so also will its deficits be carried forward as an obligation against future resources.

The third principle in this triad, stability, is important! The extent to which the RCM environment influences decisions and performance depends on local managers' understanding of the arrangement and their expectation that the rules will not change. What happens if a center runs a deficit? Fiscal responsibility will be achieved only if the discipline of retaining year-end balances—negative and positive—applies without exception. Ad hoc improvisation with the rules of income and expenditure will diminish RCM's effectiveness in motivating responsible behavior.

Coordination

The last three concepts—community, leverage, and direction—relate to coordination. The last concept, direction, is the foundation for all the others. All of the above concepts and the contrivances that derive from them are superfluous if an institution and its components lack a sense of purpose. How can good decisions be distinguished from poor ones if the direction is unclear? How can performance be evaluated except in terms of its contribution to clearly defined objectives whose priorities are established? What balance between academic programs and support services is appropriate except in the context of a mutually supportive academic and administrative plan? The raison d'être of RCM is to assist an institution in focusing its energies and resources on accomplishing its mission. If a sense of purpose and vision is lacking, the mechanism is not needed and can be a prescription for mischief.

Through leveraged leadership and sense of community, the central administration coordinates and guides the university's planning efforts for the entire institution and among centers, establishes policies and procedures defining relationships among centers, strikes a balance between academic and service functions, and allocates a central pool of resources among the primary mission units to achieve the university's overall academic objectives.

Application of the Principles

The principles provide a context in which five distinct steps are required to put RCM in place:

1. Definition of responsibility centers
2. Attribution of income to responsibility centers
3. Allocation of costs to responsibility centers
4. Determination of responsibility centers' total costs
5. Implementation

The second and third steps can occur concurrently, but dealing with one at a time constitutes a major effort of planning, analysis, communication, and coordination. The others have to happen in the sequence indicated. Each deserves a brief comment.

Definition of Responsibility Centers

How are individual operating units grouped into responsibility centers? Responsibility centers fall into three general categories:

- Academic responsibility centers charged with carrying out the institution's primary missions of teaching, research, and public service
- Responsibility centers providing supporting services to the primary mission units
- Executive management, the collection of units coordinating and guiding the university's planning efforts among centers, establishing policies and procedures defining relationships among them, and allocating

resources to achieve the overall objectives of the university's academic plan

The academic centers seem easier to define than the support centers because the former correspond to schools, colleges, or other degree-granting units. However, a single set of standards equally applicable to units in all three general categories is needed to develop a consistent arrangement of academic and support centers and executive management. Seven standards define responsibility centers.

1. Organizational Structure

The existing organizational structure of a university plays a major role in determining how operating units are grouped into responsibility centers, both academic and support. At the beginning of the process toward a move from traditional budgeting techniques to RCM, it clearly dominates all other standards. Unfortunately, as becomes clear when other standards are evaluated, the existing organizational structure does not necessarily provide an optimum configuration for responsibility centers. However, a transition has to begin at some point in time, and attempting to achieve perfection from the outset will delay progress indefinitely. As Voltaire observed, "The best is the enemy of the good."

Existing schools and colleges determine most of the academic responsibility centers. Research centers, institutes, and such operations as hospitals also are candidates. Administrative structure also dictates how support centers providing academic support, student support, institutional support, and physical plant services are defined. Executive management includes an institution's chief executive office and supporting staff.

2. Clear Definition of Management Responsibility

If a responsibility center is to operate, someone has to be in charge. This second standard is related closely to the first and sometimes conflicts with it. As programs and activities are arranged into what appear to be reasonable groups, aggregations may develop for which no one clearly is responsible. Equally possible are arrangements in which responsibilities of two or more heads of other responsibility centers are involved.

Grouping libraries, museums, galleries, computing, and audiovisual services into a support center may seem reasonable, but it is not plausible unless someone is charged with responsibility for coordinating the activities of those units. Delivering off-campus courses for degree credit presents a different issue. Who is in charge? The unit that identifies demand for the courses, finds facilities, and makes other administrative arrangements, or the academic units whose courses are being offered? Are research institutes under the purview of a dean for research and graduate development, responsible for coordinating a campus's research effort, or are they under the academic units whose disciplines are represented in the institutes' activities?

When all units feed from a common trough and are concerned only with their direct expenses, overlapping jurisdictions can be ignored, and coordination of related operations can be more casual. When earned income is to be directed to specific units, and full costs are assigned, clarification of those arrangements becomes essential.

3. Number of Centers to
Reflect Size and Complexity

The number of responsibility centers tends to increase with the size and complexity of the environment. A large, complex university can be expected to have more centers than a smaller, less complex one. However, an institution twice the size of another will not necessarily have twice as many centers. The absence of proportionality may suggest that the results are less than optimum. However, as the number of centers rises, the benefits of making improved decisions close to the point of implementation are offset by the costs of coordination and communication in a decentralized system. Experience is required to determine a proper balance and an optimum level of decentralization.

4. Approximate Parity Among Units in
Terms of Size and Complexity

Given the axiom that the effectiveness of decision making improves as the point of decision approximates the point of implementation, benefits will be maximized if centers are about equal in terms of size and complexity. If one responsibility center is twice as large or complex as all the rest, decision making in that unit is liable to be farther from points of implementation than in the smaller units. With no increase in the number of centers, decision making and implementation can be brought into closer alignment by achieving a more even balance in the size and complexity of centers.

This standard is liable to be violated by adherence to the existing organizational structure when defining responsibility centers. Tradition and considerations other than effectiveness of decision making appear to have played major roles in the development of most organizational units. If decentralization does in fact lead to improved performance and if that performance is recognized appropriately, a tendency toward centers more homogeneous with respect to size and complexity can be expected. In the absence of such demonstration of cause and effect, however, the influence of parity as a standard for defining centers is slight.

5. *Intracenter Decentralization at the Discretion of Each Center*

Differences in the size and complexity of responsibility centers becomes less of an issue if decentralization is allowed to occur within responsibility centers. Even for large centers, operating decisions can occur in close proximity to points of implementation if a center's organization parallels the RCM format. With such flexibility, familiar patterns of the existing organizational structure of a campus can be preserved while achieving a relatively homogeneous degree of decentralization. However, until the heads of responsibility centers have experience with the new arrangement, uncertainties about how it will operate can be expected to postpone further decentralization.

6. *Policy Issues*

A set of academic or support functions may not be recognized as a separate operating unit in the existing organizational structure. They may not merit center status because of their size and complexity. Nevertheless, because of an institution's priorities, generated internally or imposed externally, they may be grouped together as a responsibility center.

7. Inclusion of All Fund Groups

The sources and uses of funds for a responsibility center involve all fund groups: the general educational fund, designated funds, restricted funds, and auxiliary and service enterprises. Accounting conventions in higher education separate each of those fund groups. Under RCM, center heads are expected to manage and integrate the activities within them as a single unit.

For auxiliary and service enterprises and various designated and restricted fund units, many of the concepts associated with RCM already exist. They generate their own income, manage their expenditures within that income restraint, and retain their unspent balances at year end. Under RCM, those concepts are extended to the university's general educational fund.

Some responsibility centers will be concerned exclusively with general educational fund income, allotments, expenditures, and assessments. Others may operate exclusively within the auxiliary fund group. However, the operations of a significant number of responsibility centers will involve several and in some cases all fund groups. For heads of such centers, the interaction between activities in different fund groups will become readily apparent.

Attribution of Income to Responsibility Centers

RCM affects operating units receiving all or part of their support from general funds. For units operating as auxiliary or service enterprises, income sources are defined clearly, and actions required to generate more or less revenue are well known to unit managers. Similarly, directors of research projects receiving sponsored income recognize what they have to do to sustain their programs.

For units operating in the general fund and under traditional budgeting arrangements, the signals relating performance to resource availability often are less clear. Where revenue comes from, the form it takes, how it is produced, its amount, and its disposition are not defined. To attribute income to responsibility centers, rules for assigning general fund income to them must be specified.

General Fund Income Categories

The major categories of general fund current revenue for public institutions of higher education are the following:

State appropriation
Student tuition and fees
Other fee income
Indirect cost recovery income
Interest income
Rental income
Gifts and grants
Auxiliary service charges
Miscellaneous income

By and large, the most important component of general fund income is state appropriation. Student tuition and fees usually constitute the second most important category. The rest is generated from such sources as indirect cost recovery on sponsored grants and contracts, interest income earned on invested cash balances, and receipts from sales of service. Each category requires its own method of attribution.

1. *State Appropriation*

As the most important component of general fund income, the method of attributing state support appears to be a very important consideration. It is. But exact rules and formulae for its distribution probably should be avoided. Just as income and expenditure must balance for an institution's entire general fund, so also it must balance initially for each responsibility center. That balance is achieved by using state appropriation as a plug or balancing residual—a necessary role if no center is to be penalized or rewarded for the mere implementation of RCM. Meeting that condition, however, automatically allocates all state support in a way that represents the effect of past and current decisions and priorities—and errors of judgment.

To specify a mechanistic approach to future allocations of state support would deny central administration the leverage it needs to respond to the institution's academic plan, set priorities, and exercise judgment regarding the scope and quality of various programs. In other words, specifying exactly how state support is to be distributed probably is a mistake. A compromise between allocation rules and central administration flexibility must be developed.

On average, a large percentage of an academic center's general fund income comes from an allocation of state appropriation. That percentage represents a large dependency on a single source of income. If the entire amount is distributed at the discretion of central administration, the heads of responsibility centers may feel vulnerable and exposed to unexpected shifts in institutional priorities, changes in central management, and capricious decisions.

Furthermore, basing the entire distribution on central administration's judgment precludes reinforcing academic center behavior that promotes institutional objectives. For example, if among those objectives is strengthening sponsored research activities, a portion of state support can be linked as a supplement to indirect cost recovery or some other indicator of research programs activity paid for with outside funding. To emphasize instruction, a portion of state support can be tied to enrollments.

But not all state support should be tied to automated or defined distribution schemes. A portion should be set aside for central administration to influence and coordinate center activities in accordance with an overall academic plan. The size of that discretionary portion is a matter for collective judgment.

2. Student Tuition and Fees

After state support, student tuition and fees account for the second largest source of general fund income. I mention tuition just so people know it's here. From here on, tuition and student fees are considered synonymous. Under traditional general fund accounting and budgeting arrangements, fee income is pooled with state support and other sources of funds. Allocations for direct expenses then is made from the pool. Under RCM, fee income is attributed to the centers that earn it.

How do academic centers earn fee income? Until one attempts to attribute it, the answer to that question seems obvious. But at least two answers are possible, and probably more exist. One way of attributing fee income to academic centers is based on enrollments in the courses each of them offers. Alternatively, fee income could be attributed to the centers in which students declare a major.

The two attribution methods are likely to elicit very different reactions from the centers. In the "as taught" method, centers can be expected to welcome offering low-cost, introductory service courses to students majoring in other disciplines. Under the "as enrolled" method, providing service courses to nonmajors is liable to be viewed as charity work and not be a welcome assignment. Measuring enrollments by course and attributing the resulting income to the center offering it seems more straightforward. Nevertheless, possible behavioral reactions deserve to be kept in mind.

3. *Other Fee Income*

Not only credit hour fees but also course-related fees are attributed on an "as taught" basis. Laboratory fees, practicum fees paid by students in education and social work, and other special course fees are attributed to centers offering the courses for which those fees are charged. If a student audits a course, the center offering the course gets the fee.

Not all fees that students pay are related to instruction for degree credit. Many schools offer continuing education programs, and fees paid by participants in those activities are attributed to them. In selected disciplines, students pay special instructional fees to reflect costs uniquely associated with the pedagogy. The list of such fees potentially is endless (certainly, it tends to grow). In each case, an attempt should be made to associate the fee with the center whose instructional activity generates the income.

Certain fees paid by students are not related to any instructional program. In such cases, income is attributed to support units in charge of the activity generating it. Application fees are attributed to the admissions office, transcript fees to the registrar, and late and deferred charges, special examination fees, and charges for late program changes to the bursar who enforces their collection. Usually, support units do not generate general fund income. Those attributions represent exceptions to the usual pattern.

4. Indirect Cost Recovery Income

Attribution of indirect cost recovery income earned on sponsored research and service grants and contracts is based on their project directors. A center to which a project director is appointed receives the indirect cost recovery income. For most grants and contracts, this method of attribution matches indirect cost recovery income with the indirect costs associated with projects and allocated to centers. Exceptions are addressed on a case-by-case basis.

5. Interest Income

For the general fund, receipt of income precedes most expenditure. As a result, the general fund—even when operating on an essentially break-even basis—holds for much of the year a sizable cash balance available for investment. The interest income generated from investing cash balances is not attributed easily to any one responsibility center. For the sake of simplicity, assign it as an offset to executive management and general administration. The net assessment for executive management and general administration tends to be distributed broadly and roughly in proportion to the size of a center's operation, so the benefit of the interest income offset will be spread appropriately.

6. Rental Income

To a minor extent, space normally used for academic and administrative activities supported by the general fund is rented, sometimes to outside agencies, sometimes to university operations functioning as auxiliaries. Office and meeting room space for professional associations is an example of the former situation; bookstores are an example of the latter.

In such instances, the rental income is attributed to the unit incurring the cost of space management. In the case of an academic journal occupying space in a department, the center including that department would receive the income. If a bookstore occupies space normally used for general administration, the support center for general administration receives the income.

7. Gifts and Grants

Gift and grant income is attributed to a unit on whose behalf the university accepts. Most gifts and grants are restricted, and the recipient is designated. In those few instances where gift or grant income is unspecified, executive management and general administration get it. The benefit of the offset to cost of those two functions is widely distributed.

8. Auxiliary Service Charges

Auxiliary enterprises require services from general fund support centers. They take the form of general supervision, accounting, payroll, personnel, general building and grounds maintenance, energy and utilities. In some instances, auxiliaries are charged directly for those services; in other instances, they are not. Because all such costs are assessed by the center responsible for managing an auxiliary enterprise, auxiliary service charges, when levied, are attributed to those centers. The choice, then, of whether to levy service charges for their indirect costs is placed with center managers.

9. Miscellaneous Income

Sales and service income and other general fund income are attributed to units generating them. When the source of income cannot be associated with an operating unit, it is attributed to executive management and general administration. An example is the collection of bad debts that have been written off.

Earned Income by Responsibility Center

Under RCM, support centers have two sources of support: earned income and what we call intercenter allocations. Intercenter allocations represent charges and assessments for services rendered by support centers to other units. For the units being served, they appear as indirect cost allocations; for the units providing the service, they appear as income.

Allocation of Indirect Costs to Responsibility Centers

Under traditional general fund accounting and budgeting concepts, operating units manage only their direct costs. Direct costs can be narrowly or broadly defined. The narrower the definition, the larger the aggregate amount of indirect costs. Salaries and wages of a unit's personnel and supplies and expenses used by them constitute a definition of direct costs at the narrow end of the spectrum. Allocating to operating units the fringe benefits associated with total compensation of their personnel represents a significant—in dollar terms—broadening of the definition.

The extent to which units manage their nonpersonnel costs can vary widely. From expenditure only for direct use of supplies, it can be broadened to include travel, telephone, equipment, and—on occasion—rental space. However, whether the convention is narrow or broad, traditional accounting and budgeting arrangements do not aspire to assign all of a unit's costs to it.

Under RCM, all of a center's cost is allocated to each responsibility center. With a decentralized approach to decision making, the head of each center must recognize the effect of her or his decisions not only on the center but also on the entire institution. That perspective can be gained when total—not partial—costs of alternative courses of action are readily apparent.

When all costs are allocated, the illusion of free goods and services—goods and services that appear free to operating units but are not free to the institution—vanishes. Under traditional budgeting arrangements in which rent is seldom if ever charged, space appears free to operating units even though typically more than 10% of general fund expenditure must be allocated for the operation and maintenance of facilities. Signals given to unit managers when they are unaware of the total cost of their actions lead to decisions that do not promote the institution's objectives. If they are rational individuals, their actions will appear irrational when viewed as a group.

Cost Allocation Criteria

The distinction between direct and indirect costs is somewhat artificial. In a sense, indirect costs are direct costs that are more difficult to associate with specific activities. Because their association is less obvious, we have to adopt conventions to allocate them and conventions vary by type of cost. Adoption of conventions requires consultation. Ideally, out of consultation, consensus can emerge. In its absence, some authority has to be invoked to reach a decision.

The number of indirect costs identified and conventions adopted is a judgment call. If too few are selected, important differences in allocating costs will be ignored. Beyond a certain point, however, the sets of percentages become redundant. One distribution becomes nearly identical to another, and little information is gained for the effort.

Determination of Total Costs

Determining responsibility centers' total costs seems straightforward until we try to begin. What are the support centers' costs we are to allocate? Their direct cost? Their total cost? Or their total cost net of earned income? The correct answer to this multiple-choice question is neither all of the above nor none of the above. The correct answer is the third alternative: total cost net of earned income.

If we know total cost for the support centers, we should be able to determine total net costs. But we don't know total cost because that's what we're trying to establish for all centers—academic and support. Our problem would be simplified if support centers provided services only for academic centers. Then their direct costs would be equal to their total costs. But relationships are not that simple. Physical facilities provides services for all centers. Central administration provides services for all centers, including physical facilities. Support centers' direct costs clearly are not equal to their total costs. How can we begin?

Three ways of proceeding are available. The third, which is the most elegant, provides a better representation of the distribution of indirect costs among the centers, but all three are mentioned in case some prefer one of the other alternatives:

1. Allocating support center costs only to academic centers
2. Allocating support center costs sequentially
3. Allocating support center costs simultaneously

An advantage of the first two options is their apparent simplicity. Until the advent of electronic computing, Option 3 was not feasible. Until the advent of desktop computing, Option 3 was not convenient.

Allocating Support Center
Costs Only to Academic Centers

One way to proceed is to ignore services that support centers provide to support centers. With that simplifying assumption, each support center's direct cost—less earned income—can be distributed to academic responsibility centers in proportion to their percentages. Such an approach is entirely appropriate for support centers whose services are all or mostly directed to academic units. For centers like physical facilities and central administration, however, support center services to support centers are liable to be substantial.

Allocating Support Center Costs Sequentially

With the adoption of an artificial convention, support center services to support centers can be recognized. All we have to do is agree on the sequence of allocating support center costs. Unfortunately, the sequence adopted affects the cost allocations. But as long as the heads of both academic and support centers can be counted on to put the university's welfare ahead of their own self-interest and the welfare of their respective units, securing agreement should present no problem. If a university community were not inhabited by women and men of goodwill, allocating indirect costs based on an arbitrary sequence could be a cause of endless controversy. The third option avoids testing that assumption.

Allocating Support Center Costs Simultaneously

By expressing responsibility centers' direct and indirect costs as a set of linear equations and solving them simultaneously, we can recognize interdependence among support centers realistically and avoid protocols that are subject to challenge. Moreover, nine deans in ten will be mystified—but impressed—by the technique and unwilling to admit they do not understand what is going on.

The concepts are relatively straightforward. Each centers' total cost is equal to its direct cost plus allocated indirect costs. Its net total cost is equal to its total cost less its earned income. Its net total costs can also be expressed as its direct cost less its earned income plus the sum of percentages of each support center's net total cost—the form of the linear equations.

Determining each center's total cost involves solving all of the centers' equations simultaneously. Such a solution may seem like a major undertaking, and before the advent of electronic computing this approach had little practical significance. Now, however, it almost can be easier done than said. The calculations can be performed quickly on top of your desk (if a microcomputer sits on it).

When the calculations are completed, each support center's total costs will be matched by the sum of earned income and assessment income it receives from the other centers. That coincidence is not coincidental! The solution is one of a kind. The solution is unique. It's the only arrangement that the support centers' total allocated cost/ assessment income and earned income balance to their respective total costs. Moreover, the difference between total cost and earned income for all the academic centers will equal the only income that has not been allocated: state support.

Implementation

Virtually all of the preceding commentary on the steps toward RCM deals with mechanics. Mechanics are important. A close approximation to perfection is necessary if the transition to and operation of RCM are to proceed smoothly. Imperfections are inexcusable and not likely to be forgiven.

However, although perfect mechanical arrangements and operating systems are essential, they are not sufficient for successful implementation of RCM. The essential and sufficient ingredient for successful implementation, in my opinion, is people—people who understand RCM and who want to make it work. Even less than perfect systems can be made to work if the people involved are informed and united in their purpose. Fortunately, in making a move to RCM, educating every faculty member and every administrator is not required. Key players in the process—the executive, academic, and financial officers of a campus, the deans and their academic and financial assistants—must understand. For the others, an intensive course of study in RCM can be an elective.

In academe, there are no secrets. Attempting to implement RCM in secret is impossible in such an environment and indeed inappropriate given the approach's commitment to full disclosure. Announcing the intention to move to a new system is the only viable approach. Temptation to anything less than complete openness should be rejected. Discretion in this instance might not be sinful, but it definitely appears to be unwise.

How any university's leadership deals with making a transition to RCM depends on local circumstances and personal style.

Prerequisites for RCM

For many institutions of higher education, RCM may appear to offer an attractive alternative to existing arrangements. However great its potential advantages, it is not for everyone. Certain conditions—necessary but not sufficient—have to be in place before RCM can operate effectively in a university's environment.

Academic Leadership

Academic priorities should lead rather than follow the budget process. RCM is designed to make the budget process responsive to academic priorities. Strong academic leadership is required to identify those priorities and follow through with the allocation decisions necessary to realize them. Strong implies having moral or intellectual power. We like to think academic leadership in higher education often possesses those qualities. Among the synonyms of strong are tough and tenacious. Those characteristics seem to be less common but are essential. The rules of RCM have to be maintained and enforced. Without strong academic leadership, RCM is an idle exercise.

Administrative Support

Academic leadership is the prime mover in RCM. University administration plays the role of a facilitator. High professional standards in financial and personnel management and other service functions are required if the system is to work well. A few able individuals in central administration are not adequate. A well-trained and able administrative staff has to be dispersed to the operating units and function as part of a team with central administration.

Full Disclosure

An information-rich environment means more than lots of numbers accurate, easily retrieved, current, and subject to analysis. Under RCM, there are no secrets. And no hidden agendas. The objectives and priorities of the institution have to be common knowledge. The books have to open. No little deals on the side can be cut without everyone's knowledge. Every allocation should have an explanation. The time for allocation comes once a year during the performance evaluation and budget review process. University officers with preferences for secrecy and inscrutable arrangements should avoid RCM.

Involvement

RCM emphasizes the fact the a university is first and foremost an academic enterprise. The deans of schools and the heads of other primary mission units are key players in the enterprise and must be involved in the development of RCM and in its subsequent evolution. With involvement in the RCM's development comes not only understanding but also a sense of ownership and a commitment to its success. Their continued participation not only helps ensure orderly change but also provides a self-monitoring mechanism.

Ingredients for Success

Although strong academic leadership, a capable administrative team, full disclosure of objectives, decisions, and allocations, and involvement of the academic leadership do not ensure the success of RCM, they do make its realization possible. Such prerequisites should characterize all institutions of higher education where all the programs are strong, all the campuses are good-looking, and all the students are above average.

Note

1. Material for this chapter was extracted from Edward L. Whalen, *Responsibility Centered Budgeting: An Approach to Decentralized Management for Institutions of Higher Education* (Indiana University Press, 1991).

References

U.S. Department of Education, National Center for Education Statistics. (1992). *Integrated postsecondary education data system, 1992* (IPEDS 92 DISC). Washington, DC: Government Printing Office.

U.S. Department of Education, National Center for Education Statistics. (1994). *Digest of education statistics, 1994* (NCES 94-115). Washington, DC: Government Printing Office.

SEVEN

Funding Public Education With a State Lottery
IS EDUCATION THE WINNER?

SUSAN ROBINSON SUMMERS

Whether or not to place a bet may be the most pressing dilemma confronting Americans today concerning public lotteries. Although it is common knowledge that one is more likely to be struck by lightning than to win a lotto jackpot, billions of lottery tickets are purchased each year. In most states, lottery players are encouraged to believe that the public weal is served each time a bet is wagered. In many states, the lottery is earmarked to fund public education; even though one player each week may win a multi-million-dollar jackpot, public education is said to be the real winner because it receives a sizable share of lottery revenues every week. However, three decades of experience with contemporary American lotteries provide evidence that education never holds the winning ticket.

Three Objections to Lotteries

Early American lotteries were discontinued for the same reasons that many citizens cite today for their lottery discontent: Lotteries are an inefficient way to raise government funds, government-operated lotteries compromise political morality, and earmarked lotteries do not improve the fiscal health of the beneficiary.

First, the lottery is an inefficient method of fund-raising: Too much money is expended to raise the sums awarded to benefit the public good (Borg & Mason, 1988; Borg, Mason, & Shapiro, 1993; Gulley & Scott, 1993; Mikesell & Zorn, 1986, 1988). In the average lottery state, the revenue that can be expected to flow from lottery ticket sales is roughly equivalent to a 1-cent increase in sales tax, yet lotteries are administratively more complex.

Second, by aggressively promoting the sale of lottery tickets, state governments are promoting the concept that good fortune comes by luck, not by hard work. Household funds that are expended on lottery tickets appear to be disproportionately from economically and educationally disadvantaged segments of the American population (Brinner & Clotfelter, 1975; Clotfelter & Cook, 1990a, 1990b, 1991; Fisher, 1988; Karcher, 1989; Mikesell & Pirog-Good, 1990; Wyett, 1991); however, there is some evidence that the regressivity of the lottery may have lessened over time (McConkey & Warren, 1987; Mikesell & Zorn, 1989). Regardless of who buys the tickets, it is questionable whether a responsible government should encourage its citizens to buy quantities of what are, in essence, raffle tickets with incredibly long odds.

Third, lotteries are earmarked so as to win passage of the referendum. The voters are encouraged to believe that a vote in favor of a state lottery is a vote in favor of better funding for the beneficiary (Allen, 1991; Jones & Amalfitano, 1994). However, when the lottery is earmarked for a specific purpose, the beneficiary inevitably loses revenue from other government sources, typically through erosion of the general revenue share (Borg & Mason, 1988, 1990; Brandon, 1993; Clotfelter & Cook, 1989; MacManus & Spindler, 1989; Stark, Wood, & Honeyman, 1993; Summers, 1993; Summers, Honeyman, Wattenbarger, & Miller, 1995; Summers, Miller, & Honeyman, 1995; Thomas & Webb, 1984). Lottery supplantation of general revenue funds is well documented across the course of the lottery years. For example, based on data collected from five different lottery states from 1968 through 1973, Weinstein and Deitch (1974) concluded that lottery dollars were more likely to supplant than enhance revenues for any earmarked beneficiary.

Historical Perspective

The history of lotteries in America is an interesting story that has been extensively reported elsewhere (Clotfelter & Cook, 1989; Ezell, 1960; Karcher, 1989; Thomas & Webb, 1984). Clearly, lotteries were a common funding device used by colonial Americans. The earliest recorded fund-raising lottery in America was held in 1612 to benefit the Jamestown Settlement. Lotteries were continuously operated in some part of the United States from colonial days until the turn of the century when the Louisiana lottery was halted by federal order.

The first American lottery that was earmarked for education was held in 1746 to benefit King's College, which later became Columbia University. Thus, the use of a public lottery to benefit education in the United States is not a new phenomenon; neither is the fiscal controversy concerning the lottery revenues. Indeed, the question of whether an educational institution would, in the end, benefit from a lottery for which it was earmarked was raised in the colonial New York legislature as early as 1753, concerning a lottery to benefit King's College. Despite attempts by the college's advocates to legislatively ensure that the lottery proceeds would flow exclusively to King's College, in the final act, half the funds were diverted to corrections and health care (Ezell, 1960).

Lottery Prohibition

Although the United States is a very young country relative to the life span of many other nations, the American collective conscience has apparently forgotten that lotteries have been used on these shores for nearly 300 years. Evidently, we did not learn from the mistakes of our forebears. The following Supreme Court opinion was written in

1850, yet it speaks to the lottery disenchantment that is becoming more prevalent today:

> The suppression of nuisances injurious to public health or morality is among the most important duties of government. Experience has shown that the common forms of gambling are comparatively innocuous when placed in contrast with the widespread pestilence of lotteries. The former are confined to a few persons and places, but the latter infests the whole community; it enters every dwelling; it reaches every class; it preys upon the hard earnings of the poor; it plunders the ignorant and simple. (*Phalen v. Virginia*, 1850, p. 168)

In fact, the *Phalen v. Virginia* decision reflected the pervasive sentiment of the 19th century. By 1885, voters in 29 states had banned lotteries by state constitutional amendment (*Greater Loretta Improvement Association v. State ex rel. Boone*, 1970, p. 667). Thus, to enact the lotteries of today, it was necessary for supporters to work for passage of a state constitutional amendment through voter referenda.

The End of Prohibition:
20th-Century State Lotteries

The American lotteries that most concern education finance on the brink of the 21st century began in 1964, when the citizens of New Hampshire approved a lottery referendum. Like many of the 34 state lotteries that followed, the New Hampshire lottery was an attempt to raise additional funds for public education without passing a new tax (Allen, 1991; Fisher, 1988). In fact, 20th-century lotteries have been described as a "popular vehicle for adding a new means of 'revenue enhancement' to state tax systems," coming into vogue at a time that state income taxes were increasingly unpopular (Berry & Berry, 1990, p. 396). Lotteries were especially popular with voters throughout the 1980s; however, lottery referenda were defeated in 1993 in Oklahoma and Utah, a signal that the unattractive attributes of state lotteries had become more widely known.

Nevertheless, by 1993, 35 states and the District of Columbia had some form of state-operated lottery. Most of these lotteries were approved by referenda that linked them to some public agency as a revenue stream; the beneficiary was most often public education, especially at the primary and secondary levels. Table 7.1 lists each state and the District of Columbia, whether the state had a lottery, its year of implementation, the legal citation, and the designated beneficiary.

Lotteries Do Raise Funds

Although the success of individual state lotteries varies widely, the total amount generated is considerable. In 1990, the 32 state lotteries that were in operation generated $18.7 billion in gross revenues (Calkin, 1992). For the most part, young lotteries are more successful than those that have matured; about half the 1990 revenues came from lotteries that had been in operation for five years or less. Although states vary somewhat in the proportional allocation of prize money, administrative funds, and allocations to the beneficiary, in general about 40% of lottery gross revenue is available for state-funded projects (Allen, 1991; Brandon, 1993).

Clearly, lotteries are a common practice of raising state funds in the 1990s. They are typically promoted as a means of raising enhancement money for an existing institution or special funds for a new project. At the same time, however, the states are under pressure to raise more money to cover expenses derived from competing social concerns about health, transportation, criminal justice, and social services (Allen, 1991; Blackley & DeBoer, 1993; Jones & Amalfitano, 1993). No matter how successful it appears to be, no state lottery can generate enough revenue to meet the expectations of its backers. The revenue stream provided by a lottery is small relative to the total funds earned by other state sources and seldom constitutes more than 2% of a state's general revenue. Further, lotteries are highly elastic, unstable revenue streams, and lottery profits are relatively expensive to generate (Borg & Mason, 1988, 1990; Mikesell & Zorn, 1986, 1988; Thomas & Webb, 1984).

(text continued on p. 162)

TABLE 7.1 State-Operated Lotteries, Constitutional and Statute
Citations, and Lottery Fund Beneficiaries

State	Year Begun	Citation	Designated Beneficiaries
Alabama	None	AL Const. Art. 4, § 65	N/A
Alaska	None	AK St. § 05.15.187(f)	N/A
Arizona	1981	AZ St. § 4, 6, 5.522	Parks, transportation, commerce, and economic development
Arkansas	None	AR Const. Art. 19, § 14	N/A
California	1985	CA Const. Art. IV § 19(d), CA Code T. 2 Chpt. 12.5 Art. 1 § 8880.1	Education, all levels
Colorado	1983	CO Const. Art. 18 § 2.7	Parks, recreation, open spaces
Connecticut	1972	CT Gen. St. T. 12 Chpt. 226 12-568	Education
Delaware	1975	DE Const. Art. 2 § 17(a), DE St. T. 29 § 4815	GRF[a]
District of Columbia	1982	DC Code 1981 § 2-2501; 95 St. 1174; PL 97-91	GRF
Florida	1988	FL Const. Art. X § 15 (c)(1); FL St. 24 § 102(2)(a), § 121(5)(a-b)	Public schools, community colleges, and universities
Georgia	Pending, approved 1992	GA Code § 50-27-13(3)(b)(1), (c)(3); GA Const. Art. 1, § 2, P VIII	Educational purposes and projects
Hawaii	None	HI Organic Act 55n	N/A
Idaho	1989	ID Chpt. 20, § 1605/2	School buildings
Illinois	1974	IL Chpt. 20 1605/2	Common school fund and GRF
Indiana	1989	IN Code 4-30-1-1	Capital Improvements
Iowa	1985	IA Code T. 5 Chpt. 99E; T. 12 Chpt. 262B	Education, agriculture, university research, and economic development

TABLE 7.1 *Continued*

State	Year Begun	Citation	Designated Beneficiaries
Kansas	1987	KS Const. Art. § 15 3c; KS St. 874 8701, §8711	GRF
Kentucky	1989	KY Const. § 226; KY St. § 154A.130	Vietnam veterans' bonus, GRF
Louisiana	1992	LA Const. Art. 12 § 6	GRF
Maine	1974	ME St. T. 8 § 371	GRF
Maryland	1973	MD Const. Art. 3 § 36; MD St. Govt. 9-120	Stadium facilities, GRF
Massachusetts	1972	MA St. 10 § 24	Arts
Michigan	1972	MI Const. Art. 4 § 41	Education
Minnesota	1990	MN Const. Art. 11, § 14, MN St. § 349A.10	Environment and natural resources
Mississippi	None	MS Const. Art. 4 § 98	N/A
Missouri	1986	MO St. 313.321	GRF
Montana	1987	MT Code 20-9-343	Equalization aid for school districts, educational telecommunications, juvenile detention
Nebraska	None	NE St. § 9-1,101; § 9-507	N/A
Nevada	None	NV Const. Art. 4 § 24	N/A
New Hampshire	1964	NH Const. Part 2 Art. 6-b	Education
New Jersey	1970	NJ Const. Art. 4 § 7-2; St. 5:9	State-funded institutions, education, and senior citizens
New Mexico	None	NM St. 1978 §30-19-2	N/A
New York	1967	NY Const. Art. 1 § 9-1; NY St. FL Chpt. 56 Art. 6 § 92-c-2,3,4-b-1; NY TL Chpt. 60 Art. 34 § 1601	Public and nonpublic primary and secondary education, winter sports, physical education
North Carolina	None	NC St. § 14-290	N/A
North Dakota	None	ND Const. Art. 11 § 25	N/A
Ohio	1974	OH St. § 3770.01-.06	Education

TABLE 7.1 *Continued*

State	Year Begun	Citation	Designated Beneficiaries
Oklahoma	None	OK St. T. 21 1051	N/A
Oregon	1985	OR St. 461.543(1)	Higher education sports programs
Pennsylvania	1972	PA PL 351 no. 91	Senior citizens
Rhode Island	1974	RI Const. Art. 6, 15; RI St. 42-61-15	GRF
South Carolina	None	SC Const. Art. 17 7	N/A
South Dakota	1987	SD St. 42-7A-24	Corrections facility construction
Tennessee	None	TN Const. Art. 11 5	N/A
Texas	Pending, approved 1992	TX Civ. St. Art. 179g	GRF
Utah	None	UT Const. Art. 6 27	N/A
Vermont	1978	VT St. T. 31 654.11(d), 658	GRF
Virginia	1988	VA Code 18.2-334.3	GRF
Washington	1982	WA St. 67.70.900, 67.70.240	GRF
West Virginia	1986	WV St. 29-22-7	Education, senior citizens
Wisconsin	1988	WI Cons. Art. 4 24(6); WI St. 79.10	Property tax relief
Wyoming	None	WY St. 1-23-106	N/A

SOURCE: Summers (1993, pp. 124-128).
a. GRF = general revenue fund.

Lotteries Earmarked for Education

Beginning in New Hampshire in 1964 and ending in Georgia 30 years later, successful lottery referenda in the 20th century have usually been linked to a public institution that is most often education. As shown in Table 7.1, sometimes education is explicitly named the beneficiary, as it is in California, Florida, New York, and 10 other states. In other states, education is funded indirectly, such as in Oregon, where postsecondary athletic programs are the beneficiary, or in

Arizona, where lottery profits fund economic development grants that are available to educational institutions.

What Will a Lottery Dollar Buy?

Even in states that earmark all lottery profits for education and have high-grossing lotteries, the actual return to education is small when viewed from the context of the total education budget (Allen, 1991; Brandon, 1993; Mikesell & Zorn, 1988). For example, in Florida, public education is earmarked to receive 38% of all lottery proceeds, and the Florida lottery is one of the nation's highest producers. It generated $2.3 billion in gross sales in 1994; after funding prizes and administrative expenses, the Florida Department of Education received $870.4 million (Mann, 1995). Taken alone this is a sizable sum, yet it pales when compared to the annual cost of funding public education. The states that have high-grossing lotteries are also those with a large population of public school students. For example, in Florida, lottery profits provide only about 8% of the Florida Department of Education budget (State of Florida, 1994).

A convenient way to judge the fiscal impact of lottery dollars is to look at the number of days in an academic year that schools could operate, using only lottery dollars to fund operations. Brandon (1993) identified 11 states where primary and secondary schools were earmarked to receive lottery funds and reported the number of days schools could operate in each state, using only lottery dollars. His tabulation showed a high of 12 days in Ohio, where 7.02% of the schools' revenues come from lottery funds; the low was one day in West Virginia, where 0.53% of the schools' revenue flowed from lottery funds (p. 7). In summarizing the effect of state lotteries on school funding, Brandon concluded that "lotteries contribute only a small part of overall revenue; lottery revenues are often substituted for regular funds; the revenues are unstable; the administrative expense is high; and the lottery acts like a regressive tax" (p. 11).

Yet another perspective is to measure whether the mere existence of a lottery is predictive of the level of state support for public education. Jones and Amalfitano (1993) used this approach with 1987 national data. Their analysis found that the simple presence of a state lottery did not explain the level of state support for education. This was true whether or not the lottery was earmarked to fund education. In this study, per capita income was the variable that best explained variations in public funding for education; other explanatory variables were the proportion of the population that was nonwhite and the population density. The authors concluded, "Lottery states do spend more . . . because they are wealthier than non-lottery sates, not because they have the lottery" (p. 113).

Educators are not in the habit of turning down money. However, if presented with the opportunity to be earmarked for lottery funds, the wise choice may be to decline the offer. Thomas and Webb (1984) wrote that "earmarking lottery receipts for education is, in practice, more of a political ploy than an actual benefit" (p. 303). Brandon (1993) noted that "some revenue sources can do harm as well as good" (p. 3). In fact, a published statement by Florida lottery officials (Florida Lottery, 1993) supports the contention that lotteries may be harmful to the fiscal health of education: "The misconception that lottery dollars could solve education's funding needs has eroded support for increased education funding."

The Florida Experience

The Florida lottery is among the nation's most lucrative, in terms of gross revenues earned. Florida is also a state that has attracted attention from education finance researchers, who have studied the fiscal impact of its lottery. Proceeds are allocated by formula, such that 38% of lottery revenue flows into the Florida Education Trust Fund from which the 28-member community college system and the 9-member state university system each receive 15% and the 69 primary and secondary school districts receive 70% (State of Florida, 1994). Thus, it should be instructive to look individually at the lottery's fiscal consequences on the school districts, community colleges, and universities. Two studies conducted at the University of Florida addressed the school districts and community colleges, and a survey conducted at Florida State University examined public perception of the extent to which the Florida Lottery would fund education.

Impact on Community College Funding

In the community college analysis, one study attempted to measure whether the financial status of the individual colleges changed after the lottery was introduced as a revenue source (Summers, 1993; Summers, Honeyman et al., 1995). The study used regression analysis to examine state allocations and institutional expenditures for all 28 Florida community colleges from 1972 through 1993. The results showed that lottery dollars were negatively correlated with college expenditures; to wit, after the Florida lottery was introduced as a revenue source in 1987, the colleges had less money to spend. The results of the study further showed redistribution in the funding sources for the community colleges, with state funds contributing a declining share of total college support. Finally, the extent to which the lottery allocation was restricted, or categorical, was shown to be positively correlated with the size of the state fund allocation; thus, using lottery dollars for highly regulated, restricted expenditures resulted in a larger general revenue fund allocation than was true when lottery dollars were subject to local discretion in expenditure. The results of this study did not find statistically significant evidence that lottery funds supplanted general revenue funds; in fact, over time, lottery dollars were so small relative to the general revenue allocations that the supplantation effect was too small in magnitude to be detected by the model.

General Revenue
and Student Fee Share

A subsequent report challenged the efficacy of a state lottery as public policy (Summers, Miller, & Honeyman, 1995). The results showed that the community colleges were fiscally harmed in two different ways by being earmarked to receive lottery funds.

First, the general revenue fund (GRF) share eroded, beginning with the first full year of Florida lottery operation. Although all of Florida's education was affected, the community colleges sustained greater fiscal harm than the state's educational system as a whole. Figure 7.1 shows that, even though the Florida Department of Education (DOE) as a body lost GRF share, the community college erosion was greater. In fiscal year (FY) 1984, the community college system received 5.32% of the Florida GRF; in FY 1994, the community colleges received 3.63%, an erosion of nearly 32% over a 10-year period. By comparison, the DOE received 61.48% of GRF in FY 1984 and only 50.42% in FY 1994, an erosion of 18%. The result is that, because of the loss of GRF support, lottery dollars are even more critical to funding the Florida community colleges than the public school districts; given the flat performance of the state's lottery throughout the 1990s combined with the increasing enrollment, this is cause for concern. In FY 1994, the lottery allocation was 18.5% of the community college system's budget but only 8% of the budgets of the primary and secondary school districts (Mann, 1995). Figure 7.2 shows that, in current dollars per full-time-equivalent (FTE) student, the community college lottery allocation was fairly flat from FY 1991 to FY 1994, at about $650 per FTE student. At the same time, the GRF allocation per FTE student was also flat at about $2,300 and still has not regained the peak of $2,936 in GRF per FTE student the colleges received in FY 1988. During this period, the state experienced an increase in GRF available to the legislature for allocation.

Second, after the lottery became a revenue source for Florida's community colleges, student fees rose both in dollar value and in proportional share of total per-student funding. In-state fees for Florida's community college students have traditionally been very low by design, using the model of the junior college as an extension of secondary school (Witt, Wattenbarger, Gollattscheck, & Suppiger, 1994). Figure 7.2 shows that while GRF and lottery allocations per FTE student were flat and at times declined since FY 1987, FTE student fees rose steadily in both dollar value and proportion of total FTE student funding. In FY 1987, student fees contributed $798, or 20.8% of the FTE student funding; in FY 1993, they comprised $1,134, or 27.2%.

In conclusion, the authors of the Florida community college finance studies proposed that the lottery allocation to community colleges be restricted entirely to fund student financial aid. Alternatively, they proposed that all earmarking be removed, so that the Florida lottery would fund the general treasury as it does in many of the lottery states.

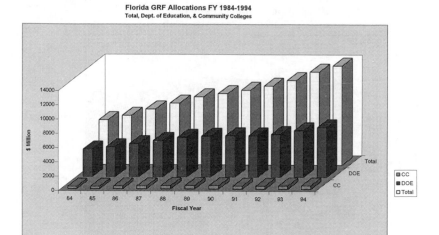

Figure 7.1. Florida general revenue fund (GRF) allocations to all agencies (TOT), the Department of Education (DOE), and the community college system (CC), FY 1984-FY 1994

SOURCE: Summers, Miller, and Honeyman (1995, p. 30). Copyright 1995, Florida Association of Community Colleges, Talllahassee. Used with permission.

Supplantation of School District Funds

A separate study conducted at the University of Florida concerned funding for primary and secondary school districts in Florida (Stark et al., 1993). This study examined whether the lottery fund allocation of FY 1989 supplanted general revenue funds. Regression analysis was used with financial data from FY 1973 through FY 1989 to address the question of whether the lottery allocation of FY 1989 suppressed the GRF allocation of the same year. In effect, did Florida lottery funds substitute for state funds that were, in turn, diverted to other agencies? The results of the study showed that lottery funds were used to supplant, or substitute for, GRF dollars. Stark et al. (1993) concluded that 43.2% of the FY 1989 lottery funds were, in fact, new funding, or enhancement dollars; the remaining 56.8% of the lottery allocation was a substitute for GRF dollars, or existing resources. This finding was problematic for at least two different reasons. First, Florida

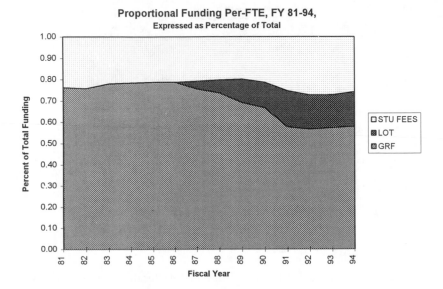

Figure 7.2. Proportional funding per full-time-equivalent (FTE) student, FY 1981-FY 1994, from student fees (STU FEES), lottery funds (LOT), and the Florida general revenue fund (GRF).

SOURCE: Summers, Miller, and Honeyman (1995, p. 31). Copyright 1995, Florida Association of Community Colleges, Talllahassee. Used with permission.

Statute 24.102.2.a clearly states that lottery funds are to be used for enhancement of public education: "That the net proceeds . . . be used to support improvements in public education and . . . not be used as a substitute for existing resources." Second, the supplantation reported in this study occurred in only the second full year of Florida lottery operation, providing evidence that supplantation is inevitable.

Public Delusion

A separate, although related, issue from supplantation of existing resources is the fact that being earmarked to receive lottery funds gives the general public a misconception about the extent to which the lottery will fund the beneficiary. This misconception is understandable, considering that the lottery advertising campaigns emphasize what a boon the lottery funds will be. Thus, the loss of general revenue share is accompanied by a public perception that the beneficiary is, in fact, better funded than ever. A study conducted at Florida State University in 1989 attempted to measure public perception of the extent to which Florida's lottery would fund education.

Allen (1991) reported the results of a survey conducted by the Policy Sciences Program at Florida State University. The results of this study illustrated the general misconception about the extent to which a state lottery will fund the beneficiary. Of the more than 1,000 persons surveyed, most believed that the lottery would provide a greater share of total education funding than was in fact the case. Allen reported that, although 17% of respondents said they did not know what proportion the lottery would contribute to education's funding, 40% believed lottery funds would contribute less than 10% of the total education budget. In contrast, 42% believed the lottery would contribute from 10% to more than 50% of the education budget: 23% believed the lottery would contribute from 10% to 25% of the total budget, 14% of respondents believed the lottery's share was 25% to 50% of the education budget, and 5% believed lottery funds would constitute more than 50% of the education budget (p. 305). Allen quoted Florida Education Commissioner Betty Castor as saying, "The false perception that the lottery will pay for all education damages our effort to keep Florida on a path toward excellence in education" (p. 304).

Conclusion

Lotteries are here to stay. From the long view, they have been a part of the fiscal armament of this nation from the Jamestown Settlement to the present day, with only a brief respite beginning at the turn of the century when the Louisiana lottery ended until startup of the New Hampshire lottery in 1964. It is a fact that a state lottery is an inefficient way to raise public funds, but it is a method that is acceptable to the citizens of most states and is well entrenched in the American experience.

Therefore, it is unlikely that state governments will discontinue their involvement in the lottery business. Instead, I suggest that earmarking be stopped. States that operate a lottery should use those revenues for the general treasury, not for any beneficiary. This solution would eliminate the problem of supplantation of general revenue funds with lottery allocations. Because such beneficiaries as Florida's community college system are so heavily dependant on lottery funds, the earmarking should be gradually discontinued over a period of several fiscal years. Second, the promotion of state lotteries should not include any reference to public well-being that would accrue as the result of the purchase of lottery tickets. State lotteries should, instead, follow the standard set by states where liquor is sold in state stores: Buy a ticket if you so choose but do not be deluded that society is better off because you wagered a dollar or two.

References

Allen, P. J. (1991). The allocation of lottery revenue to education in Florida, California, Michigan, and Illinois. *Educational Policy, 5*(3), 296-311.

Berry, F. S., & Berry, W. D. (1990). State lottery adoptions as policy innovations: An even history analysis. *American Political Science Review, 84*, 395-415.

Blackley, P. R., & DeBoer, L. (1993). Explaining state government discretionary revenue increases in fiscal years 1991 and 1992. *National Tax Journal, 46*, 1-12.

Borg, M. O., & Mason, P. M. (1988). The budgetary incidence of a lottery to support education. *National Tax Journal, 41*, 75-85.

Borg, M. O., & Mason, P. M. (1990). Earmarked lottery revenues: positive windfalls or concealed redistribution mechanisms? *Journal of Education Finance, 15*, 289-301.

Borg, M. O., Mason, P. M., & Shapiro, S. L. (1993). The cross effects of lottery taxes on alternative state tax revenue. *Public Finance Quarterly, 21*, 123-140.

Brandon, D. P. (1993). *State-run lotteries: Their effects on school funding.* Arlington, VA: Educational Research Service.

Brinner, R. E., & Clotfelter, C. T. (1975). An economic appraisal of state lotteries. *National Tax Journal, 28*, 395-404.

Calkins, S. (1992, March 23). Lotteries: Has a growth industry failed? *Tax Notes, 54*, 1563-1566.

Clotfelter, C. T., & Cook, P. J. (1989). *Selling hope: State lotteries in America.* Cambridge, MA: Harvard University Press.

Clotfelter, C. T., & Cook, P. J. (1990a). On the economics of state lotteries. *Journal of Economic Perspectives, 4*(4), 105-119.

Clotfelter, C. T., & Cook, P. J. (1990b). Redefining "success" in the state lottery business. *Journal of Policy Analysis and Management, 9*, 99-104.

Clotfelter, C. T., & Cook, P. J. (1991). Lotteries in the real world. *Journal of Risk and Uncertainty, 4*, 227-232.

Ezell, J. S. (1960). *Fortune's merry wheel: The lottery in America.* Cambridge, MA: Harvard University Press.

Fisher, R. C. (1988). Revenue for state and local governments. *State and local public finance* (pp. 99-280). Glenview, IL: Scott, Foresman.

Florida Lottery. (1993). *When will the Florida lottery solve education's funding needs?* Tallahassee: Author.

Greater Loretta Improvement Association v. State ex rel. Boone, 234 So.2nd 665, 42 A.L.R.3d 632 (FL 1970).

Gulley, O. D., & Scott, F. A., Jr. (1993). The demand for wagering on state-operated lotto games. *National Tax Journal, 46,* 13-22.

Jones, T. H., & Amalfitano, J. L. (1994). *America's gamble: Public school finance and state lotteries.* Lancaster, PA: Technomic.

Karcher, A. J. (1989). *Lotteries.* New Brunswick, NJ: Transaction.

MacManus, S., & Spindler, C. (1989). Florida's lottery: How long education's sacred cow? *Florida Policy Review, 4*(2), 1-4.

Mann, M. (1995, Winter). Lottery sales up, though colleges down. *FACC Current,* p. 16. Tallahassee: Florida Association of Community Colleges.

McConkey, C. W., & Warren, W. E. (1987). Psychographic and demographic profiles of state lottery ticket purchasers. *Journal of Consumer Affairs, 21,* 314-327.

Mikesell, J. L., & Pirog-Good, M. A. (1990). State lotteries and crime: The regressive revenue producer is linked with a crime rate higher by 3 percent. *American Journal of Economics and Sociology, 49*(1), 8-19.

Mikesell, J. L., & Zorn, C. K. (1986). State lotteries as fiscal savior or fiscal fraud: A look at the evidence. *Public Administration Review, 46,* 311-320.

Mikesell, J. L., & Zorn, K. (1988). State lotteries for public revenue. *Public Budgeting & Finance, 8,* 38-47.

Mikesell, J. L., & Zorn, K. (1989). A note on the changing incidence of state lottery finance. *Social Science Quarterly, 70,* 513-521.

Phalen v. Virginia, 49 U.S. 163 (US 1850).

Stark, S. D., Wood, R. C., & Honeyman, D. S. (1993). The Florida education lottery: Its use as a substitute for existing funds and its effects on the equity of school funding. *Journal of Education Finance, 18,* 231-242.

State of Florida, Department of Education. (1994). *The Florida lottery and the educational enhancement trust fund.* Tallahassee: Author.

Summers, S. R. (1993). *An examination of supplantation and redistribution effects of lottery allocations to a community college system.* Unpublished doctoral dissertation, University of Florida. (Ann Arbor, MI: University Microfilms International, Document No. 9505844)

Summers, S. R., Honeyman, D. S., Wattenbarger, J. L., & Miller, M. D. (1995). An examination of supplantation and redistribution effects of lottery allocations to a community college system. *Journal of Education Finance, 21,* 236-253.

Summers, S. R., Miller, M. D., & Honeyman, D. S. (1995). The Florida education lottery: A lotto nonsense or a wise bet for Florida's community colleges? *Visions: The Journal of Applied Research for the Florida Association of Community Colleges, 1*(1), 10-13.

Thomas, S. B., & Webb, L. D. (1984). The use and abuse of lotteries as a revenue source. *Journal of Education Finance, 9,* 289-311.

Weinstein, D., & Deitch, L. (1974). *The impact of legalized gambling: The socioeconomic consequence of lotteries and off-track betting.* New York: Praeger.

Witt, A. A., Wattenbarger, J. L., Gollattscheck, J. F., & Suppiger, J. E. (1994). *America's community colleges: The first century.* Washington, DC: American Association of Community Colleges.

Wyett, T. A. (1991, Spring). *State lotteries: Regressive taxes in disguise.* Section on Taxation, America Bar Association, 44 Tax Law 867 (WESTLAW Document Reproduction Service).

EIGHT

Funding for Community Colleges
CHANGING PATTERNS OF SUPPORT

DALE F. CAMPBELL

LYNN H. LEVERTY

KAREN SAYLES

Since their development almost 100 years ago, community colleges have been particularly adaptive to the social and economic challenges facing communities, states, and the nation. The first community colleges were two-year additions to secondary schools and provided a link between the elementary/secondary and baccalaureate systems. The growth in community colleges was rapid, especially after World War II. Public community colleges have nearly tripled in number since 1960, increasing to nearly 1,300 institutions (Vaughan, 1995, p. 1). These colleges now enroll half of all beginning college students. Having shed their K-12 roots, community colleges today take various forms, ranging from comprehensive community college districts and systems to two-year campuses of universities to vocational-technical colleges.

Vaughan (1995) cites five commitments that characterize the community college:

- Serve the postsecondary needs of all segments of society regardless of their level or preparation—better known as open access.
- Provide comprehensive educational programs.
- Serve the nontraditional educational needs of the community for cultural, recreational, and other programs.
- Emphasize teaching.
- Permit access to education through lifelong learning.

The community college commitments promise much. More people are recognizing the responsiveness of community colleges to their needs and the benefits provided by a community college education. Most critical to the delivery of the services a community college can provide is sufficient resources. Today, this is no small business. Community colleges nationwide have a total budget that exceeds $18 billion.

Hauptman (1993) suggests that the fiscal issues confronting higher education in the 1990s can be viewed from two basic perspectives: how higher education institutions obtain funds and how the funds obtained are spent. Although finance issues have traditionally been analyzed from this dichotomy, trends today indicate that questions of obtaining and spending funds are increasingly related.

Honeyman, Bruhn, and Sayles (1995) conclude that the pressures on public funds for all services have made the balance of benefits, as the ratio of public to other funding of higher education, fluid. Financial support for higher education is increasingly being affected by types of calculations that includes the rates of return to society and the individual. These returns include the monetary value to the individual, monetary value to society, social value to the individual (skills, sensitivity, and knowledge), and social value as defined by the efficient functioning of society. The ratio of benefits between society and the individual has never been defined clearly enough to produce uniform public support of higher education by the federal government, among states, or even in individual states from year to year.

The purpose of this chapter is to analyze the changes that have occurred in community college appropriations, enrollment, and tuition from 1990 to 1995, discuss the tensions in state legislatures concerning support for higher education, report on responses to the shifts in funding by college administrators, and discuss the implications for the future.

Sources of Funding

Historically, there have been five major sources of financial support for higher education: the federal government, state government, local government, tuition and fees, and other. Honeyman, Williamson, and Wattenbarger (1991) identify the distribution of the various sources of funding for community colleges in 1988 as approximately 58% state, 13% local, 22% student fees, 3% federal, and 4% other. Cohen and Brawer (1996) reported that in 1992 the distribution of sources of funding had changed to 46% state, 18% local, 20% tuition and fees, 5% federal, and 3% other (p. 140). Two additional categories of funding were reported: private gifts and grants (1%) and sales and services (7%).

Support for community colleges from the federal government has been limited, and this type of funding is restricted. The federal government largely funds financial aid, training programs and support services for disadvantaged students or special populations and research programs of interest to particular federal agencies. Federal funds that may be used for general operating support of institutions are channeled to the institutions as tuition. Most often, federal programs are funded on a contract basis where specific services are expected. Legislation is pending in Congress that could change dramatically in the area of workforce-related programs by consolidating many of the categorical programs and distributing funding to the states through block grants.

State governments are the largest sources of funds for public institutions including community colleges. Although many states fund financial aid programs that may be used at both public and private institutions, most state support is provided as general operating support for public institutions.

State funding for higher education reflects each state's preference for higher education among other services funded by the states.

Layzell and Lyddon (1990) describe the state budget as a "unique product shaped by a unique environment interacting with a dynamic process" (p. 53). Zumeta (1995) refers to the traditional role of higher education as a "budget balancer." Higher education is the largest area of state funding that is not constitutionally mandated, dictated by matching federal dollars or otherwise required. As a result, it is the area that can be "readily cut or held to small increases" (p. 73).

According to Layzell and Lyddon (1990), state funding for higher education is a product of the historical, political, economic, and demographic variables in the states. These variables are processed by the various players in the budgetary process, including governors, legislators, and state higher education leadership or coordinating agencies as well as the institutions themselves, and are eventually translated into a level of state funding.

In an effort to find a logical basis for higher education funding, 33 states used funding formulas to fund higher education in 1992 (McKeown & Layzell, 1994). This is an increase of 1 from 1988 (McKeown, 1989). Although these numbers appear stable, a few of the states using formulas in 1988 were not using them in 1991, and others had begun to use them, so the consistency of the count does not reflect the whole picture.

Some states use formulas as a statement of need or a desirable level of funding in the request process, others use them as methods of allocation, and still others use them as both a statement of need and then as an allocative mechanism for the amount of funds finally appropriated.

State funding formulas for higher education vary widely in complexity, but most serve to link mission with funding. The most clear and frequently used link is that of credit-based enrollment with funding. This poses a problem for community colleges because significant portions of the mission of these institutions (e.g., continuing education and public service) are not associated with enrollment or credit hours. Community colleges are often expected to sustain the noncredit portions of their mission on a self-supporting or fee-for-service basis.

Support for higher education from local government is almost exclusively for community colleges. The use of local funding for the community college reflects its roots in the school district, where the revenue source is usually the property tax, most often the only revenue source permitted to localities. Illinois and Texas, which have two of the oldest community college systems, combine local and state support for their districts. In Texas, the state funds the academic component, and the district funds facilities. The community college systems in Florida and Massachusetts, which were largely formed in the late 1950s and early 1960s, are wholly state funded.

The final major sources of higher education funding are tuition and other fees. If higher education is the budget balancer at the state level, tuition and fees are, in many cases, the budget balancer at the institutional level.

There has been and continues to be much discussion over demand relative to price in higher education. In keeping with the perspective of community colleges as open-door institutions, there is much concern regarding the barrier to access to higher education presented by tuition. The "sticker shock" of tuition may dissuade individuals from pursuing higher education despite the availability of financial aid. For this reason, many states have a low tuition policy to maintain access, especially at the community college level. For example, California did not implement a tuition policy for its community colleges until the 1980s.

To ensure access, many state governments retain control over tuition by dictating specific tuition rates or ranges within which an institution may set tuition and by setting or limiting the other fees for services such as student activities, labs and materials, or computer support that a college may charge.

Finally, available to both public and private institutions are funds from private individuals or foundations. Although these funds represent growing portions of campus budgets, most gifts are not available for general operating expenses but have specific purposes specified by the donor.

In this context, our analysis focuses on the largest portions of funding for community colleges that are also those shared by most states: state appropriations and tuition and fees. In addition to the inconsistency of data on the other sources, the disparity of use of those other sources makes a trend comparison less useful. Also, from a policy perspective, these aspects, which are largely controlled at the state level, are far easier to influence.

1990-1995 Analysis

State appropriations for community colleges increased by only 3% over the five years reviewed. Enrollment over the comparable period increased by 11%, and tuition increased by 47%. Assuming even a modest 1.5% annual cost increase over the same period, real state support for community colleges actually decreased across the period. Three states, California, Connecticut, and Maine, show decreases in state appropriations over the five-year period. Three other states, Michigan, Montana, and West Virginia, show enrollment decreases over the period. All states show tuition increases over the period, ranging from 14% in Louisiana to 208% in California.[1]

Figure 8.1 graphs the annual percentage changes in appropriations, enrollment, and tuition over the period. Tuition increased every year, ranging from 9% to 14%. Nationally, appropriations fell in consecutive years 1992-1993 and 1993-1994. Three states, California, Minnesota, and New York, experienced consecutive appropriations decreases, and 16 others experienced an appropriations decrease in one of these two years. The year 1994-1995 brought increased appropriations to 37 of the 43 states with community colleges.

However, the national data are skewed by the trends in one state—California. Representing at least 22% and as much as 25% of the enrollment in this study and at least 14% and as much as 26% of the appropriations, California deserves special attention. Excluding California from the data, state appropriations for community colleges actually increased by 17% over the five years reviewed. Enrollment over the comparable period increased by 12%. The increase in tuition in California cannot be subtracted from the national average reported above.

Figure 8.2 graphs the annual percentage changes in appropriations, enrollment, and tuition over the same period but excluding California. The trend for state appropriations is significantly different. The consecutive years of decrease were completely driven by California. This graph shows annual increases in appropriations over the period, ranging from 2% to 7%. As would be expected, the enrollment trend is also more moderate.

Both graphs show an enrollment decrease from fall 1992 to fall 1993. Because the enrollment and tuition data cover the same years, it would appear that the largest tuition increases were accompanied by the

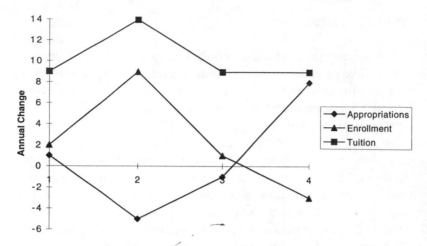

Figure 8.1. Annual Percentage Change in Appropriations, Enrollment, Tuition

largest increases in enrollment, followed by declining enrollment as tuition increases moderated. Further research is needed to determine the relationship between higher tuition and enrollment trends. Factors such as comparable increases in senior college tuition, unemployment, and workplace demands for training must be taken into account.

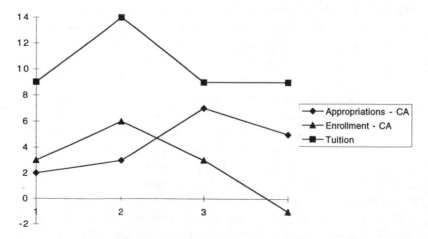

Figure 8.2. Annual Percentage Change in Appropriations, Enrollment, Tuition—Excluding California

Even in examining the trend of support without California, state funding has barely kept pace with enrollment growth. Individual states experienced decreases in appropriations in the face of rising enrollments. Considering the volatility of annual funding within the five-year period examined, holes in the resource fabric of community colleges may have been created that have not been mended by the 1994-1995 funding increases.

Context of the Changes in Financial Support

The generally conservative political climate of the United States in the 1990s has particularly affected higher education due to the conservative fiscal stance taken. The reluctance to raise taxes at all levels of government in the face of increasing demands for public services has severely constrained public resources. As the budget balancer, most of the fiscal stress has been exhibited in reduced support of higher education.

Recent congressional actions in Washington, D.C., indicate that states will have more responsibility for federal programs and policies. Michael Garber of the Educational Excellence Network has observed that, if this trend continues, the real action is going to occur in the nation's state houses where community colleges derive the majority of their funding (McClenney, 1995, p. 2).

Declining resources and increased competition for funding will become more critical, especially for states experiencing rapid growth in their schools as well as the college-age population or significant economic shifts. For this reason, state legislatures are attempting to impose accountability on all public and publicly supported institutions by moving toward performance-based budgeting. Many states have instituted a form of performance-based budgeting in which funding is tied to specific outcome measures. For community colleges, these outcomes often include student graduation rates and the number of students employed in their fields after graduation. These and other measures have been difficult to develop, quantify, and report in terms that are meaningful and which the legislature and the public can understand and use effectively. The difficulty in defining adequate performance measures is typified by the widespread discussion concerning the definition of a full-time student in an era where many students vary their enrollment from semester to semester or even drop out for a period of time due to financial or family problems. The issue is exacerbated for many community colleges where the majority of students are part-time and do not intend to pursue a degree.

Legislative concern about the costs of remediation necessary for college students is also increasing. Due to inadequate high school preparation, many entering college students and returning adults do not have the skills to successfully complete college-level work without remediation. Concern over the number of underprepared students prompted filing of a bill in the 1996 Florida legislature that would require degree-seeking students applying to community colleges to meet the admission requirements of universities to be admitted. The bill did not pass, but it was a clear concern to community colleges committed to preserving their mission as open-door institutions. Other states are looking at options that would remove remediation from the college setting and require local school districts to provide and pay for necessary skill development.

Institutional Responses

Recalling Hauptman's (1993) parameters for higher education finance, community colleges can adjust to their resources situation by increasing revenue or addressing costs. As documented above, many states have raised revenue by increasing tuition. Yet tuition across the nation varies widely. The 200% increase in tuition in California was against a base of just $100. In 1993-1994, tuition and fees ranged from $350 to just over $2,300. Legislative interest in shifting the burden of paying for community college costs to the students in many states has been tempered by concerns from employers and students about restraining access.

Despite the potential problems concerning increased tuition, higher education institutions across the nation have asked their legislatures for the ability to set their own tuition and even to vary tuition depending on degree programs as one means of raising revenue. Florida's legislature last session enacted legislation enabling community college boards to raise tuition up to 7%. Local boards will work with the college and community leadership to determine the rate of increase for individual institutions.

Colleges also are placing greater emphasis on developing partnerships with business and industry and conducting contract training through continuing education programs or shadow colleges. These initiatives are usually self-supporting, free of bureaucratic red tape, and do not have the same limits in staffing or collective bargaining agreements as the regular institutions. These growth areas of the college not only can meet the training and retraining needs of business and industry, they also have the potential to become a revenue producer for the institutions (Leverty & Campbell, in press).

Efforts to accommodate growth and cut costs have also resulted in a large increase in part-time, non-tenure-track faculty members. This trend has been alarming to faculty groups and many educators and students. However, it has been viewed as positive by bonding companies rating the financial strength of the colleges. Standard and Poors recently cited the financial strength of community college bonds by crediting their use of part-time faculty as an effective cost-containment tool (White, 1994).

Alan E. Guskin (1994), chancellor of the Antioch university system, believes that advances in technology will challenge faculty members to integrate the world of simulation and interactive technologies with their roles as mentors, coaches, facilitators, and teachers of student learning. Restructuring and downsizing are realities for all institutions in today's economy, and he feels that if community colleges do not reduce costs creatively it will be done for them by federal and state governments or the marketplace. Colleges and legislatures alike are looking to technology as an effective means to extend access and reduce costs. The Colorado community and technical college system has created the virtual community college. In a public/private partnership with Jones Education Network, the colleges offer the associate degree via cable. Technology may be one way for many institutions to respond imaginatively, although start-up costs for equipment and training can be high. Also, early initiatives indicate that even though distance learning increases student access it might not decrease costs for the institution.

Changes in the way educational services are delivered will reverberate throughout public institutions and the governmental structures that support them. Distance learning provides one clear example of ways in which systems may have to change. The fundamental component of most higher education funding formulas relates students in a classroom with a teacher for a certain number of hours each week to calculate funding. The basic relationship between colleges, government, and the public will need to be substantially redefined to accommodate alternative delivery of learning.

Accountability will continue to be a major issue. Public funders will continue to seek a relationship between revenue and cost, defining costs as a function of what is done and how it is done. One of the current difficulties is defining what community colleges, and higher education in general, are expected to do. "The establishment of goals and objectives for higher education is by definition a process of consensus building among the primary constituencies: policy makers, administrators, faculty, students and the public" (Layzell & Lyddon, p. 58). Waggaman (1991) attributes the basis of criticism of higher education costs and quality to the conflicting goals and expectations of higher education. Expectations, particularly on the part of the public, are changing in ways that are yet to be clearly defined.

Implications for Leadership

Kay McClenney (1995), vice president of the Education Commission of the States, predicts that the following will be the key issues affecting higher education at the state level:

- Reduced or restricted taxpayer support
- Access pressures
- Productivity and restructuring
- Workforce preparation
- Performance and accountability

She cites recent public opinion polls by Harris, Gallup, the Education Commission of the States, and the American Council on Education that found that, by and large, the American public continues to hold higher education in high regard and views the college degree as the passport to the "good life." Yet the surveys also indicate that the public knows very little about higher education and tends to put more emphasis on individual education for a specific career goal rather than expressing support for a well-educated citizenry (McClenney, 1995, p. 3).

There is philosophical agreement that, for anyone who is motivated and capable, economic status should not be a barrier to advanced education. Yet the public believes that a lot of people "don't belong there" and would be better off in trade or technical schools rather than universities. There appears to be increasing concern about the cost of a college education and the need to ensure that only serious students who plan to get a degree or certification as quickly as possible and then find a job immediately are enrolled. As discussed earlier, remedial education is under fire at all types of higher education institutions, and general education is generally viewed with increasing disdain except among certain groups of university graduates (McClenney, 1995, p. 3).

Based on polls and discussion groups, the public supports the following principles to address higher education issues. First, more costs should be borne by the consumer, and there should be more low-interest loans and opportunities for students to work. Second, giving more money to institutions is not necessary. Instead, public money should be used to create more alternatives to traditional college that would lead to a skill and gainful employment. These alternatives include short-term certification programs, training through distance learning, and enhanced continuing education opportunities. Finally, there is general agreement that more emphasis should be placed on accountability and the return that taxpayers get for their investment in higher education (McClenney, 1995, p. 4).

Elected officials are sensitive to public opinion polls such as these in formulating state policy. The implication for leadership is the need to clearly define and communicate the community college mission to the public and to policy makers in ways that can be understood and supported.

Community colleges need to work with their communities to increase support and understanding of higher education when there is no crisis. McClenney's (1995) research clearly indicates that the public does not understand or appreciate the role of higher education in today's society. All institutions need to actively find ways to tell the larger community about the benefits of higher education. An example of an effective communication effort is in the Maricopa Community College District, which received the 1996 Bellwether Award for its strategic conversation initiative. Monthly public meetings encourage participants to discuss a topic of strategic importance to the college. The internal college community and the public are learning together, resulting in new policies adopted by the governing board and increased public support (Institute of Higher Education, 1996).

/ Community college leadership should continue to strengthen its efforts to demonstrate value to the community and learner to assist state officials in supporting continued funding for colleges from state appropriations rather than continuing to pass the cost to individuals through increased tuition. If community colleges begin to take charge of the public debate on higher education, the emphasis can be shifted from the continuing justification for higher education and the fight over the allocation of scarce resources to the broader and more important issues of what students need to know, how they should learn it, and how colleges will continue to adapt and be responsive to their respective communities' needs.

Note

1. Information on state appropriations come from data collected by Edward R. Hines and published in *Chronicle of Higher Education* annually in October, except for 1990-1991 and 1991-1992 that come from the State Higher Education Executive Officers (SHEEO) publication prepared by Dr. Hines, *State Higher Education Appropriations, 1992-93*. States have the opportunity to update the data reported to Dr. Hines between its October publication and the *Chronicle* and the completion of his annual publication. The state appropriations data are, therefore, substantially but not strictly comparable. The data used cover the period 1990-1991 through 1994-1995. Appropriations data are specifically reported in a category for community colleges.

Tuition and fee data come from the almanac issues of *Chronicle of Higher Education*, 1991-1995. The data used cover the period from 1989-1990 through 1993-1994. These data are classified in a category called "public two year."

Enrollment data are also taken from the almanac issues of the *Chronicle* from the category "public two year" and cover the period from fall 1989 to fall 1993. The enrollment data are examined to observe both the demand against appropriations and as a test of price elasticity with regard to tuition increases.

States without appropriation data specifically reported from community colleges in each of the five years were eliminated from this analysis, leaving 43 states. The states omitted—Alaska, Indiana, Kentucky, North and South Dakota, and Vermont—comprise less than 2.5% of the public two-year college enrollment in any given year of the study, ranging from 2.1% in fall 1989 to 2.4% in fall 1993. In the annual *Chronicle* report, appropriations data for the community colleges in Hawaii and Kentucky were reported with the university systems of which they are a part. Hawaii and Kentucky represent half of the omitted enrollment data in any of the years of the study. The omission of these 7 states should not significantly affect the trend for appropriations and enrollment. The national average on tuition data, however, does include these states and could not be recalculated.

The time periods covered by the data substantially overlap, but are not completely synchronous. Appropriations are specifically reported for public two-year colleges that may include university branch campuses or vocational technical schools that are not community college equivalents in their states. The effect will be to somewhat overstate enrollment and tuition. The preponderance of community colleges as the identified public two-year offering in most states and the fact that enrollment will not be related to appropriations on a per-student basis mean that the interpretation of trends should still be valid.

References

Cohen, A. M., & Brawer, F. B. (1996). Finances: Sustaining and allocating resources. In *The American community college*. San Francisco: Jossey-Bass.

Davis, G. W. (1995). Tuition and fee increases and community college enrollments. *Community College Journal of Research and Practice, 191*, 13-21.

Guskin, A. E. (1994, September/October). Restructuring the role of the faculty. *Change*, p. 25.

Hauptman, A. M. (1993). *Higher education finance issues in the early 1990s.* New Brunswick, NJ: Consortium for Policy Research in Education.

Honeyman, D. S., Bruhn, M., & Sayles, K. (1995). *The financing of higher education.* Manuscript submitted for publication.

Honeyman, D. S., Williamson, M. L., & Wattenbarger, J. L. (1991). *Community college financing, 1990: Challenges for a new decade.* Washington, DC: American Association of Community and junior Colleges.

Institute of Higher Education. (1996). *Bellwether award winners announced.* Gainesville, FL: Author.

Layzell, D. T., & Lyddon, J. W. (1990). *Budgeting for higher education at the state level: Enigma, paradox and ritual* (ASHE-ERIC Higher Education Report No. 4). Washington, DC: George Washington University, School of Education and Human Development.

Leverty, L. H., & Campbell, D. F. (in press). *The politics of higher education: Communicating with policy makers and the public.* In A. M. Hoffman & Y. Neumann (Eds.), *Handbook on college and university management.* Maryville, MO: Prescott.

McClenney, K. M. (1995, Summer/Fall). Public expectations and political realities shaping the future of community colleges. *The Bottom Line*, pp. 2-4.

McKeown, M. P. (1989). State funding formulas for public institutions of higher education. *Journal of Education Finance, 15*, 101-112.

McKeown, M. P., & Layzell, D. T. (1994). State funding formulas for higher education: Trends and issues. *Journal of Education Finance, 19,* 319-346.

Vaughan, G. B. (1995). *The community college story: A tale of American innovation.* Washington, DC: American Association of Community Colleges.

/ Waggaman, J. S. (1991). *Strategies and consequences: Managing the costs in higher education* (ASHE-ERIC Higher Education Report No. 8). Washington, DC: George Washington University, School of Education and Human Development.

White, L. (1994, November). Presentation to the National Council of Community College Business Officials, Hawaii.

Zumeta, W. (1995). State policy and budget developments. In National Education Association (Ed.), *NEA 1995 almanac of higher education* (pp. 73-96). Washington, DC: National Education Association.

NINE

Funding the Multipurpose Community College in an Era of Consolidation

JAMES C. PALMER

Today's community college system is a product of the publicly subsidized move to mass higher education during the 25 years following World War II. When the President's Commission on Higher Education (1947) issued its landmark report advocating free schooling through grade 14 for all who could benefit, 315 public junior colleges enrolled 216,325 students (Palmer, 1987). By the time the Carnegie Commission on Higher Education (1970) published *The Open-Door College*, 847 public community colleges enrolled 2,366,028 students (Harper, 1971). Between the publication of these two reports, which anchor both ends of American higher education's greatest growth period, the proportion of individuals between the ages of 18 and 24 who were enrolled in college (two-year or four-year) rose from 12% to 32% (U.S. Bureau of the Census, 1975, p. 383). During the same time period, total government revenues to public institutions of higher education (in current dollars) increased from $453 million annually to $9.2 billion (U.S. Bureau of the Census, 1975, p. 384).

Although enrollments continued to grow after 1970, rising to 5.5 million students in 1992 (Snyder & Hoffman, 1995, p. 177), community college claims to increased public subsidies have been more intensely scrutinized. Lombardi (1973) notes that the "golden era of community college financing peaked in the mid-sixties" as the public became more distrustful of social institutions generally and as access to education became a less urgent priority in light of other "local and national concerns . . . crowding education for first demand on public money" (p. 110). The change in fortunes experienced by the community college was characterized by Lombardi as "its most serious crisis since the Great Depression" (p. 111) and was mirrored globally as countries throughout the world found that postwar rates of growth in tertiary education became fiscally unsustainable in the 1970s (Eicher & Chevaillier, 1993). The result for American community colleges is documented in Table 9.1: Between 1977 and 1992, tuition revenues per full-time-equivalent (FTE) student increased by 32%, while state and local appropriations per FTE student decreased by 12% and federal appropriations per FTE student decreased by 58%.

The current era, then, is one of consolidation, marked by an effort to prioritize the purposes of mass higher education and to achieve ever greater operating efficiencies as demand continues to outpace public revenues. The primary fiscal question of the past 25 years has not been "Will the community college survive?" Indeed, the institution remains a well-established part of American higher education and in the 1990s has often enjoyed higher percentage increases in state appropriations than those enjoyed by four-year colleges and universities (Hines, 1994, p. 10). The more important question, rather, is "On what basis will public subsidies be made?"

Answers have been made from two standpoints. Scholars with close ties to the community college movement have responded from a policy viewpoint, arguing that state funding plans should be consistent with the tenets of open access, curricular comprehensiveness, local control, low cost to students, and responsiveness to local needs (Martorana & Wattenbarger, 1978; Wattenbarger, 1985). Their goal is to preserve the expanded access to education that emerged in the immediate postwar decades. Economists have applied theoretical constructs. Examples include Breneman and Nelson (1981), who weigh institutional claims for public subsidy against the competing values

TABLE 9.1 Current Fund Revenues per Full-Time-Equivalent Student (in 1994 constant dollars) at Public Two-Year Colleges, by Type of Revenue Source: Academic Years Ending 1977 Through 1992

Academic Year Ending	Total	Tuition and Fees	Federal Appropriations	State and Local Appropriations	Federal Grants and Contracts	State and Local Grants and Contracts	Private Gifts	Endowment	Sales and Services of Educational Activities
1977	$5,727	$962	$114	$4,153	$330	$112	$29	$4	$23
1978	5,744	925	102	4,212	317	132	28	3	24
1979	5,864	928	114	4,262	353	146	27	4	30
1980	5,790	933	78	4,201	365	151	27	5	30
1981	5,516	928	68	3,957	345	154	27	6	31
1982	5,454	980	59	3,911	285	156	29	6	27
1983	5,109	985	41	3,650	221	148	29	7	27
1984	5,243	1,023	45	3,725	229	154	31	8	28
1985	5,719	1,091	43	4,055	265	194	35	8	28
1986	5,981	1,111	37	4,268	268	218	38	8	34
1987	6,059	1,121	45	4,269	251	292	39	9	35
1988	5,905	1,105	43	4,163	240	275	42	5	31
1989	6,052	1,155	40	4,159	254	361	48	6	30
1990	5,904	1,157	39	3,997	249	373	51	6	32
1991	5,891	1,206	41	3,971	246	336	53	6	31
1992	5,743	1,269	48	3,743	260	331	56	5	31

SOURCE: Smith et al. (1995, p. 407).

of market efficiency and social equity, and Garms (1977), who analyzes state funding plans against nine criteria that stress tax equity, access for those unable to attend four-year colleges, minimal duplication of effort between educational sectors, and internal college efficiency.

This chapter takes a different approach, analyzing the question of public subsidy from the standpoint of educational purpose, for at the heart of today's funding controversies lies the often unrecognized problem of reconciling the conflicting economic imperatives inherent in the community college's multiple educational roles. One role is that of the *flexible institution*, meeting the diverse and idiosyncratic educational needs of local citizens. A second role is that of the *scholastic institution*, leading students to degree completion or to successful entry into higher levels of the graded education system. A third role is that of the *social service agency*, executing government programs that address economic or social ills through education or training. Each offers the public a different picture of the return it can expect (both to individuals and to society at large) on its investment in the community college.

The Flexible Institution

Although community college catalogs describe curricula leading to degrees and certificates, students use the institutions for their own purposes. For example, studies of transfer students reveal wide variations in the ways students use community colleges on the path to the baccalaureate. Some take only one course at the community college either before or after matriculation into the four-year college, whereas others earn well over 100 semester hours of community college credit; the linear sequence of two years at the community college followed by two years at the university applies only to a minority of students (Palmer & Pugh, 1993; Palmer, Stapleton, & Ludwig, 1994). In the vocational arena, students also exhibit diverse patterns of study. Except in allied health and other areas that require licensure, relatively few students complete the associate's degree; student association with the college may range from enrollment in one semester to completion of two or more programs over an extended period of time (Cohen & Brawer, 1989, pp. 215-216).

It can be argued, therefore, that besides maintaining access to degree programs, investment in community colleges (with their relatively loose entry and exit policies) yields the advantage of an institutional flexibility needed for ad hoc, complementary, or even serendipitous learning. Ad hoc learning is undertaken to meet the need for new skills or understandings. An example might be a student who enrolls in a computer science course to cope with new technologies on the job. Complementary learning is undertaken in conjunction with degree programs offered elsewhere. A common example is the university student who concurrently enrolls in a community college course either to remediate skills or to complete a required course that is oversubscribed at the four-year institution. Serendipitous learning involves spontaneous discovery and redirection, as in the case of students who enter a program in one field but discover that they would like to study something else. Adelman (1992) documented these and other patterns of idiosyncratic use in the college-going behavior of respondents in the National Longitudinal Study of the High School Class of 1972 (NLS72), concluding that community colleges are facilitators of "occasional" learning with only a minimal credentialing role. "What the community college does," he maintained, "is to canonize and formalize the many decisions we make as adults to engage in learning for either limited, highly focused purposes or for general purposes" (p. 22).

Why Invest in the Flexible Institution?

The benefits accrued to individuals through this institutional flexibility are difficult to calculate because the uses and outcomes of the institution are as varied as the students who attend, but at least four types of benefits might be assumed. One is access to education. As Adelman (1992, p. 22) points out, four-year institutions usually have a "culture of credentialism," with an attendant adherence to academic calendars, making it difficult for them to serve occasional learners. Without the community college, these individuals might presumably find few opportunities for structured study.

The second potential benefit, implied in the first, is learning efficiency. The university student who takes a community college course in the summer may decrease the time to degree. Similarly, the employee who takes a computer course to enhance job skills may learn those skills in a more timely and efficient manner with the guidance of an instructor.

The third benefit to individuals entails enhanced earnings. Kane and Rouse (1995a, 1995b) offer evidence of the wage benefits of course taking without earning a credential. Their analysis of the incomes of NLS72 respondents suggests that "both men and women earn more than comparable high school graduates after attending a two-year college whether or not they complete the [associate's] degree" (Kane & Rouse, 1995a, p. 219). Grubb (1995) concurs but argues that much depends on the type of credit earned. His analysis of the same data set suggests that the wage benefits of nondegree holders accrue only to those who earn vocational credits and not academic credits.

Beyond ex post wage differentials, however, Kane and Rouse (1995b) also note the probability of a fourth benefit: an "option value" accrued to those who complete courses without earning a credential. As they explain,

> When one is uncertain about the prospects of completing college before entry, there will be value attached to enrolling in order to discover whether one is "college material." . . . Those who do not exercise the option of completing college and leave after only a few credits may enjoy only small wage differentials. However, it would be inaccurate to describe college as not having been worthwhile for this group, because the *ex ante* returns may indeed have been large enough to justify the public and private investments. (p. 611)

Presumably, the students' future educational investments will be made on the basis of better-informed judgments.

To the extent that individuals enjoy these benefits, society may also gain through positive externalities. Without flexible community colleges (or institutions like them), individuals would presumably underinvest in the occasional learning (above and beyond employer-provided, on-the-job training) needed to remain employable in a rapidly changing economy. Aggregate consumer investment in postcompulsory education would be less efficient because consumers would not have the insights gained through the opportunity to experiment by taking occasional courses. (It would be as though consumers in the automobile market were asked to make purchasing decisions without test drives.) Society might also lose the net increase in educated citizens that presumably results with the freedom afforded by community colleges to test one's educational intentions and skills in a low-risk atmosphere that facilitates easy entry and exit. Romano (1986b) implies this benefit in his suggestion that discount rates used in the calculation of the return on investment in education at two-year and four-year colleges should include a "risk factor" that recognizes the tendency of the former to attract students for whom traditional baccalaureate-granting institutions are intimidating. As he explains, "If . . . the risk of going to a 4-year college is perceived to be higher . . . than that of going to a 2-year college, then the future stream of earnings for the 4-year choice would have to be discounted at a higher rate" (p. 162).

Funding the Flexible College

Given the presumption of societal benefits, a case can be made for public subsidy of the flexible community college. These subsidies would ideally be made in ways that encourage the maintenance of easy access and exit, rewarding enrollment of any kind regardless of the student's length of association with the institution. Because the educational needs of area citizens will presumably vary between localities, funding mechanisms should, in Garms's (1977) words, "enhance, rather than impede, the ability of the community college to respond to the particular needs of the community it serves" (p. 38). Local administrators should be given a high level of autonomy in setting academic policy and administering funds, points that have been emphasized by many community college leaders (Martorana & Wattenbarger, 1978; Wattenbarger, 1985).

Effectiveness in the use of funds would be measured in terms of consumer satisfaction with the college experience. Indicators of the extent to which idiosyncratic student goals have been met might also be emphasized.

Those who would tie funding to the college's role as a flexible institution nonetheless face the challenge of defining priorities among a potentially infinite set of individual training and education agendas that students bring with them. To do otherwise is to suggest that society offer the colleges a blank check, subsidizing the enrollment of all comers. But whose agenda is more worthy of public support? Economic analysis leads to conflicting views. For example, Breneman and Nelson (1981) claim that vocational education yields few positive externalities and should be paid for by students and their employers, who are the presumed beneficiaries of such training. Yet Romano (1986a) cautions that public subsidy of vocational education might be required in the face of employer fears that workers will move or change jobs, thereby making it difficult for businesses to recoup their training costs. These fears might limit employer contributions to training, leading to the possibility "that in the face of no publicly-financed training programs, fewer people would be trained than is economically justified" (p. 12).

Even if priorities were made, the colleges would still face the difficulty of pigeonholing students into priority categories. Which of the students in a photography class, for example, are honing job skills and which are pursuing a personal avocation? Answers to these types of questions remain as elusive as the goals of the students themselves. In the end, flexible responsiveness to idiosyncratic educational agendas becomes an ever more infeasible institutional purpose as the need to prioritize those agendas increases. The natural fallback is to the prescriptive stance of the degree-granting scholastic institution.

The Scholastic Institution

Advocates of a scholastic focus for the community college, notably Cohen and Brawer (1987, 1989) and Eaton (1994), question the supposed benefits and efficiencies of the flexible institution. They emphasize the importance of student placement and guidance through sequenced degree programs, arguing that students may otherwise wander through the curriculum without demonstrable results. Attention to sequenced learning according to prescribed curricula, they maintain, is also necessary to sustain transfer opportunities for baccalaureate-seeking students. From the scholastic viewpoint, the flexible institution offers what Cohen and Brawer (1989) call a "nihilistic curriculum represented by students taking classes at will" (p. 386). All efficiencies are lost: "This is chaos, not college" (p. 386).

The scholastic philosophy figures heavily in policy responses to the fiscal problems of the post-1960s. For example, McCabe (1981) called on community colleges to follow the lead of Miami-Dade Community College: tightening matriculation processes through rigorous entrance testing and placement, insisting that students master basic skills prior to enrollment in college-level courses, providing continual feedback to students as they progress through their programs, and strictly enforcing standards of academic progress with the understanding that public subsidy of a student's education will be discontinued if those standards are not met. In California, the exigencies of a declining state economy were met during the 1980s and 1990s with policies that reflect many of McCabe's precepts. The state instituted a matriculation program emphasizing testing, placement, and the mutual responsibility of college and student to work toward the completion of educational goals (California Community Colleges, 1984). As the gap between enrollment demand and available funding expanded in the 1990s, a task force convened by the board of governors of the California community colleges drafted recommended registration guidelines that give first priority to matriculated students who intend to transfer, earn a credential (associate's degree or certificate), acquire entry-level job skills, or upgrade job skills. Among matriculated students, priority was to be given first to continuing students, followed by recent high school graduates, other new or returning students, and new students who already hold the baccalaureate (Walters, 1994).

Why Invest in the Scholastic Institution?

These measures emphasize individual and societal returns on investment in degree attainment. Some are economic, dealing principally with the earnings advantages that accrue to at least some degree holders. Although Kane and Rouse (1995a, 1995b) show that college dropouts earn higher wages than high school graduates who accumulate no college credits, their analysis of NLS72 respondents also suggests a sheepskin effect for women who earn the associate's degree and for men who earn the baccalaureate. In these cases, those who hold the credential enjoy higher earnings than similar students who earn the equivalent of two or four years' college credits but who do not earn, respectively, the associate's degree or the baccalaureate. Analyzing the same data set, Grubb (1995) comes to a similar conclusion but again cautions that much depends on the student's curriculum. He argues that the sheepskin effect enjoyed by women applies only to those who earn vocational degrees and not to those who earn associate's degrees in academic fields. Obviously, much depends on whether the degree is an entry-level requirement for job seekers. As Kane and Rouse (1995b) note, the sheepskin effect enjoyed by women earning two-year degrees probably reflects "the value of the associate's degree in nursing, since one-quarter of the associate's degrees for women [in the NLS72 study] were awarded in the field of nursing" (p. 605).

A second and potentially more compelling set of considerations, however, lies in the intrinsic value of the bachelor's degree within a society that views the four-year credential—rightly or wrongly—as the principal mark of achievement in undergraduate education. The high visibility of the bachelor's degree, which contrasts sharply with the obscurity of the relatively unknown associate's degree (Adelman, 1992, pp. 25-26), places considerable pressure on the community college to maintain its place in the graded system of education, offering students the maximum opportunity for transfer to baccalaureate-granting institutions. From this standpoint, the scholastic stance offers important advantages. Its emphasis on matriculation, guided progress through a sequenced curriculum, and enforcement of academic standards reinforces the goal of degree attainment, promising efficiency for students who will proceed purposely rather than haphazardly toward the baccalaureate; for individual community colleges, which will minimize the costs associated with continually reregistering students who attend sporadically; and for state higher education systems, which will be characterized by greater linkages between two-year and four-year institutions. Because of the disproportionally large numbers of minority and low-income students at community colleges (as opposed to four-year colleges), it can also be argued that the scholastic stance promotes equity, offering a path to the baccalaureate for those who have been underrepresented in the ranks of bachelor's degree graduates (Palmer & Eaton, 1991, pp. 19-20).

A third set of potential benefits is pedagogical in nature, based on the assumption that adherence to prerequisites and academic standards throughout the curriculum may limit faculty tendencies to cope with wide-ranging student skills by watering down expectations for learning. Richardson and Rhodes (1985) take this stance, arguing that "open access defined as the opportunity to take all but the limited-seat, high-cost technical programs" has diminished instructional quality, thereby limiting educational opportunity (p. 286). They maintain that "qualified students who wish to earn legitimate college and occupational credentials are handicapped by college-level courses that are taught at less-demanding levels in order to accommodate underqualified students" (p. 286). This view has been supported by interviews and ethnographic research that portray the community college faculty as casualties of an acculturation process that leads many new teachers to compromise their commitment to academic standards (London, 1978; Richardson, Fisk, & Okun, 1983; Seidman, 1985; Weis, 1985). Without the corrective measures of the scholastic stance, the result may be a diminished return on societal investment in the community college as an avenue for educational advancement.

Funding the Scholastic Institution

Besides employing registration priorities favoring matriculated, degree-seeking students (as has been recommended in California), funding systems designed to yield the benefits and efficiencies implied in the scholastic framework would have three features that make them radically different from the fiscal structures that support community colleges today. One would be a performance-based approach to funding that ties subsidies (at least partially) to documented evidence of student learning. This performance-based approach would rest heavily on assessments of curriculum effects, demonstrating the extent to which program completers have the knowledge and capacities that are expected of graduates.

A second feature, inherent in the first, would be the diminution of enrollment in the calculation of subsidies. Noting that enrollment-based funding mechanisms were developed to cope with the rapid growth of the 1950s and 1960s, McCabe (1981) suggests that they have become detrimental in the subsequent, less affluent era. He argues that the colleges have "become entrapped by an essential need to sustain enrollment in order to remain economically viable" (p. 8), often to the detriment of the institution's academic viability. "Legislators who demand improved quality and higher standards," he maintains, "must help by freeing the colleges from the bondage of enrollment-driven funding formulas" (p. 10). This stance would be heartily approved by those who feel that faculty efforts to maintain high expectations for students are thwarted by an enrollment-at-all-costs attitude.

Finally, the scholastic stance demands the fiscal and administrative separation of the credit curriculum, which leads to degree completion, from the continuing education curriculum, which accommodates occasional learning. Cohen and Brawer (1989) have argued that the intermingling of these two functions, which have essentially different purposes, diminishes each and confounds education for personal consumption with education for the benefit of society. They maintain that students pursuing occasional learning should be enrolled in a self-supporting college extension division and not in credit classes, which should be offered in a separate subsidized program for degree seekers. Their approach models those employed in universities and in the higher education systems of foreign countries, aligning funding intent with educational purpose:

> Other nations have been more vigorous in steering . . . personal interest students to self-pay activities or government funded programs provided through community education structures and operated through local government agencies. American universities tend to shunt them to their extension divisions. Community colleges function in a shadow world of enrollment-driven, program differentiated funding for students whose aspirations

are as mercurial as their use of the institutions is indistinct. (Cohen, 1993, p. 74)

The Social Service Agency

Largely unmindful of the philosophical distinctions and fiscal nuances of the flexible and scholastic viewpoints, legislators are nonetheless intent on demonstrating the utility of their appropriations. One approach has been the use of categorical funds that underwrite college efforts in economic development projects or other social programs. In Illinois, for example, formula-derived funding for the community colleges is augmented by economic development grants and other special appropriations that support small business centers, training programs for displaced workers, and other projects that are designed to boost the economy of local communities or enhance the skills of the local workforce (Illinois Community College Board, 1994). Such nonformula components have seen increasing use in state funding plans nationally (McKeown & Layzell, 1994, pp. 321-322). Between 1977 and 1992, the constant-dollar revenues per full-time-equivalent (FTE) student received by community colleges in the form of state or local grants and contracts increased by 196%, the largest increase in any of the eight revenue categories tracked by the United States Department of Education (see Table 9.1).

This trend is wholly in line with Lombardi's (1973) prescient observation that "slowly but surely community colleges are becoming dispensers of social welfare" (p. 114). The acceptance of and active competition for government contracts to carry out economic development and social welfare programs has been accelerated by a perceived need on the part of colleges to diversify their funding base. For example, fiscal uncertainties in California led Newmyer and McIntyre (1992) to recommend, among other policy initiatives, the pursuit of "a greater share of [federal] funds for vocational education, such as the Perkins Act and JTPA" (pp. 24-25). Community college leaders have also used economic development projects, particularly those that are developed in partnership with area businesses, to enhance the institution's image and utility. Zeiss (1989) maintains that linkages with business

could be the vehicle that erases the identity problem of community, technical, and junior colleges that has so long endured. . . .
By examining their frame of reference, focusing on a target market, and promoting a point of difference, community colleges can
easily become recognized as a vital part of their communities,
states, and nation. (pp. 3-4)

Why Invest in the College as Social Service Agency?

From the economic perspective, public investments in these projects imply efficiencies in the production of social benefits, such as net
increases in employment, reductions in welfare dependence, or reductions in the rate of small business failure. For example, the Illinois
Community College Board reports annually on the estimated number
of jobs that are saved, retained, or created through investment in
economic development grants (see, e.g., Illinois Community College
Board, 1996). So long as these jobs represent a net increase in employment and not simply the economic gain of Illinois at the expense of
employment in other states (a potential danger pointed out by Grubb,
1989), they presumably reflect a positive return on public investment.

A second, more subtle benefit lies in the potential efficiencies of the
funding mechanism itself; because contracts target funds for specific
purposes, usually requiring rigerous assessments of results, they avoid
the vagaries of general institutional support. Eicher and Chevaillier
(1993) note the attractiveness of this direct funding to policy makers
worldwide who feel that subsidies for the general operation of institutions (such as those subsidies awarded simply on the basis of
enrollment) offer few incentives for increasing productivity or reduc-
ing costs. They point out that such doubts are less frequently raised
in the case of "specific support given only on a temporary basis and
subject to evaluation. . . ." Hence, "funding based on contracts and
signed between the government and each institution recently has been
advocated at the higher education level" (p. 484).

Finally, community college leaders and commentators have raised
the possibility of increased efficiency in government delivery of social
services. They argue that the nation's community colleges, with their

commitment to vocational training and their ethos of responsiveness to local needs, constitute an established adult education system that can consolidate and coordinate the delivery of diffuse government programs for human resource development. For example, Katsinas and Swender (1992) and Katsinas (1994) suggest that these advantages are not always understood by administrators who oversee government manpower development programs, with the result that funding is inefficiently spread across several community-based organizations (CBOs), sometimes involving community colleges, sometimes not. Hence, "community colleges must actively promote a national strategy of human resource policy development that places them in a primary brokering role, extending and in many cases replacing those functions previously performed by CBOs" (Katsinas & Swender, 1992, p. 22). This picture of the community college is one in which the institution is at the center of government workforce development efforts, coordinating credit programming with "non-FTE-based employment and training, welfare-to-work, and adult literacy systems" (Katsinas, 1994, p. 25). The inefficiencies inherent in the overlapping regional jurisdictions of adult literacy agencies, regional economic development councils, and other agencies that administer programs funded by the Job Training Partnership Act (JTPA) and the Family Support Act of 1988 (such as the JOBS program) would be eliminated as community college districts become the service regions for all.

Funding the Community College as Social Service Agency

The desired advantages of these funding arrangements may not be realized if hidden costs remain unrecognized in funding mechanisms. These costs are incurred through the paperwork burden of government contracts, the strictures within legislative mandates that impede responsiveness to local needs, and the tendency to involve colleges in noneducative work for which the institution may be ill suited. Each should be avoided.

Paperwork documenting compliance with contract obligations cannot be avoided. But it can lead to inefficiencies when it makes unwarranted demands on staff time (potentially to the detriment of clients) or when the information it generates has only marginal utility. For example, college staff working with public aid recipients may devote a great deal of time to collecting and reporting data that say more about the month-to-month compliance of clients with public aid rules and regulations than about the progress the students make in their educational programs. Clearly, the data collection mandates imposed on the colleges, although required by law, may be of little or no use to the colleges in their attempt to help public aid recipients.

College action can also be restricted by legislative prescriptions that preclude creative responses to local problems. For example, Katsinas (1994) urges community colleges to become local coordinators for the federally funded JOBS programs. But does the JOBS program as developed in the Family Support Act of 1988 offer an optimal welfare-to-work mechanism? Herr, Halpern, and Conrad (1993) say no, pointing to research evidence suggesting that its emphasis on education limits its utility for all but the most able public aid recipients. They maintain that "the welfare-to-work transition is not a single leap from education to employment" (p. 115). For some individuals, it is a long and difficult period of adjustment because "at a more basic level, it is about personal growth and change" (p. 115). Hence, they question the utility of immediately placing welfare recipients in education programs and suggest alternative approaches that may not be fundable under the current law.

If this analysis is correct, community colleges may buy into a flawed mechanism, offering their curricula as the path out of welfare for area citizens who have more immediate, noneducational needs. In the extreme, the ideal of community responsiveness could be turned on its end as colleges develop programs whose starting points are legislative mandates rather than community nuances. Because these mandates change constantly, there is the added danger that college services to local communities will evolve incoherently, thereby thwarting the efficiencies seen by Katsinas (1994) in government use of community colleges as a nexus for social service programs. Eicher and Chevaillier (1993) have noted that "specific grants do not ensure the long-term stability that institutions need, and they can be given more in accordance with passing priorities and fancies of elected bodies than with a thought-out pattern of development" (p. 513).

The recognition that solutions to social problems entail more than formal education also leads to the question of how far community colleges should stray from their traditional educative roles. If the colleges are viewed as *the* solution to social ills rather than *part of* the solution, expectations of the colleges may rise exponentially. Welfare-to-work programs that start with an emphasis on education may add on services related to personal counseling, legal advice, or reference and referral to emergency housing shelters. It quickly becomes evident that success of the college program requires careful coordination with other community-based agencies. Otherwise, the college may go beyond its expertise and endanger its reputation as an educational institution. As Vaughan (1991) notes, college leaders should protect the educational core of the community college mission:

Waiting at the edge of the mission are any number of problems that need solutions. Indeed, the problems are too numerous to be addressed effectively by any single entity in society. Thus, priorities must be established. . . . To try to be all things to all people is both to dissipate the mission beyond recognition and to pull so many resources from the core that the community college no longer functions as an institution of higher learning. Once this happens, the community college has trouble justifying funds from the sources that normally finance higher education. (p. 32)

All of these cautions point to imperatives in contracted funding for college economic development or social welfare programs. First, reporting requirements, although necessary, should yield useful information about program success and not be so burdensome as to reduce client services. Although colleges must remain accountable, there is clearly a point of diminishing returns at which staff investment in paperwork endangers program effectiveness. There is also a point at which legislative strictures diminish college responsiveness to local needs. This responsiveness will be endangered to the extent that funding is tied to specific, centrally prescribed actions rather than to desired outcomes. Piland (1995) notes this danger in California, arguing that if the state's community colleges are to fulfill their potential as catalysts of local economic development they must be freed of regulatory and legislative micromanagement.

Finally, special purpose contracts should not expect more from the community college than the institution can deliver. Gottschalk's (1977) observation that community colleges "provide the educational component of solutions to social problems" (p. 9) is a useful rule of thumb, suggesting that contracted funds will yield the greatest return when targeted to educational services. At the most, community colleges might serve as brokers, funneling funds to community-based organizations for noneducative services. But success in this role presupposes minimal political conflict between CBOs and community colleges. This conflict is rarely discussed by those calling on community colleges to coordinate government social welfare programs.

Balancing Means and Ends
in a Multipurpose College

Although each can be discussed separately, the flexible, scholastic, and social service philosophies are thoroughly intertwined in today's community college as it serves the diverse constituency of mass higher education. The flexible institution, evident in and encouraged by enrollment-driven subsidies, benefits occasional learners. The more prescriptive scholastic institution, evident in curriculum structures outlined in college catalogs (and tacitly supported by state policies that allow funding for enrollment in credit programs only), recognizes the needs of degree-bound students. The social service agency, evident in the growing use of special purpose contracts that involve colleges in social and economic development programs, recognizes the needs of displaced workers, public aid recipients, and others who can profit from a coordinated "one stop" approach to the receipt of government subsidized education and training benefits.

But it is hard to see how the three can be combined in ways that allow each to flourish to its full potential (Cohen & Brawer, 1989, pp. 277-278). College funding mechanisms necessarily represent a trade-off (by default or design) between the benefits of the flexible, scholastic, and social service institutions. For example, the benefits derived from citizens' opportunity to engage in occasional learning are diminished to the extent that colleges introduce matriculation policies or other initiatives that stress sequenced learning and degree completion. Similarly, increased use of special purpose contracts that involve community colleges in economic development programs divert at least some administrative attention away from more traditional service areas.

As the public seeks ever greater returns on its investment, it is appropriate to ask how the lost opportunities inherent in these trade-offs can be minimized. One potential answer lies in the argument that these lost opportunities are (in aggregate) the inevitable cost of a greater good: the presence of a community-based institution that can meet local needs as they change over time. Efficiencies are maximized through administrative judgments that, based on study of these needs, offer the most appropriate mix of the flexible, scholastic, and social service approaches.

Another answer, however, lies in the conviction that the attempt to mix educational functions is inherently wasteful and that the community college must be fundamentally changed.

Eaton's (1994) call for a collegiate emphasis is an example. She would concentrate community college efforts on postsecondary degree programming, leaving remedial education, workforce development, and other noncollegiate functions to other agencies that are more capable of carrying out these ends; the colleges would be funded accordingly with the goal of maximizing the efficiencies and benefits of the scholastic institution. Cohen and Brawer (1989) offer a compromise approach to the same end, maintaining institutional comprehensiveness but insisting on clear fiscal and administrative divisions within the college that separate units with different educational functions. For example, the unit serving degree-seeking students would be separate from the unit serving ad hoc learners; each unit would be funded separately because each takes on an entirely different task for students pursing different ends.

These answers imply a more reasoned, means-ends approach to funding than is usually the case in the public arena. Cohen (1993) has correctly observed that "as always, the nature of college services is driven less by intramural educational philosophy than by the ability to sustain revenues" (p. 74). It remains to be seen whether the contemporary period of consolidation and fiscal parsimony will lead to decisions that are driven more by considered debate about institutional purpose than by fiscal opportunism.

References

Adelman, C. (1992). *The way we are: The community college as American thermometer.* Washington, DC: Office of Educational Research and Improvement, U.S. Department of Education.

Breneman, D. W., & Nelson, S. C. (1981). *Financing community colleges: An economic perspective.* Washington, DC: Brookings Institution.

California Community Colleges, Board of Governors. (1984). *Student matriculation: A plan for implementation in the California community colleges.* Sacramento: Author. (ERIC Document Reproduction Service No. ED 261 738)

Carnegie Commission on Higher Education. (1970). *The open-door college.* New York: McGraw-Hill.

Cohen, A. M. (1993). Trends and issues in community college finance. *Community College Review, 20*(4), 70-75.

Cohen, A. M., & Brawer, F. B. (1987). *The collegiate function of community colleges.* San Francisco: Jossey-Bass.

Cohen, A. M., & Brawer, F. B. (1989). *The American community college.* San Francisco: Jossey-Bass.

Eaton, J. S. (1994). *Strengthening collegiate education in community colleges.* San Francisco: Jossey-Bass.

Eicher, J.-C., & Chevaillier, T. (1993). Rethinking the finance of post-compulsory education. *International Journal of Educational Research, 19,* 445-519.

Garms, W. I. (1977). *Financing community colleges.* New York: Teachers College Press.

Gottschalk, K. (1977). Can colleges deal with high-risk problems? *Community College Frontiers, 6*(4), 4-11.

Grubb, W. N. (1989). *The developing vocational education and training "system": Partnerships and customized training.* Washington, DC: Office of Vocational and Adult Education, U.S. Department of Education. (ERIC Document Reproduction Service No. ED 329 680)

Grubb, W. N. (1995). Response to comment. *Journal of Human Resources, 30,* 222-227.

Harper, W. A. (1971). *Junior college directory.* Washington, DC: American Association of Junior Colleges.

Herr, T., Halpern, R., & Conrad, A. (1993). Changing what counts: Rethinking the journey out of welfare. *Applied Behavioral Science Review, 1,* 113-149.

Hines, E. R. (1994). *State higher education appropriations, 1993-94.* Denver, CO: State Higher Education Executive Officers.

Illinois Community College Board. (1994). *A fiscal profile of the Illinois public community college system: Fiscal years 1966-1994.* Springfield: Author.

Illinois Community College Board. (1996). *Workforce preparation grant report for fiscal year 1994.* Springfield: Author.

Kane, T. J., & Rouse, C. E. (1995a). Comment on W. Norton Grubb, Grubb, "The varied economic returns to postsecondary education: New evidence from the class of 1972." *Journal of Human Resources, 30,* 205-221.

Kane, T. J., & Rouse, C. E. (1995b). Labor-market returns to two- and four-year college. *American Economic Review, 85,* 600-614.

Katsinas, S. G. (1994). Is the open door closing? The democratizing role of the community college in the post-cold war era. *Community College Journal, 64*(5), 22-29.

Katsinas, S. G., & Swender, H. J. (1992). Community colleges and JTPA: Involvement and opportunity. *Community, Technical, and Junior College Journal, 62*(6), 18-23.

Lombardi, J. (1973). Critical decade for community college financing. In J. Lombardi (Ed.), *New directions for community colleges: Vol. 2. Meeting the financial crisis* (pp. 109-120). San Francisco: Jossey-Bass.

London, H. B. (1978). *The culture of a community college.* New York: Praeger.

Martorana, S.V., & Wattenbarger, J.L. (1978). *Principles, practices, and alternatives in state methods of financing community colleges and an approach to their evaluation, with Pennsylvania as a case study.* Report no. 32. University Park: Center for the Study of Higher Education, University of Pennsylvania.

McCabe, R. H. (1981). Now is the time to reform the American community college. *Community and Junior College Journal, 51*(8), 6-10.

McKeown, M. P., & Layzell, D. T. (1994). State funding formulas in higher education: Trends and issues. *Journal of Educational Finance,* 319-346.

Newmyer, J., & McIntyre, C. (1992). *Funding gap study.* Sacramento: California Community Colleges Board of Governors. (ERIC Document Reproduction Service No. 351 066)

Palmer, J. C. (1987). *Community, technical, and junior colleges: A summary of selected national data.* Washington, DC: American Association of Community and Junior Colleges. (ERIC Document Reproduction Service No. ED 292 507)

Palmer, J. C. (1995). *Results of a formative evaluation of the opportunities program.* (Available from the Illinois Community College Board, 509 South 6th Street, Room 400, Springfield, IL 62701)

Palmer, J. C., & Eaton, J. S. (1991). Building the national agenda for transfer: A background paper. In J. S. Eaton (Ed.), *Setting the national agenda: Academic achievement and transfer* (pp. 17-52). Washington, DC: American Council on Education.

Palmer, J. C., & Pugh, M. B. (1993). The community college contribution to the education of bachelor's degree graduates: A case study in Virginia. In J. S. Eaton (Ed.), *Probing the community college transfer function* (pp. 45-70). Washington, DC: American Council on Education.

Palmer, J. C., Stapleton, L., & Ludwig, M. (1994). *At what point do community college students transfer to baccalaureate-granting institutions: Results of a 13-state study.* Washington, DC: American Council on Education.

Piland, B. (1995). Facing the 21st century: California community colleges at the crossroads. *Community College Journal, 65*(3), 24-28.

President's Commission on Higher Education. (1947). *Higher education for American democracy.* Washington, DC: Government Printing Office.

Richardson, R. C., Jr., Fisk, E. C., & Okun, M. A. (1983). *Literacy in the open-access college.* San Francisco: Jossey-Bass.

Richardson, R. C., Jr., & Rhodes, W. R. (1985). Effective strategic planning: Balancing demands for quality and fiscal realities. In W. A. Deegan & D. Tillery (Eds.), *Renewing the American community college* (pp. 284-302). San Francisco: Jossey-Bass.

Romano, R. M. (1986a). An economic perspective on the public financing of the community college. *Community College Review, 14*(2), 8-13.

Romano, R. M. (1986b). What is the economic payoff to a community college degree? *Community/Junior College Quarterly of Research and Practice, 10,* 153-164.

Seidman, E. (1985). *In the words of the faculty.* San Francisco: Jossey-Bass.

Smith, T. M., Perie, M., Alsalam, N., Mahoney, R. P., Bae, Y., & Young, B. A. (1995). *The condition of education, 1995* (NCES Report No. 95-273). Washington, DC: Office of Educational Research and Improvement, U.S. Department of Education.

Snyder, T. D., & Hoffman, C. M. (1995). *Digest of education statistics, 1995.* Washington, DC: Office of Educational Research and Improvement, U.S. Department of Education.

U.S. Bureau of the Census. (1975). *Historical statistics of the United States: Colonial times to 1970.* Washington, DC: Author.

Vaughan, G. B. (1991). Institutions on the edge: America's community colleges. *Educational Record, 72*(2), 30-33.

Weis, L. (1985). *Between two worlds: Black students in an urban community college.* Boston: Routledge & Kegan Paul.

Walters, J. E. (1994). *Registration priorities: A report.* Sacramento: Chancellor's Office, California Community Colleges. (ERIC Document Reproduction Service No. ED 374 878)

Wattenbarger, J. L. (1985). Dealing with new competition for public funds: Guidelines for financing community colleges. In W. A. Deegan & D. Tillery (Eds.), *Renewing the American community college* (pp. 253-283). San Francisco: Jossey-Bass.

Zeiss, T. (1989). Roles of community, technical, and junior colleges: Positive image opportunity. In T. Zeiss (Ed.), *Economic development: A viewpoint from business* (pp. 3-6). Washington, DC: American Association of Community and Junior Colleges.

TEN

Competition for Limited Resources
REALITIES, PROSPECTS, AND STRATEGIES

RICHARD L. ALFRED

Throughout this decade, colleges and universities have seen their financial resources and public esteem plummet and their costs and challenges skyrocket. On the surface, the causes are evident: economic uncertainty, changing demographics with an increasingly nontraditional student body, an apparently unbreakable cycle of higher tuition and higher student financial aid, and unaffordably large administrative overhead and costs. Underneath, however, a whole new dynamic of changing demands, changing customers, changing competitors, and new technologies is forcing institutions to devise strategic responses at warp speed. These responses have entailed rounds of reform, retrenchment, and reengineering. From Yale to Miami-Dade Community College and the University of Maine to the Minnesota state college and university system, institutions have slashed budgets, cut positions and personnel, and eliminated programs. Critics have asked tough questions about not only whether colleges and universities are doing things right but whether they are doing the right things.

Consider for a moment an article on college costs published by *Newsweek* in its April 29, 1996, issue. Ostensibly, the article focused on the high costs of college attendance. In actuality, however, it raised serious questions about higher education as an industry, and it noted that a combination of sticker shock and questions concerning faculty productivity and workload is shaking the foundations of higher education (Morgenthau & Nayyar, 1996).

To address changing markets and cost-conscious policy makers, colleges and universities must implement new cost and revenue strategies. Burdened with high fixed costs and competing for limited resources, institutions are caught in a vortex of change that threatens to undermine their competitiveness. Tinkering will not be enough. The only way out will be to formulate strategies that create new forms of value and, in so doing, enable colleges and universities to compete more effectively for shrinking resources. The purpose of this chapter is to describe strategies that institutions can use to create new resource markets. The chapter begins by looking at some of the forces leading to compression of support for colleges and universities. It then describes different strategies for procuring dollars. Creating resources through new approaches to cost and revenue will be a critical challenge for management. This challenge is acknowledged and framed in a series of competitive goals that institutions will need to tackle to create new resource markets. The chapter concludes with several questions that leaders must ask to determine the readiness of their institutions for competition.

Compression of Public Support

From heady growth and incremental budgeting to calls for accountability, colleges and universities have entered a period of resource constriction. College administrators now routinely identify financial issues as the greatest challenge facing their institutions (El-Khawas, 1991). Some factors influencing the availability of resources are beyond the control of institutions, others can be controlled. Jaschik

(1990), for example, identified uncertainty in the national economy brought about by fluctuations in the stock market; continued regional economic problems in states dependent on manufacturing; downsizing of service industries; and the reluctance of governors and legislatures to raise taxes in an election year as factors beyond institutional control. Fischer (1986) described the effects of fluctuating enrollment on budgets as a controllable factor in resource availability.

Regardless of the causes of resource decline and whether or not they can be controlled, there is a general acknowledgment among college leaders that a decline in the availability of economic resources heightens institutional sensitivity to financial issues and their causes (Smith, 1995). Skolnik (1986) briefly summarized the direct relationship between the weakening of an institution's financial situation and its leadership's emphasis on financial matters. Cohen and Brawer (1989) described specific high-level steps that colleges have implemented when faced with the prospect of unbalanced budgets. Temple (1986) detailed institutional compromises effected in the face of financial difficulty and cautioned against acts of academic hypocrisy that may be invoked in attempts to offset financial difficulties and enrollment declines. Finally, Alfred and Carter (1996) described the growing interest of college leaders in external scanning activities and competitor analysis to identify root causes and consequences of financial decline.

Structured Competition

Competition can assume many forms, work in different arenas, and involve a variety of organizations. Some competitive arenas are more "structured" than others insofar as the rules of competition are clear-cut, service concepts better defined, organizational boundaries more stable, and constituency needs more precisely measurable. Colleges and universities annually engage in structured competition for public funds with K-12 schools, prisons, mental health, and a host of other agencies. The basis or "structure" of this competition are guidelines established by government agencies regulating the flow of resources. What are the competitive strategies of public agencies, and how do they work to compress support for colleges and universities?

The impact of changing federal government policies (e.g., student financial aid, entitlement grants, and direct institutional support) on economic resources available to higher education is well documented. Less well understood are the views of state legislators and their impact on college and university budgets. In a decade characterized by state control of higher education through block grants, the views of state legislators are important as an index of public support. Recent research shows that legislators are bifocal in their views of higher education. State lawmakers believe that undergraduate education should be a priority in their states, they expect tuition and fees to increase, and they plan to strengthen the relationship between state funding and educational outcomes. These findings, summarized in a National Education Association (NEA) report titled "The Politics of Remedy: State Legislative Views on Higher Education" (Ruppert, 1996), were drawn from in-depth interviews conducted in 1995 with 58 House and Senate Education Committee chairs in 49 states. In general, legislators see themselves as knowledgeable, action oriented, and discontent with tinkering with the status quo. They indicate a commitment to expanding the use of technology, but they are not inclined to support spending on new buildings or campuses. Among other findings in the survey impacting institutional finances are these:

- Legislators want less bureaucracy and politics in the governance of higher education. They desire more autonomy for institutions and state systems, but that autonomy will come with a price—higher levels of accountability and efficiency.
- Legislators want to remove the perception that colleges and universities are an ivory tower and link elementary-secondary, voc-tech, and higher education all together as one unit of education from early childhood through graduate work.
- Fifty-six percent of state lawmakers feel the current level of funding for education is inadequate to meet current needs, and 75% feel the current level of funding is inadequate to meet future needs.

Nongovernment agencies are also part of the structured arena of competition. K-12 schools, prisons, mental health, public colleges and universities, environmental protection, and human services are known competitors that use predictable arguments for state support.

Each of these agencies can advance compelling arguments for support through information that differentiates them from competitors. For example, faced with a real or potential decline in state support, a likely array of arguments advanced by competitors are the following:

- K-12 schools would raise the specter of additional support needed for technology and special programs to improve basic skills.
- Human services would argue for more support to help youths at risk and a growing number of economically disadvantaged adults.
- Corrections would use arguments keyed to public concerns about "safety and security" to support new prison construction and modernization of facilities.
- Transportation agencies would cite studies showing infrastructure deterioration to support highway and bridge construction projects.
- Environmental protection agencies would supply reams of pollution data supported by analyses of risk to build support for waste water treatment facilities.

The price of success experienced by any one agency will often be compression of support for the others.

The likelihood of intensifying competition for resources in the structured arena raises important questions for colleges and universities. What kinds of information can public colleges and universities provide to support requests for state aid? What are the "benefits" to the public if these requests are supported and the liabilities if they are not? What benefits will be gained by providing proportionally greater support to public colleges and universities in periods of economic growth, uncertainty, or stagnation? Competition for limited resources is an inclement business. Human service organizations will respond to cutbacks and rising competition for state funds through deinstitutionalization strategies—lowering fixed costs for operations through reduction of the number of clients served. Restrictive admissions and early release programs are deinstitutionalization strategies commonly employed by state prisons and hospitals to produce cost savings and evidence of negative impacts to counteract a shortfall in operating resources (Alfred, 1985). What countervailing strategies can colleges and universities develop to compete in periods of resource decline? Institutions must build meaningful strategy; the alternative is a compression of public support.

Unstructured Competition

Structured competition involves predictable relationships among known competitors in a stable market. However, unpredictable and turbulent change can come to any market, and new opportunity arenas are almost always unstructured. New competitors are emerging and are fast at work reshaping the postsecondary education market. Five in particular will have a significant effect on college enrollments and finance, yet have not been met with adequate responses:

- Companies and corporations providing on-site programs for current and future workers
- Corporate giants in the communications industry with a capability for distance delivery into homes, workplaces, shopping centers, and areas where people congregate
- Supplementary education providers, such as private tutoring companies, that use proven techniques to produce positive learning outcomes in students
- K-12 schools partnering with business and industry to prepare work-ready youths
- Temporary service agencies using training programs to prepare flexible workers for many different jobs (Alfred & Carter, 1996; Alfred & Rosevear, in press)

Figure 10.1 depicts the nature of structured and unstructured competition for resources in postsecondary education. Although agencies like prisons, transportation, and human services can make exceptional resource requests in the structured context, most of their resource acquisition behavior follows a prescribed pattern. In the unstructured context, the situation is different; there are no rules and no prescribed patterns of behavior. Competitors operate outside existing boundaries by creating *value* in ways that surpass colleges and universities.

Value can take many forms, including some that have not been considered by college faculty and administrators. It can be created in the form of *cost*, which makes education more affordable for students through operating procedures that control costs. Community colleges, for example, can build a competitive advantage in relationship

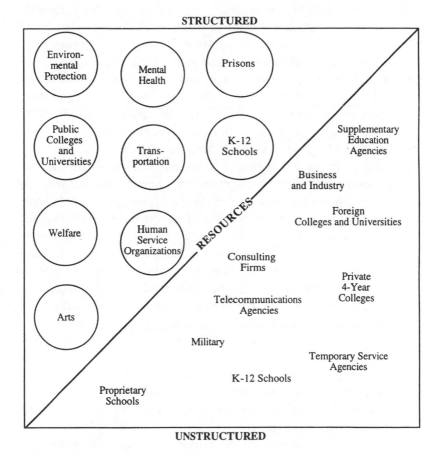

Figure 10.1. Structured and Unstructured Competition for Resources in Postsecondary Education

to higher-cost four-year colleges because they have multiple funding sources and instructional strategies which enable them to keep student tuition low (Alfred & Carter, 1996). Or value can be realized as *convenience* that makes access easy by bringing courses and services directly to the customer. Potentially, telephone and cable companies are in a strong position to make education convenient for students through distance delivery into homes, community centers, shopping malls, and just about anywhere people congregate. Or value can be created in the form of *great programs and services* that attract students because of their distinctive design and delivery. Take, for example the skill of corporations with high-powered training programs (e.g., Motorola and General Electric)—first in identifying employee needs, next in high-quality program design, and then in fast program development. These capabilities transform otherwise pedestrian training programs into niche programs that can be delivered outside company walls and bring the corporation that developed them into the business of education. Or value can be achieved through *customer intimacy*—operating practices that distinguish one institution from another because they reach out and identify beneficiary needs and find ways to help them achieve important goals. Some proprietary schools have succeeded in competition with established colleges through student intake procedures (i.e., admissions and financial aid) that are custom crafted to students and support services that provide a direct linkage between education and work. Finally, value can be created in the form of *maverick ideas* that provide a competitive advantage to organizations that invent totally different ways of delivering education and surprise and outstrip traditional institutions. K-12 schools partnering with business and industry in the primary grades to introduce children to technology and education/work linkages could potentially reshape college enrollment patterns by preparing students directly for work in corporations. These students would appear on college campuses as part-time learners already engaged in a career, not as full-time students seeking a career.

Value, whatever its form, will be the vehicle that determines success for organizations competing for enrollment and resources in the postsecondary education market. Organizations that succeed will find new ways to create value that enable them to deliver programs, courses, and services better and more economically than other organizations. Motorola, for example, possesses a range of resources that could yield a competitive advantage in the delivery of postsecondary education. Using the interplay of values such as convenience, customer intimacy, and maverick ideas, Motorola could choose to partner with a telecommunication firm and deliver high-quality courses to "customers" in homes, workplaces, and other locations. It could establish its own form of credit for these courses and circumvent the traditional accrediting apparatus by connecting credit with important

known competitors, new competitors will emerge to gain market share and create new resource markets. In the future, competition for resources will take place at five levels (see Figure 10.3). Colleges and universities will need to understand the nature of competition at each level and take appropriate steps with strategy, structure, systems, and organizational culture to effectively compete for resources.

Level 1: Analyzing the Competition

The goal of Level 1 competition is to determine what competitors are doing and their relative advantage or disadvantage in the resource market. This competition will take place in the delivery of value—the advantages of education provided by an institution that make it more or less desirable. Value comes in many forms, some of which are identified below.

| | FORMS OF VALUE | | | | |
COMPETITORS	Low Cost	Convenience	Great Programs and Services	Customized Services	Maverick Ideas
Traditional					
Colleges and universities					
Proprietary schools					
Corporate "universities"					
Consulting firms					
Emerging					
K-12 schools					
Temporary service agencies					
Telecommunication companies					
Learning systems companies					
Other					

Farsighted institutions will have up-to-date knowledge of what their competitors are doing to deliver value, where they want to compete, and what they need to do to win. Ultimately, they will use the results

Figure 10.3. Competition for Resources

of competitor analysis to find ways to deliver programs, courses, and services more economically than other organizations. In so doing, they will maintain or increase market share and open up new resource markets.

Level 2: Building Strategy

College leaders have focused much attention on the problem of acquiring resources to support a cumulative base of programs and services. For most institutions, resource growth is the primary criterion for measuring the strength of strategic position. But what is the meaning of resource growth in a market that will be much different tomorrow? The goal of competition in Level 2 will be to build strategy for the future that will maximize opportunities for institutional growth and development. The question that must be addressed through this strategy is, Given our current strengths and weaknesses, what opportunities are we likely to capture in the future? This question leads to others: What new programs, services and delivery systems do we need to build? How will our definition of student and resource markets need to change to capture a larger share of future opportunities? What resources can be acquired to support growth tomorrow that are not available today?

To gain resources in the future, new competencies must to developed. To know which competencies to build, college leaders must be prescient about the broad shape of tomorrow's opportunities (Hamel & Prahalad, 1994a, 1994b). Institutional strategy must focus as much on maximizing opportunities as on maximizing market share. This means a commitment to build competencies in new areas, long before the precise form of future markets comes into view.

Level 3: Changing Organizational Structure and Systems

The third level of competition will occur around organizational structures and systems—concepts that can help or hinder a college in the quest for limited resources. A college's stake in current structures and systems is economic as well as emotional. For an established institution, the definition of student and resource markets, the production of educational outcomes, the particular configuration of programs and services that yields those outcomes, and the supporting administrative structure and systems together constitute a well-tuned engine. Although this engine may perform superbly in one educational market, any change in that market could threaten the engine's efficiency (Hamel & Prahalad, 1994a, 1994b). Investing in existing administrative structures and systems (e.g., the academic semester) may render them useless in another set of conditions (e.g., distance delivery through technology). New technology and maverick educational delivery strategies used by competitors have reduced the efficiency of college and university administrative structures and systems (see Table 10.1).

Administrative structures and systems are different from strategy: They encompass deep-seated loyalties to particular ways of doing business; they are also a source point of resistance to change. To illustrate, faculty have invested entire careers in an educational delivery system built around fixed entry/fixed exit, a 14-week academic semester, academic credits, and grades based on academic performance. They have also become accustomed to a 9-month contract, fixed workload, and compensation based on length of service. It would be a flight into fantasy to expect them to readily embrace a different system based on open-entry/open-exit, modular curricula, skill certification in contrast to credits, a 12-month contract, flexible workload, and incentive-based pay. Colleges that want to successfully compete for resources in the future will need to constantly alter their structure and systems to meet new needs. Tinkering with a new campus registration system is not enough if a competitor has developed a distance delivery system that voids the need for registration. Every college must sooner or later design new systems to maintain market share and stay in the hunt for resources.

Level 4: Cultural Change

In an environment of turbulent change, redesigning administrative structures and systems is not enough. Implementing new systems without faculty and staff involvement and support is a recipe for

TABLE 10.1 Current and New Systems in Colleges and Universities

Systems	Today	Tomorrow
Educational delivery		
Strategy	Fixed entry/fixed exit	Open entry/open exit
Time	Semester based	Modular
Awards	Credits	Certification
Evaluation	Grades	Skills/competencies
Method	Single mode	Multimodal
Instruction		
Instructors	Content deliverers	Content managers
Focus	Teaching	Learning
Method	Single mode	Multimodal
Curriculum/		
development	Specialized faculty	Cross-functional design team
Support services		
Delivery	Centralized	Decentralized
Customer	Students/staff	Students
Time	Periodic/episodic	Continuous
Staff		
Faculty contract	9 months	Year round
Workload	Fixed	Flexible
Compensation	Formula	Incentive based
Hiring	Integrated	Integrated/virtual
Planning		
Process	Prescriptive	Exploratory
Goal	Incremental improvement	Create new futures
Unit of analysis	Existing market/ competitors	Market foresight
Model of analysis	Benchmarking	Challenging orthodoxies
Assessment		
Timing	Periodic/episodic	Continuous
Customer	Faculty/staff	Students/community
Unit of analysis	Programs/services	Institution

failure. Neither is it enough to employ a reactive approach moving to design new systems only when faculty are ready. A college that waits for the "right time" to implement change will quickly find itself behind competitors in the race for market share and new resources. Leveraging a college to compete for resources calls for an entire community to become involved in questions related to fundamental rethinking and redesign. Why do we do what we do? What is the purpose of this process? How dramatically different should our core processes related to teaching and support services be? The goal of competition at Level 4 will be to transform the culture of a college through embracing change. Engaging faculty and staff in initiatives such as structural change and systems development that make a college more competitive is contingent on accepting that change is essential. In many colleges, there is a significant group that believes that change is neither necessary nor desirable. If given a disproportionate voice, this group can subvert and hamper the competitive capacity of the institution—particularly its capacity to build new resource markets.

Leaders face the challenge of ensuring that individual players are aware of the need for, and implications of, change. Often, this involves management strategies that produce results ranging from a healthy level of anxiety to a dysfunctional environment paralyzed by fear. One college president referred to this challenge as "creating constructive chaos" to inform, engage, alert, convert, or simply warn resistors that change is under way.

Level 5: New Leadership Approaches

The goal of competition in Level 5 will be to develop approaches to leadership suitable for a transformed organization—an organization capable of competing for resources because it has interwoven a compelling strategy with redesigned systems and a flexible culture. The dimensions of the organizational transformation task faced by most colleges were established by leaders who tinkered with structures and systems using established road maps. Having failed to reinvent the institution 5-10 years ago and lacking a unique point of view about the future, these leaders have temporized. In short, for many colleges, leadership has been reactive rather than proactive.

All of this prompts one to ask how much of a transformation agenda college and university leaders are actually working on today. Although resource constriction and cost containment dominate the top management agenda in many colleges, to create new resource markets a college must be capable of recreating its market. To recreate a market, a college must have leaders with vision, to enact vision it must have resources, to have resources it must have a strategy to compete for resources and to compete for resources, it must have leaders with ideas. The primary task of leadership in the future will be to create new resource markets by reinventing the institution.

Looking Ahead

This chapter opened with a reference to a recent article in *Newsweek* (Morgenthau & Nayyar, 1996) that posed serious questions about higher education as an industry. The article suggested that colleges and universities may have lost sight of both their educational mission and their historically lofty ideals. Now that the landscape in which institutions will compete for resources has been considered, a second set of questions is necessary.

- Do senior executives have a clear and collective view about how the future will or could be different?
- Is top management allocating as much time and intellectual energy to creating new resource markets as to competing in today's markets?
- Is the college exercising an influence over the evolution of the postsecondary education market that is disproportionately large given its resources?
- Do faculty and staff share an aspiration for the institution and possess a clear sense of goals they are trying to achieve?
- Is there a significant amount of stretch in that aspiration—does it exceed current resources by a substantial amount?
- Does the college's opportunity horizon extend sufficiently far beyond the boundaries of existing service markets?
- Have all potential opportunities for resource leverage been fully exploited?
- Have new resource markets been identified that will carry the college into the future?

These questions present a point of view about competition and resources strategy that push a college into the future rather than hold it in the past. They focus more on building than maintaining, long-term possibility more than short-term feasibility, leveraging resources more than allocating resources, and creating new markets more than managing existing markets. In higher education, as in business, what distinguishes market leaders from laggards and resource growth from decline is the ability to uniquely imagine what could be.

References

Alfred, R. L. (1985). Emerging issues in public policy and financial administration. In D. F. Campbell (Ed.), *Strengthening financial management* (New Directions for Community Colleges, No. 50). San Francisco: Jossey-Bass.

Alfred, R. L., & Carter, P. (1996). Inside track to the future: Strategies, structures and leadership for change. *Community College Journal, 66*(4), 10-19.

Alfred, R. L., & Rosevear, S. (in press). Organizational structure, management and leadership for the future. In A. M. Hoffman & Y. Neumann (Eds.), *Handbook on college and university management*. Maryville, MO: Prescott.

Cohen, A. M., & Brawer, F. B. (1989). *The American community college* (2nd ed.). San Francisco: Jossey-Bass.

El-Khawas, E. (1991). *Campus trends*. Washington, DC: American Council on Education.

Fischer, R. (1986). California community college libraries: Spiraling downward. *Wilson Library Bulletin, 60*(8) 15-19.

Hamel, G., & Prahalad, C. K. (1994a). Competing for the future. *Harvard Business Review, 94*(4), 122-128.

Hamel, G., & Prahalad, C. K. (1994b). *Competing for the future: Breakthrough stategies for seizing control of your industry and creating the markets of tomorrow*. Boston: Harvard Business School Press.

Jaschik, S. (1990, October 24). States spending $40.8 billion on colleges this year: Growth rate at a 30-year low. *Chronicle of Higher Education*, pp. A1-A26.

Morgenthau, T., & Nayyar, S. (1996, April 29). Those scary college costs. *Newsweek*, pp. 53-54.

Ruppert, S. (1996, April). The politics of remedy: State legislative views on higher education. *National Education Association*.

Skolnik, M. L. (1986). If the cut is so deep, where is the blood? Problems in research on the effects of financial restraint. *Review of Higher Education, 9*, 435-455.

Smith, R. K. (1995). Building budgets for effective resource utilization. In *A handbook on the community college in America*. Westport, CT: Greenwood.

Temple, R. J. (1986). Weak programs: The place to cut. In B. W. Dziech (Ed.), *Controversies and decision making in difficult economic times* (New Directions for Community Colleges, No. 53). San Francisco: Jossey-Bass.

Treacy, M., & Wiersema, F. (1995). *The discipline of market leaders: Choose your customers, narrow your focus, dominate your market*. Reading, MA: Addison-Wesley.

APPENDIX

American Education Finance Association Board of Directors, 1996-1997

OFFICERS

Lawrence O. Picus, *President*
Eugene P. McLoone, *President-Elect*
George R. Babigian, *Executive Director*
Mary P. McKeown, *Immediate Past President*

DIRECTORS

1997 Term

Anne L. Jefferson
Michael O'Lloughlin
Kathleen C. Westbrook
Terry Whitney
R. Craig Wood

1998 Term

Patrick Galvin
Carolyn Herrington
Maureen McClure
John Schneider
Stephanie Stullich

1999 Term

Mary F. Fulton
Robert K. Goertz
Stephen L. Jacobson
Richard A. King
Barbara LaCost

Sustaining Members

Jewell C. Gould
Edward J. Hurley
Chris Malkiewich
Michael A. Resnick
Donald I. Tharpe

Mary F. Hughes, *AEFA Journal Executive Editor*
Kathleen C. Westbrook, *AEFA Newsletter Editor*

Index

CORWIN
PRESS

The Corwin Press logo—a raven striding across an open book—
represents the happy union of courage and learning. We are a
professional-level publisher of books and journals for K-12 educators, and we are committed to creating and providing resources that
embody these qualities. Corwin's motto is "Success for All Learners."

Components of Strategy	Controlling Costs	Leveraging Existing Resources	Maverick Revenue Strategies	Bifocal Strategies
Method	Basic quality at low cost	Implementing strategies to improve resource flows from traditional revenues sources	Locating and tapping into totally different resource markets	Using leverage and maverick strategies to generate resources
Organizational structure	Central authority: finite level of empowerment	Top management determines and carries out strategy	Leaders at all levels identify novel ideas about revenue	Decentralized authority; flexible and loosely knit
Systems	Standard operating procedures	Match institutional programs and benefits with external priorities	Value different ways of doing things and underwrite risk	Reward creativity and put innovations into practice
Culture	Concern for balancing quality and cost	Values responsive to external priorities	Permits freedom for maverick managers to pursue and implement ideas	Experiments and thinks outside current practice
Leadership	Emphasis on controlling costs	Emphasis on improving performance to meet external expectations	Emphasis on innovation and supporting risk	Focus on generating resources through multiple strategies employed with multiple markets

Figure 10.2. Resource Strategies for Tomorrow

create new revenue markets. One method for doing this is to use existing resources to build new resources—a strategy known as leveraging. Colleges that use this strategy will identify the priorities of funding agencies and allocate resources to programs that fit these priorities. But matching up with today's priorities is not the same thing as anticipating needs tomorrow. Needed will be a strategy for tapping into entirely new markets through *maverick ideas* that change the shape of competition. Competition in tomorrow's market will take place outside the boundaries of postsecondary education as leaders know them. Moreover, although benchmarking the successful practices of today's competitors is sufficient to gain or maintain a competitive advantage, tomorrow it will be the minimum price of market entry. Keeping score of competitors and a college's advantages or disadvantages is not the same thing as inventing new advantages. Therefore, it may be appropriate for colleges to look beyond their rivals in the quest for resources and to challenge themselves by looking at opportunities on the horizon and creating radical designs to pursue these opportunities.

Maverick strategies for resource development require ideas and an organization that support risk. Many colleges are not organized to encourage risk—centralized decision making continues to prevail, and faculty participation in out-of-classroom activities is fluid and situational. A more realistic strategy, therefore, may be one involving continued reliance on traditional revenue sources and the creation of new resource markets as opportunities permit. This involves a *bifocal* strategy. As part of this strategy, leaders must decide where to devote the bulk of their time and attention: everaging existing resources, or creating new resource markets? Experience suggests that both are important, but administrators spend a disproportionate amount of time focusing on the known—that is, working with existing markets.

Leveraging Colleges for Competition

Earlier, the observation was made that competition for resources will be unstructured in the future. Whereas competition today is structured involving predictable strategies for acquiring resources by analysis will provide only a map of today's competitive arena. Of what use are the traditional tools of market and competitor analysis to leaders racing to understand the opportunities created by changing boundaries, or to faculty and staff trying to adapt to new technology and delivery systems? How can a college possessing only a map of the present and past, make an intelligent decision about what value to deliver, which core competencies to build, which programs and services to offer, which alliances to form, and—most important— which resource strategies to use in the future? Colleges that see resource strategy as primarily a positioning exercise in an existing market are apt to overlook important opportunities for resource generation; they are also likely to be at a disadvantage in the competition for limited resources.⌉

Resource strategy is as much about understanding tomorrow's market as it is about competing in today's market (Hamel & Prahalad, 1994a, 1994b). Competition for resources within today's market raises issues such as these: What changes should be made in programs, services, and delivery systems to attract and hold students? How can we improve our marketing? What new initiatives should we undertake with legislators to increase our share of state aid? Competition for resources in tomorrow's market will raise deeper questions such as these: Whose concepts for program and service delivery will prevail? How will partnerships form to new markets, and what will determine each organization's share of the resources? And, most critically, what new revenue sources can be tapped in the unstructured playing field that will characterize tomorrow's market?

These questions point to vision as a key determinant of resource strategy. Because most colleges have not developed a long-term vision focused on resources—their origin, volume, and durability—an important task is to forge strategy that will help define the future. The framework in Figure 10.2 depicts different approaches to resource strategy. At the most basic level, strategy can amount to *controlling costs* and *leveraging existing resources.* Essentially, the goal here is to preserve the base of the institution by gathering sufficient revenue to offset expenditures. As competitors using innovative delivery systems begin to bite into market share, this strategy will yield diminishing returns.

To gain an advantage over competitors, colleges and universities will need to develop creative arguments with existing markets or outcomes (e.g., jobs, job skills, and advanced technology training). The academic semester and credit hour would become irrelevant and so would when, where, and how a course is taught (Alfred & Carter, 1996). Most important would be value created for the customer. Success would be determined through creating competitively distinct value and deploying it in a well-conceived strategy.

What is astonishing about these new competitors is their focus on the "customer" and their speed in serving new and existing markets. Research has shown that five factors contribute to their success (Treacy & Wiersema, 1995):

- Well-developed core competencies that serve as launch points for new services
- An ability to fundamentally renew or revitalize by periodically changing the services they deliver and delivering new ones
- A focus on "operational excellence" that in some way distinguishes the programs and services offered by the organization from those offered by other organizations
- A flattened decentralized organization that enables staff to identify and respond quickly to changing needs
- A dedication to "customers" and "suppliers" that enables the organization to "live" the customer's problems; it understands that the best program or service is not the best value if the customer is unable to use the program or service effectively

The new competitors have ways of creating and delivering *value* that set them apart from colleges and universities. They focus on *learning* required to make *transformational changes*—changes in basic assumptions needed to succeed in today's fast-moving, often turbulent market. Using technology and innovative student intake systems, they can create immediate problems in enrollment and longer-term problems in finance for institutions using conventional delivery systems.

Financial Strategy for Tomorrow

Strategies for resource acquisition must by necessity be driven by a market structure analysis of existing competitors and the delivery systems they will use to attract students and resources. However, this